Nelson English

Literature & Media 9

Activity Authors

Martha Di Leonardo
Lilia D'Ovidio
Michelle Fletcher
Paul Frawley
Pauline Mallan
David Opiola
Mary Lou Tollis

Media Consultant: Pauline Mallan

Equity Consultant: Ken Ramphal

Anthologizers
Linda Sheppard
Steven Beattie
Todd Mercer

Advisory Panel Members
Bill Anderson, Toronto DSB
Sandy Bender, Ottawa-Carleton CSB
Mike Budd, Greater Essex DSB
Anne Carrier, Toronto DSB
Owen Davis, London DCSB
Anthony De Sa, Toronto CDSB
Rocco Di Ianni, Halton CDSB
Lilia D'Ovidio, Dufferin Peel CDSB
Joanne Folville, Halton CDSB
Jean Godfrey, Greater Essex DSB
Maureen Maloney, Durham CDSB
Nora Quinn, Niagara CDSB
Denis Stokes, Nipissing-Parry Sound CDSB
Lisa Taylor, Durham DSB
Mary Lou Tollis, Hamilton Wentworth CDSB

Editorial Consultant: Anthony Luengo

A special thanks to the teachers who attended the Ontario Council of Teachers of English Conference for the over 200 suggestions which helped shape Nelson Canada's Grade 9 English literature and language resources

TABLE OF CONTENTS

SHORT FICTION

Humour, sadness, mystery, real life, horror, action. These are some of the broad themes that can be found in the short-fiction selections you are about to read. Stories in this anthology reflect a variety of cultures and times, from the great myths of the ancient Greeks and the Ibo people of Nigeria to the stories of contemporary society where technology can sometimes seem to reign supreme. All stories, regardless of the period in which they are set or the topic they explore, have much to teach us about human behaviour.

No matter how much the selections vary in time, place, or genre, each story is structured around a central idea or main point. In some stories, the idea can be suggested in the title. In other stories, you will have to "read between the lines" of the characters' words and actions. Each selection invites you, as a reader, to enter another world, a world created by the short-story writer.

CHARACTERISTICS OF SHORT FICTION

A work of short fiction
- will be based on a central idea
- may contain a number of elements, such as setting and mood, characterization, conflict and plot, but will often emphasize only a few of these elements to achieve particular effects
- will be written from the first- or third-person point of view

VISITORS

by Sarah Ellis

WE STARTED up the rocky streambed trail. The stones shifted under my boots. My right big toe was not happy, and my pack already felt heavy. A coalition of my legs and stomach decided to report to me that this hike was a dumb idea. Ahead of me Ellen was setting an ambitious pace.

"Hey, Ellen, slow down a bit. And just remind me. I forgot for a minute. Why is it fun to haul your body up the side of a mountain?"

One thing about old friends. You can count on them to be sensitive and sympathetic when you are needy or troubled.

"Come on, droop-head, you're always like this for the first 20 minutes. Don't forget. No pain, no gain."

I trudged along, wondering when I could suggest a gorp break. Then I fantasized about how much I would like to hike the Grand Canyon, where you get to go down first. And then I thought for about the eleventeenth time how amazing it was that Ellen and I were here at all.

In our minds it was the "weekend hike to the cross-country ski hut." In our parents' minds it was mission intergalactica or something. They thought of many dire fates that awaited us. Ellen and I have seven parents between us. That's a lot of interparental phone calls. But finally we persuaded them. My wild card was that I reminded my mother that she was only one year older than me when she set off to Europe on her own. It is a good idea to pay attention when parents are discussing their youths. It can often make useful ammunition. Really, though, I think they let us go because my parents think Ellen is very responsible and Ellen's parents, well, they let Ellen do pretty well what she wants. They're a bit scared of her ever since she was in hospital.

Ellen was still setting a "we have to be at K3 before nightfall" kind of pace.

"Hey, Ellen, if each of our parents phoned each of our other parents, how many calls would that be?"

Ellen paused. "The formula would be number of parents minus one plus number of parents minus two and so on. In our case it would be, let's see, six plus five plus four plus three plus two plus one equals twenty-one."

Ellen's mathematical pause gave me a chance to catch up and get out my mountain mix before she could set off again.

The trail got steeper. Ellen led and I caught up. This is more or less how our friendship had been since we met in Tiny Tutus for Twos. According to Dad, Ellen grabbed my hand the first day of ballet and showed me exactly what to do. I don't remember this. I don't remember a time when I didn't know Ellen.

After about half an hour my body parts stopped whining and the trail widened out. Sun splashed through the trees and the only sound was the scuff of our boots. I tried to cover everything with snow to turn it into the familiar ski trail. But this was a new world, of dark and pale green and the soft warm smell of forest dirt.

After lunch we got a case of the early afternoon stupidos, and we started talking without our tongues. This is a method of talking that Ellen invented in grade 4. The idea is that you leave your tongue limp on the bottom of your mouth and try to talk. Ellen recited the "Tomorrow and tomorrow and tomorrow" speech from *Macbeth*. Then I sang "On Top of Spaghetti." Then we both fell on the ground.

There are probably some people who think we should have out-grown dead-tongue talk by now. But it can really be a riot. Go on, try it. Rest your tongue on the bottom of your mouth and sing. "With glowing hearts …" No? Well, maybe you had to be there.

My favourite moment hiking is when you come up above the tree line. Everything opens up and becomes light outside and inside, and you feel like the discoverer of the top of the world. It was about five o'clock when we left the forest behind us. The air was suddenly crisper, and I gulped it in.

"I feel like I'm breathing helium."

"If you were breathing helium you would sound like Donald Duck," said Ellen, who knows many odd facts. "We should be at the hut in about an hour."

My legs were just starting to ask questions again when we arrived. The hut looked different in the summer, naked without its cover of snow. But inside there were ghosts of winter, the faint smells of wet woollen socks and soup-in-a-mug.

I was all for an immediate supper, but Ellen wanted to unpack first. As she laid out the contents of her pack on one of the wooden benches along the wall, I was treated to a vision of minimal packing at its most intense. We had discussed travelling light, and I felt I had made the ultimate sacrifice by bringing only two books. But Ellen had brought an individual portion of toothpaste, screwed up in a piece of waxed paper, and a single length of dental floss.

I left her in her organizational mode and went around to the back of the cabin. There was a clearing, a big flat piece of rock covered in moss and lichen. The orange warning flashers that the ski patrol puts up in the winter to keep people from skiing off the edge were gone. I went to the edge and sat with my feet hanging over. I tossed a small stone and it went tumbling down the rocky slope, bouncing and ricocheting. I looked out over the deep green valley. And then I flopped onto my back. The moss was soft, and the warmth of the sun-heated rock radiated through the thin covering and onto my arms and the back of my knees.

I turned my head and looked through one eye at the moss world. A dozen shades of green and brown and little stems with flowers. I made myself the size of a ladybug and went on a hike. Pale green lichen like frost-flowers. I closed both eyes and the world tipped slightly. I took off my boots, stripped off my sweaty socks, and wiggled my toes in the helium air.

For supper we had sandwiches. I ate three plus a chocolate bar and a peach yogurt. Ellen ate a few bites of yogurt and the filling out of one sandwich. She fed the bread to a whisky jack. Three more birds appeared, looking with greedy and unafraid eyes at our provisions. I kept a protective hand over the granola bars.

After supper we sat on the bench at the back of the hut and played insult alphabet. Ellen had just called me a quisling and I was about to call her a reprobate when they came around the corner of the cabin.

I didn't see them clearly at first because I was looking right into the setting sun. A moviemaker couldn't have done it better—the sun lighting them from behind, their red-blond hair glowing like haloes. They were tall. They looked remarkably alike. And they were beautiful. Cheekbones, symmetry, sea-green eyes, hair like polished silk. We're not talking cute here. We're talking stare and be stunned.

"Hello," said one, the male one. "Can we visit?"

They didn't look like the drug-crazed axe murderers that our seven parents had warned us about, so I said sure. Ellen didn't answer.

They walked across the clearing and sat down on the ground next to us. They didn't seem to sit down so much as to float to ground level. Their clothes, layers of pale light cotton, settled around them. I wondered if they were dancers.

Afterwards Ellen and I couldn't remember what we talked about with them. We tried to piece together what we knew about them and it wasn't much. Their names were Sith and Bab. They were brother and sister. Not twins, although they sure looked it. They were camping somewhere "over there"—one waved toward Salmonberry Flats. They didn't go to school.

There was only one bit of conversation I remember clearly. Sith slid down onto one elbow and said, "I have a white coat, an inner case of velvet, and gold at the heart."

I tried to catch Ellen's eye. Was this guy on something or what?

But she was staring at him with that look she sometimes gets in math class. Concentration, admiration, and challenge.

"An egg," she replied.

Again I tried to roll my eyes at Ellen. How corny. We hadn't played riddles since about grade 3. I stretched back to find one. What's green and plays the guitar?

Ellen beat me to it. "I have a fat little body, six arms, no legs. I can cover the mountains and fill the valleys and some day I could become a man."

I was just as glad she had beaten me to the draw. Elvis Pickle was seriously outclassed in this company. I elbowed my way in. "It's a spider, right? Like, it could become a man. Spider-man. And covering the mountains. Like that could be a whole bunch of spiders. Is that it?"

Bab and Sith looked at each other and at Ellen. There was an invisible cobweb joining them, a sparking electrical current that definitely didn't include me. They weren't even listening to me. I wanted the visitors to go away.

Then Bab and Sith each gave a little explosive sigh at the same time, as though they had been holding their breaths. These guys obviously took their riddles seriously.

"A snowflake," said Bab.

Sith gave a little smile, but only with his mouth. "It is higher than the highest thing, lower than the lowest thing, better than God, worse than the devil. The dead eat it but if you eat it you die."

Ellen was thinking so hard I could almost see her head glow. Finally, she seemed to slump. I wondered if I could lighten things up with my Alexander the Grape riddle. Probably not.

"I give up," she said.

"You'll know later," said Sith.

The sun went down and Ellen and I put on sweatshirts, but the visitors didn't seem to feel the cold. And then, just at the moment I wanted to go in and light the stove in the hut, Sith took out a mouth organ. He started out with that sucking sound that mouth-organ players seem to warm up with. I always think it sounds like a train in the distance. When he started to play, it went right into my feet, bypassing my brain entirely. I slipped my boots back on. Bab grabbed the spoons from our empty yogurt containers and licked them, the way people lick the last of their ice-cream cones. Then she began to tap them together, running them over the fingers of one hand and against her thigh.

Before I had decided to, I was on my feet dancing around that rocky place like a crazy person. Ellen, too. We couldn't stop. And I wasn't tired at all. My legs were like springs. I just wanted to dance harder and faster and longer and never stop. Sweat broke out on my scalp. We danced the sun down and then, still dancing, I went into the hut and got a couple of candles and the matches. I moved a piece of kindling into the middle of the rocky clearing and drip-attached two candles to the wood. The night was so still that only the wind of our dancing made them flicker.

There was no moon, and the green valley turned into a dark pit. The whole world was there in that circle of candlelight. The visitors danced with us. Sith pulled his shirt out of his pants, and it billowed as he whirled. Bab's skirt stood out like a bell. We danced in ones and twos and threes and all together. The candle shadows sharpened their faces. Their eyes disappeared into deep shaded sockets.

Sweat ran down into my eyes, and drops flew off the visitors through the light into the darkness. I was doing a step of my own invention, a sort of clogging, hip-hop fusion, when I put my foot down hard on the edge of a loose rock, and pain flashed across my ankle. I tried to keep dancing, but each step was worse. So I hopped over to the bench and collapsed onto it. Nobody seemed to notice. I considered feeling left out and sorry for myself, but I couldn't do it. Not with that music swirling around the candlelit circle, around my brain. My pounding heart calmed down, and I lifted my hair off my neck and held it on top of my head.

I wondered if I had broken my ankle. I thought about having to be rescued by helicopter. *Whappity, whappity, whappity.*

Then Sith yelled something, one word, and the music seemed to flip into a higher gear of speed and volume. He sure could get an amazing sound from that little mouth organ.

Ellen and Bab were holding hands and whirling in a tight little circle around Sith. Then Ellen let go for a moment and slid off her flannel shirt, hurling it out of the circle. Underneath she was wearing a dark tank top, and when I squinted at her I could merge the top and the surrounding darkness, so that she looked like a head and arms with no body. Then she danced closer to the light and I got a flash glimpse of her upper arms and I felt cold. They were like dowels. She was still so skinny.

Three years ago Ellen stopped eating. She nearly died. And I nearly stopped being her friend. I nearly stopped because I started to be too careful.

Have you ever noticed how often you mention food in the course of an ordinary conversation? "What's for dinner?" "I'm starving." People don't with Ellen. Like when we were planning this trip. Bryce said (Bryce is my father number two), "What are you planning to do about food?" And when he asked, there was a little pause, a little hairline crack between "about" and "food." A little icy hairline crack.

After Ellen got out of the hospital, she started eating again. Well, sort of. But because she nearly died, I was scared of her. So I was really careful, too. But those little hairline cracks widened, and soon she was on the other side of the Grand Canyon.

Our friendship was saved by fajitas. We had been out to a movie. It was a weeper. We used a pack of Kleenex each. Tragedy always gives me an appetite and it felt so much like before—both of us crying in a movie—that I suggested we drop into, tentative little pause, the Sunshine Cafe. Ellen gave a little wince but said okay.

Ellen wouldn't look at the menu so I ordered fajitas for both of us. They were fabulous, full of sautéed peppers, red and yellow, big sweet pieces of fried onion, all smothered in melted cheese and sour cream. I finished mine off in about four transcendent bites. But Ellen just kept pushing hers around the plate.

And suddenly I had had it. I wanted that fajita. I was furious with Ellen. Furious with her for nearly dying and for wasting her fajita.

"If you're going to treat that thing like a dead rat, give it to me."

First of all Ellen tried that "how cruel of you to say such a thing to me" look, but she couldn't keep it up. Her mouth started trembling and then she was laughing and snorting and crying again. She had to blow her nose on her napkin. "Dead rat," she kept repeating.

She impaled the fajita with her fork and sailed it across the table to my plate. Then she looked deep into my eyes and said, "If I had only one dead rat I would give it to you."

Since then I haven't been careful with Ellen.

But seeing her stick-like arms did make me feel a bit cold in my stomach. What had she actually eaten today? Almost nothing.

Nothing.

Hey!

"Nothing!" I yelled it out. "Nothing."

The dancers didn't hear me. I pivoted off the bench and hopped over. Ouch.

"Nothing," I bellowed.

Still they carried on. What, were they deaf or something? I ducked under their dancing arms and blew out the candles. The music stopped.

"The answer to the riddle is nothing."

"Katie." Ellen's voice was furious. "What did you do that for? What's with you?"

It's a lot darker out on the mountain at night than it is in the city. I heard confused movement and then Ellen said, "I'm going to get the flashlight."

I stood on one leg in the dark quiet, and then the flashlight beam cut across the darkness. It scanned the whole circle.

"Bab? Sith?" Ellen yelled, and her voice echoed across the valley.

"They've gone," I said.

She shone the light into my eyes. "Thanks a lot."

"Well, it's not my fault if they take off just because I guess their dumb riddle."

I expected Ellen to argue with me, to tear a strip off me, but instead her voice got small. "Why did they have to go so soon?" She shone the flashlight out over the valley, where its thin beam was eaten up by darkness.

We crawled into our sleeping bags without speaking, without taking off our clothes. Our silence filled the room like roaring. I tried to think of the one right thing to say, but in the middle of thinking I fell into sleep, abruptly, like falling off the edge of a cliff.

The next morning Ellen shook me awake. The minute my eyes opened I felt like a scumbag.

"Are you mad? I'm sorry. I was really feeling left out and...."

But Ellen reached over and put her finger on my lips. "Shh. I've got something to show you. Come on."

I slid out of my sleeping bag and followed her out the door and around to the back of the cabin. The ground was cold on my bare feet, and my ankle was a bit stiff but it seemed to work.

A light mist was moving across the clearing as dew steamed off the moss and rock.

And then I saw it. A circle. A circle where dancing feet had worn away the moss. A circle whose outer edge was a hand's-breadth away from the crumbling cliff edge.

I swallowed. There was something in my throat. "Who were they?"

Ellen shook her head. Then her face fell apart. Ellen, who doesn't cry except at movies. She pushed the words out between sobs. "I got up early. And I hiked over to Salmonberry Flats. There's nobody camping there. So I came back. I was just going to sit here. So I could see them again. Like they were last night. Perfect. I wanted them to be here. And then I noticed."

Ellen's arms were rigid at her sides, her hands clenched. I stepped up close behind her and rested my head on her shoulder. A whisky jack bounced out of a tree, did a fly-by through the clearing looking for breakfast and then, with a complaining cry, flew out over the deep green valley.

MOONFACE

by Richardo Keens-Douglas

IT WAS A BEASTLY HOT JULY a long time ago and the sound of laughter came drifting across the cornfield on the little bit of breeze that was in the air. It was coming from Moonface Wellington and his friends. It was Moonface's thirteenth birthday and his parents had thrown him a party. And everyone was having the time of their lives, as they usually do whenever Moonface was around. They were playing hopscotch, rounders, hide-and-seek, Jacks. Some children were even playing doctor under the watchful eye of the older folk from a distance. Everybody loved this little boy named Moonface. His real name was Maurice, but he had the roundest face and the biggest and brightest eyes this side of the mountain. Just like a full moon. So affectionately they called him Moonface.

Now the following year just before his fourteenth birthday Moonface started to get sick. But no one really took it on, because he was a strong boy and he always bounced back in a couple of days. But this sickness didn't seem to want to leave him this time. They tried every remedy in the book, but nothing appeared to work. They took him to the local doctor, even that seemed futile.

Then one morning like magic he got up and was as well as well can be. The sickness had disappeared just like that, and he was back with his friends doing all the things he loved to do.

But about a month later, bam, the sickness returned. This time it came back with a vengeance. He got weak, he started to lose weight, his eyes dimmed. Some days he couldn't even move. He just wasn't the old Moonface everybody knew. Eventually they brought in a specialist who discovered he had a fatal disease that there was no cure for. It was a disease that was spreading throughout the world at a rapid pace, and somehow Moonface contracted it. Well, when people heard Moonface had this illness, everybody immediately became magicians and slowly started to disappear. His best friends stopped coming out to his farm to play because their parents wouldn't allow them.

Then curiosity got the cat. They all wanted to know how he got the disease. His parents said, "It's not important how he got it. The fact remains he has it and we have to deal with it." His parents told them over and over it's not an easy disease to catch. You cannot get it from touching, or from a glass, or from caring and showing some love. His mother told them all the ways the illness is spread. Gave them all the material necessary for educating. But that wasn't enough. The people of the town wanted Moonface out of the school, out of the playground, out of the gym, out of the pool. They picketed. They stopped buying corn from Moonface's father. Their faces changed. Moonface couldn't understand it. People that he loved and played with all his life, all of a sudden, didn't want to be around him.

Then strange little things began to happen. One day the family went into town to do some shopping and when they came out of the store the tires from their car were slashed. One night they were coming home from a little night drive and as they were approaching their farm they saw a red sky. It was the toolshed. Someone had set it alight. Thank God it wasn't close to the house and the wind wasn't high that night. The three of them just stood there and watched. They didn't even make an effort to put out the fire. They just sat on the porch and watched the shed go up in smoke. "The human race is a strange race," the mother said. And they calmly went inside and had a cup of cocoa.

Moonface became weaker and lonelier as the months went by. His parents didn't know what to do. It was the saddest farmhouse this side of the mountain.

Then one night Moonface was lying in his bed, and the way he had positioned his bed, he could see right through the window all the way up to the moon and the stars. And you could tell the moon was keeping him company that night because the beams were shining right back onto his face, lighting up the room. That became one of his favourite pastimes. Painting pictures with the stars.

Then all of a sudden that night there was a quick darkness that flashed across the moon. He jumped up and ran to the window. And what he saw was a ball of light speeding toward the earth. It looked like a million candles rolled into one. And it just kept falling and falling until it disappeared behind the little hill across from the cornfield. Well, right away Moonface got excitedly curious. He quickly bundled up himself, put on his hat, and out the house he crept trying his level best not to wake his parents. And across the field he trotted like a tired little pony.

When he got to the top of the hill he thought he was going to faint. It was the most energy he had used all week. His head started to spin. He had to sit down. Slowly he reached for the ground, and as his bottom touched the grass he noticed a figure coming up the other side of the hill toward him, shining a light. It was a strange-looking light, filled with bright magnificent colours, similar to a rainbow. As the figure got closer and closer to him, Moonface noticed that it was just a little boy the same size as him, and the beautiful light was coming not from a flashlight but from the palm of his hand.

Well, Moonface was so surprised to see a little boy coming up the hill with light beaming from the palm of his hand that he didn't have time to get frightened. And in the blinking of an eye, the little boy gently lifted his hand and shone the light right into Moonface's eyes, and the next thing Moonface knew they were both sitting on top of the hill chatting and laughing, and he never remembered anything about the light shining from the boy's hand. It was quite extraordinary. It was as if they had been friends from the day they were born.

Moonface asked him what he was doing out in the fields at this time of the night, and if he had seen a ball of fire falling from the sky. The little boy said he didn't see the ball of fire, and that he was a new neighbour. They sat on that hill and the little boy asked about a thousand questions and Moonface answered about a thousand and one. Time just seemed to stand still for a little while.

They planned to meet the next day at the same spot. The following morning after breakfast he was back on the hill. His parents couldn't understand the sudden strength Moonface had gotten. This went on for about two weeks. Every time he came back from playing with his new friend on the hill, he would come back stronger and happier than when he left.

Then one day he brought the little boy home to meet his parents. The parents were happy because the change in Moonface was because of his new friend. But they found it quite strange that every time they asked him where he lived, he would casually lift his fingers to the heaven and say, "Out there." So the parents thought that that was just some modern-day young people's slang for "Don't ask me my personal business." And so the case was closed.

Then one day Moonface and his friend decided to go into the town. Something Moonface had stopped doing since the day his father's car tires were slashed. Moonface was having a great time showing his friend around the sights. Then all of a sudden, he noticed people were staring at them. He heard a familiar voice say, "He must have the same disease as little Moonface. That's why they are friends." Moonface's heart just sank. Because he had never told his friend that he was sick. And sweat started to form above his lips. His friend noticed the change and asked, "What's the matter?" Moonface looked at him and, with all the honesty in his heart, said, "Once I used to have many friends. You see, I'm going to die. I have an illness that there is no cure for as yet. And I was afraid if I told you ..." And before he could finish saying what he had to say, the little boy put his hand up, smiled and said, "I know you are ill." Then he put his arm around Moonface's shoulder and they kept on walking through the town.

After they strolled in silence for a little while, Moonface asked, "How did you know?"

"Come to the hill tonight around midnight," the little boy said, "and I will tell you."

That night when Moonface got to the top of the hill, there his friend was waiting. His friend took him down the other side of the hill and they headed through a wooded area until they came to a clearing.

Then the little boy looked at Moonface and said, "Remember that night you saw the ball of fire?"

"Yes," Moonface said.

"Well that was my ship. I'm from out there."

"I knew it," Moonface shouted. "I knew it."

"I knew you knew it," said the little boy. And they started to laugh.

"You can't see it, but it's over there, hovering above the clearing."

And all of a sudden the rainbow beam started to shine from the palm of the little boy's hand, and he aimed the beam toward the space above the clearing, and very slowly, very slowly, a ship started to appear, flooded with beautiful blue lights. Then at the top of the ship a huge door began to open, as if it had all the time in the world. And like magic, a silver-green ramp just floated out of the ship and came to rest upon the ground. All by itself.

The little boy stepped onto the ramp and he said, "I must go back to my home now. Come with me." And immediately Moonface started to remember the wonderful times he used to have before people became scared of him. The time he used to swim in the streams, fish with his friends, play tag, or simply pick the corn in the field. Moonface stepped onto the ramp and started to follow his friend. Then his friend stopped and without turning he said, "But you know one thing?"

"What's that?" Moonface asked.

And very slowly his friend turned and looked at him and said, "We will never come back this way again you know. If you come with me, you will never be able to return to earth. Because when I leave this galaxy I cannot return. I came here by accident."

And Moonface just kept walking toward him. It was as if he didn't understand or hear what his friend had said. Then all of a sudden Moonface stopped, and tears began to form in his eyes, and he turned and started to head back down the ramp.

"Come with me," the little boy said. "Where I'm going no one will scorn you. Where I'm going there's a cure for what ails you."

Moonface stopped, turned around and their eyes met. "No. I can't," he said.

"Why?" asked the little boy.

"Because I have to give them a chance."

"But they don't love you because you are sick, different."

"I know," said Moonface. "But one day they will. One day they will come to understand. And they won't be frightened anymore. And I also believe we will find a cure."

And his friend looked at him and smiled and said, "Ah, my little earthling, you do have faith in the human race. I'm glad you are the one I met."

And all of a sudden the ramp started to float up to the sky, and slowly descended to the ship. And just before it disappeared, Moonface shouted out, "Stop!" And the ramp stopped. Moonface ran closer to the ship. The lights powdering his face with a blue tint. "What is your name?" he shouted. "We never exchanged names."

"Where I am from they call me Moonface," said his friend.

"That's my name too!" screamed Moonface with laughter.

"I know," said the little boy.

And the ramp continued down into the ship and the door closed. With a sudden spark the ship just shot up into the sky like a million candles rolled into one. Moonface stood there for the longest while just looking up into the starry darkness. And with a smile on his face he calmly turned and went back to his home.

MOVING DAY

by Helen Porter

I SUPPOSE IT SHOULDN'T have come as such a shock to me really. I mean, all I heard at the University for the whole year was centralization, resettlement, relocation—the professors had a real field day, especially the ones in the Sociology Department. And the newspapers, too, it was a godsend for them. As for the politicians—well. In fact the only people who haven't had too much to say about it are the ones who are really involved in the thing. But anyway, as I said, I shouldn't have been so surprised when I heard that everybody from Grassy Island was going to move to Carlisle. It was Karen who brought it up.

"But why didn't Mom and Dad tell me?" I was talking to myself although Karen was sitting right next to me on the train.

"They probably wanted to surprise you with the good news when you got home." Karen is from Carlisle herself and of course she thinks there's no place like it.

"I can think of more pleasant surprises," I told her, and then I changed the subject. Somehow I didn't want to discuss it with Karen.

When I got home, though, I lost no time in bringing up the matter, I can tell you. They were all on the wharf to meet the boat, all except Mom and Nan, that is. It took the two of them to look after the big Welcome Home Dinner. I couldn't get a word in edgeways going up the hill, what with Cavell and Charlie asking a thousand questions. Dad didn't say much. He never does.

But when we were all sitting around the table, after Mom had hugged me and Nan cried I let go.

"What's all this I hear about leaving Grassy Island, Mom?" It was a long time since I'd had chicken and salt meat on the same plate, but I wasn't as hungry as I'd expected to be. "It's not true, I hope."

You know how they always used to say in old-fashioned books "Her face fell"? Well, that's what happened to Mom's face then. "Yes, it is true, Jenny," she said slowly, "I thought you'd be glad."

Well after that everyone got into the act—Nan telling Mom that "everybody is not in such a rush to get away as you is, Martha," and Cavell and Charlie both saying they didn't know what anyone could see in a place like Carlisle. Even Dad had his say. "It's the women that's doing it," he told me. "If it was left to us men we'd all be content to live out our lives here."

And didn't Mom go for him when he said that—all about the men being away in the lumber woods or on the Labrador when things were really rough on the Island, and how she was sick and tired of not being able to get a doctor when she needed one, and of having her children go to a one-room school under teachers too young or too stupid to get a job anywhere else. Then when Nan said she didn't see how Mom could go away and leave the place where dear little Tommy was buried—well, that was too much even for Mom. Tommy was my little brother, died when he was three years old, pneumonia, I think it was. But Dad took up for Mom then and reminded Nan that if she was the good Christian woman she was supposed to be she'd know it wouldn't matter where the poor little body lay. The next thing I knew I was up in my room bawling my eyes out. It wasn't a bit like the kind of homecoming I'd been looking forward to for months.

I suppose I must have fallen asleep, for the next thing I knew the house was quiet and Mom was standing in the doorway just looking at me. When she saw that I was awake she came in and sat on the bed, not even pushing back the spotless white spread she always ironed so carefully.

"Try to see it my way, Jenny," she pleaded, and it did seem strange to hear Mom plead. She was usually so sure of herself.

"I'm sorry, Mom, I shouldn't have been so upset. But I can't imagine any home except this one, and I don't know how I can live if I don't have this place to come back to."

"To come back to. That's just the point, Jenny." Mom stood up then, and walked over to the window. I couldn't see her face. "I wouldn't mind coming back here for the rest of my life. But it's *living* here, day in, day out, season in, season out, year in, year out, that I can't take any longer. It was bad enough when there were 20 or more families here, but now there's only eight left, and more going all the time. Things'll get worse instead of better." She ran her hand along the shiny-painted window sill. "If you had to settle down here yourself, Jenny, you'd know what I mean."

She did have something there, though I wasn't willing to concede it then. I had never considered settling down on Grassy Island myself, but I'm going to be a teacher, after all, so I'll *have* to go away. And then, when I do marry Ralph, he'll probably still be working in Corner Brook, where he is now, so I'll have to live there. But I had always counted on Grassy Island as being *there* when I needed it. I would never be able to feel the same way about Carlisle.

Well, somehow things got back to normal after that first awful day. It was as if we had all made up our minds, on our own, not to bring the matter up. Everything was finalized, anyhow, so what was the use? Evidently Mom had been one of the instigators of the whole project and this was what was annoying Nan. But Nan didn't have much left to say, except a scattered word under her breath and Mom ignored that.

We had a wonderful summer. Even the weather cooperated, for once, and we spent more time outdoors than in. Between the boats and the berries, the grass, and the gardens, we didn't have an idle minute. It was like we couldn't get enough of it all. But you know, even though Mom didn't say another word to me about moving, except what she had to in the way of preparation, sometimes I couldn't help seeing her side of it. I still couldn't picture myself in Carlisle, but after all, I wouldn't be there very much, and it *would* be better for Mom. I had never really realized before how much she must have hated the isolation of the island all those years. It would probably turn out to be good for Cavell and Charlie, too. As for Dad, well, he seemed closer to being reconciled than he had been at first. One night I even caught him looking at the pictures of modern kitchens in Eaton's catalogue. He always did like carpentry work next best to fishing.

Mom was quieter than I ever remembered her. Sometimes I'd catch her looking at me, as if she was about to say something and then she'd change her mind. She had a lot of work to do of course, and although Cavell and I helped she had her own way of doing things and didn't want to be interfered with too much. One night, when she was taking a batch of bread out of the oven of the old coal stove, Dad laughed and said to her, " ... I suppose that bread'll taste better when we gets electricity, Martha," and she snapped right back, "Are you trying to tell me I don't make good bread, Peter Mead?" But most of the time she was unusually silent. I figured it was because she had her sights set on Carlisle and was almost afraid to breathe for fear something would go wrong with the plan.

But nothing did, and almost before we could turn around it was moving day. We were all standing on the wharf watching Dad load our gear aboard Uncle Job's boat. Some of it had gone ahead of us, but there were certain things that we wouldn't take until the last day.

Cavell and Charlie were horsing around, threatening to throw each other overboard, and Nan was sitting on an overturned barrel, her ankles tightly crossed, looking almost as if she was enjoying the excitement.

"Where's your mother?" she asked suddenly. "I thought by the way she been dyin' to get out of here that she'd be the first one on board."

"She must have gone back to the house for something. Run up and get her, Jenny, we're almost ready," Dad said, and I was off like a flash.

Mom was just standing in the middle of the kitchen when I got there, and I had the "Hurry up" formed on my lips before I got a good look at her. Even though her back was toward me, the sight of her shoulders was enough to make me swallow the words I was about to say. Quiet though she was, I knew that she was sobbing her heart out.

I slipped out of the house and hurried back to the wharf. I felt I shouldn't hang around. "Mom'll be down in a minute," I told Dad. "She's just—having a last look."

I wondered if I should tell him more but just at that moment his eyes met mine, and I could see there was no need. "I'll go and get her myself, Jenny maid," he said, and our eyes followed him as he ran up the path. Even Nan didn't have a word to say.

LOATHE AT FIRST SIGHT

by Ellen Conford

"YOU ARE DRIPPING on my toes."

"I'm sorry. I was admiring you from afar, and I wanted to admire you from a-near. From afar you looked terrific."

"Oh, thanks a lot. Meaning, up close I look like a toad."

"That's not what I meant at all! You look good up close, too. I love your bathing suit."

"Then why do you keep staring at my toes?"

"It's that stuff you've got on them. What do you call that?"

"Nail polish."

"I know, I know. I meant, what colour is it?"

"Rosy Dawn. Look, what is this with my toes?"

"Rosy Dawn. That's kind of romantic. I would have thought it was just pink."

"Will you stop talking about my toes? What are you, weird or something?"

"No! Oh, boy, this whole conversation has gotten off on the wrong foot. Wrong foot—ha! Get it? Foot, toes?"

"Ha ha."

"Just a little humour to lighten up a tense situation. I thought you'd appreciate a good joke."

"I do appreciate a *good* joke."

"I just thought it was too early in our relationship to make personal comments about how great you look in a bathing suit."

"Our relationship? *What* relationship?"

"The one we're going to have."

"Oh really? Have you always been this unsure of yourself?"

"Have you always been this sarcastic? Look, I just wanted—"

"And besides, toes are personal. Personal comments about toes are just as—as personal as comments about how I look in a bathing suit."

"Well, all right, do you want me to tell you how I think you look in your bathing suit?"

"No. I'm really not interested in your opinion of how I look in my bathing suit."

"Okay, then. How do I look in mine?"

"Wet."

"Picture me dry."

"Please. I already had a nightmare last night."

"That's not very nice."

"Look, I'm sorry, but you just walk up to me, drip on my feet, and start raving about my toes and have the gall to make this incredible assumption that I'm going to be so devastated by your wit and charm—"

"And my good looks."

"—and your *modesty*, that I'll fall madly in love with you."

"Well, actually, I didn't expect you to fall madly in love with me in the first five minutes of our relationship."

"See, that's just what I mean! We don't have a relationship."

"I'm working on it. How'm I doing so far? Say, on a scale of one to ten."

"Minus three. Look, would you please move? You're standing in front of the sun and I'm going to have a big white stripe right in the middle of my back."

"Okay."

"I didn't mean for you to sit down. I meant for you to go away."

"But you didn't get a good look at me yet. All you could see when I was standing up was my knees. They're not necessarily my best feature. This way, you can look straight at me."

"Goody."

"Now, come on. I'm really pretty nice-looking."

"You're really pretty conceited."

"I'm just repeating what other people have told me. Some people think I look a lot like Burt Reynolds."

"Some people think the earth is flat."

"I'm getting this definite impression that you're not being dazzled by my wit and charm."

"How very observant of you."

"That's the first nice thing you've said to me."

"I was being sarcastic."

"I know, but I'm grasping at straws. I thought for sure if the wit and charm didn't work, I could always fall back on my good looks."

"You can fall back on your head, for all I care."

"This isn't going exactly as I planned it. Could we start all over again? Hi, there, my name's Alan. What's yours?"

"Hepzibah."

"... Hepzibah?... I see. And what do your friends call you?"

"Hepzibah."

"Uh, I don't want to insult you or anything, just in case your name really is Hepzibah, but I have this funny suspicion you're putting me on."

"Flurge."

"I beg your pardon."

"My last name. Flurge."

"*Hepzibah Flurge?*"

"Right."

"You're going to burst out laughing any minute, I can tell. Come on, look me straight in the eye and tell me your name is Hepzibah Flurge."

"My name is Hep—Hep—"

"I knew it! You can't even keep a straight face. You can't even say it.... You know, you have beautiful eyes. What colour are they exactly?"

"Brown."

"I know, but there are little specks of something in them that—"

"Probably sand."

"Now, come on, don't go all cold and sarcastic on me again. We were doing so well a minute ago."

"I hadn't noticed."

"Sure, you were laughing and everything. Really sort of loosening up, know what I mean? You were right here; you wouldn't have missed it. What's your name, really?"

"Anne."

"There, that's better. Mine's Alan."

"You told me."

"I know, but I'm running out of ideas. I did all my best stuff already."

"That was your best stuff? You're in trouble."

"Well, help me out. What kind of a person are you to leave me floundering around for something to say like this? I mean, this is really embarrassing. The least you could do is hold up your end of the discussion."

"I didn't start this ridiculous conversation—if you can even call it a conversation. I don't see why I have to take any responsibility for keeping it up."

"What kind of an attitude is that? What if everybody felt that way? What kind of a world would this be?"

"Quiet."

"Boring."

"Peaceful."

"Not necessarily. If nobody communicated with anybody else there'd be wars all the time."

"There *are* wars all the time."

"… Uh, yeah. Well. Good point. Would you—um—like me to rub some suntan oil on your shoulders?"

"No, thank you."

"Would you like to rub some on mine?"

"Not particularly."

"Look, Anne, I'm getting desperate here. Where did I go wrong? Did I come on too strong?"

"Yes."

"A little heavy on the wit and charm?"

"Hey, I like wit and charm as much as the next person, but—"

"I overdid it."

"Yes."

"It was the toes, wasn't it? I really turned you off with that stuff about your toes."

"Yes."

"It was just what you call a conversational gambit. You know, an ice-breaker. I mean, not that I don't think your toes are extremely attractive—"

"*Alan*—"

"All right, all right, I swear I'll never mention your toes again. From this minute on, as far as I'm concerned, your toes don't exist. It's just— well, what *should* I have said?"

"What's wrong with hello?"

"Hello? Just hello? But what about after that? What happens after I say hello?"

"Who knows? If you don't try it you'll never find out."

"All right. Here goes. But I don't think this is going to work.... Hello, Anne."

"Hello, Alan. How's the water?"

"Uh, it's very cold when you first go in, but it warms up after a while."

"A lot of things are like that, don't you think so, Alan?"

"I … I think I see what you mean."

"I felt certain you would …"

DOING SOMETHING

by R. P. MacIntyre

IT'S ONE OF THOSE beautiful days. If it was music, it couldn't be metal or rap, it'd be a great ballad with slow clean guitar riffs. The sky is blue, the trees are green, and the lake is calm as glass. It's so perfect and beautiful it makes your eyes hurt. It's the perfect day for doing something. The question is, what?

"I don't care what you do," Dad says, getting into the car, "just don't touch the boat."

"But ..."

"Don't even *think* about it," says Dad.

"And be careful," says Mom. The car rumbles off.

Mom always says that to me, ever since last summer when I broke my knee in Jansen's back yard. This is when I took up guitar. Something to do while I was hobbling around in a cast. The knee's fine now, but every now and then when I'm walking and when I least expect it, it does a vanishing act, just pretends that it's not there, and I wind up on my face. It's embarrassing sometimes but no big deal.

Anyway, everybody else is doing something. Dad and Mom have gone golfing. My sister, Karen, and her friends are practising to be movie stars (good luck). My bud, Snake, has gone north fishing with his Uncle Jack. My other bud, Jodie, is back in town going to his orthodontist. And I'm stuck here alone. With nothing to do. I can't even play guitar. It's at the shop getting fixed. Broken neck.

When I say my sister is practising to be a movie star, I'm not kidding. She and all her other 16-year-old friends have all gone gaga over these two dudes who pulled into the Stones Throw Restaurant and Motel in a black van with Sunrise Films Inc. written on it. I follow them.

They have sort of long hair and sunglasses. One of them needs a shave. They immediately started wandering around for "locations," places where the scenery is best and that sort of thing. That's what they tell me. I tell them that around here that shouldn't be a problem because most of the scenery is like out of a movie anyway, except for the dump and Jansen's back yard.

The other thing they do is put a notice up on the board outside the Stones Throw Restaurant. It says,

EXTRAS NEEDED
For Television Commercial
Ten females, ages sixteen to twenty.
One male, sixteen to twenty.
Apply in person for audition, Room 16, Stones Throw Motel
10 A.M. to 2 P.M. Tuesday, July 8.
Sunrise Films Inc.

And now everybody wants to be a movie star. Except me. I won't be 15 till next month.

The two guys disappear into the motel and I wander down to the lakeshore just to see if anything's happening and to kind of look at the boat that's been declared out of bounds while Dad's not around. It's not exactly built for speed, but it goes all right with the 90 horse Merc flat out. I mean, at least it makes waves, and does a pretty good job towing skiers. But not today. There's nobody to ski with anyway. What a waste.

All that's around is a couple of little kids playing in the sand. They don't even look up, they're so into building a sandcastle. I almost want to join them. I find a good flat skipper and see how many times I can bounce it on the water. I throw. It hits. Perfect. Fourteen skips! It's got to be a record!

Big deal. There's nobody here to see it. The little kids didn't even notice. I could jump in the lake and drown and nobody would notice.

I cut through the woods to get up to the road, thinking that I might as well go to the Stones Throw. Maybe something is happening there. It's the only place to hang out if you're not at the lake itself.

In the motel parking lot sits the black van with Sunrise Films Inc. on it. As I enter the restaurant, a woman with the clipboard smiles at me on her way out. I try to smile back but she is gone before I get a chance. So I'm actually all the way in the <u>restaurant</u> before I notice what I'm in the middle of.

Girls.

There's more girls here than I knew existed, I mean at the lake. I want to say they're every different size and shape, but they're not. They're all the same. The smell of hair spray just about knocks me out. I feel like I'm in the middle of a rock video without the band. All these girls, and every one of them wants to be a movie star. There's two or three guys here too. I guess they're <u>auditioning</u> for the 16-year-old-guy part. The girls are looking at me, like, what am I doing here? I've got to get out.

I turn to leave, I take a step, but … my knee isn't there!

So I'm laying on the floor. I open my eyes and above me I see a blurry circle of tanned wanna-be-movie-star faces. They're staring at me like I was a car accident, when one of them leans out and says, "Oh, it's Kenny! Are you okay?" It's one of my sister's friends.

"I'm fine," I say, "I'm fine," but on the way down to the floor I guess I banged my head against the counter and I can feel the egg growing. The truth is I'm woozy as heck.

But Karen's friend is helping me to my feet saying, "Your sister's over there. I'll help you." And she does. She half hauls me across the restaurant full of wanna-be-movie-stars to where Karen is sitting with somebody in a booth.

Karen is not wearing her glasses, so she doesn't know it's me—yet. Karen is one of those people who <u>would</u> prefer to squint and be blind than wear her glasses and see.

When she finally <u>recognizes</u> that it is me, she is not pleased. I know what she's thinking. She's thinking I did this all on purpose, just to get some attention, just to wreck her day, her chance to be a movie star. She is giving me one of her Kenny-can't-you-ever-do-anything-right looks.

I sit down next to her, holding the lump on my head with my right hand. I look across the table.

And there she is, the girl of my—okay, I'm not going to say dreams, because not only is it such a cliché, but I've never seen anyone like this before, not even in my—dreams. For all future dreams, this is the face in place. Anyway, the sound you hear is probably my jaw hitting the table.

"What happened?" asks Karen.

I pick up my jaw. "Nothing. I fell." My voice doesn't even crack. Victory! A small one, I admit. I wipe the drool from my chin.

In the middle of all these wanna-be-movie-stars is a face that could actually be one. A Vision. Her angled features cut the air like drum beats cased in black hair. Her lips are like full long notes on a slide guitar. Her eyes—I can't see her eyes. She's wearing shades.

"Who is this?" asks the perfect Vision across the table.

"Oh," says Karen. "This is my brother Kenny. He's always falling."

"Yeah," I agree like an idiot. "Or slipping. I slip a lot too." Something I'm doing right now.

"Oh, I'm Cynthia," says Cynthia the Vision. "How are you?"

She presents her perfect hand across the table. She wants me to shake it. I can't believe this. *None* of Karen's friends ever want to talk to me much less touch me, willingly, with their hands. If I were a puppy dog, I'd be peeing on the floor right about now. But I'm not and I don't. Instead, I reach for her hand as calmly as I can. I grasp it, gently, trying not to sweat. Her hand is warm and dry. Golden brown. The back of it feels like butterfly wings.

"Fine," I say, but something is wrong. Something is uncomfortable about this handshake.

"Oh," she says, "the hand of a musician."

Well if I wasn't already a bowl of jelly, I'm right now a pool of goo.

"How did you know?" the goo manages to ask.

"The calluses on your fingers."

I've given her my *left* hand, the wrong hand! The one with leather-tipped fingers from playing guitar. That's what's wrong with this handshake! My *right* hand is still propping up my stupid head.

"Oh, yeah," I say, recovering my hand from her, "I play guitar. But it's broken."

"Is it two yet?" asks Karen.

X Cynthia, hardly looking toward her watch, sort of brushes it with her long fingers. "Five to," she says.

"I've got to go," says Karen. "My audition. How do I look?"

"Fine, I hope," says Cynthia.

Explain "Yeah, why am I asking you?" says Karen. I take this to mean that Karen is admitting she doesn't have much hope in front of the most beautiful girl in the world. "Wish me luck," she adds.

We do. She's going to need all the luck she can get. Squeezing by me, and squinting to see which way the door is, Karen leaves. Me alone. With my tongue in knots. I try not to ogle at Cynthia.

A fly lands on the table in front of us. Something to focus on. It strolls over to a grain of sugar and starts doing something. An hour passes. Maybe two. I've got to untangle my tongue, so I ask a question.

"What do flies do anyway?" I ask as casually as I can.

"I beg your pardon?"

"Oh nothing," I say. I realize that this might be the stupidest question ever asked on the planet earth.

Another hour passes. The fly buzzes off.

"It's a beautiful day," says Cynthia the Vision.

"Yeah, yeah, it's beautiful." I couldn't agree more.

"We should be doing something," says Cynthia the Mind Reader. "I mean on a beautiful day like today."

"Exactly what I was thinking!" I say, practically jumping off the seat.

"Any ideas?" she asks.

"Ideas. I've got tons of ideas," I lie. Now I've got to name one. "Like we could go for a walk or something."

"I don't think so," says Cynthia. Her lips go into a kind of curious pout.

I've got to come up with something big, or I'm going to lose her before she realizes I'm here.

partial truth

"How about a boat ride? In my boat."

"You have a boat?"

"Well it's not actually mine. It's my dad's. He sort of left me in charge." He did leave me in charge, in charge of not touching it.

"Are you sure you'd like to take me?"

"Sure? Of course I'm sure!" She doesn't know how sure. I'll be grounded for a week, but who cares. This is the chance of a lifetime. A beautiful girl and me, alone, on the boat. If we just happen to run out of gas on the middle of the lake …

"Well if you're sure, let's go then."

"Great!" I say, a little too loud. I look around at all the wanna-be-movie-stars. A thought occurs to me.

"But what time is your audition?"

"What audition?" asks Maid Cynthia.

The one that everybody's going to, that Karen went to."

"I'm not going," says Cynthia.

"No? Why not?"

"I'm blind, Ken, in case you haven't noticed."

I haven't noticed. I haven't noticed anything. She's just been sitting there. For all I know, she doesn't have any legs. I find myself wanting to look underneath the table, to check. I restrain myself. I panic instead. If I had an expression on my face, it's probably one with lots of teeth, a broken smile I'm trying to fix.

"You're blind?"

"I'm blind," says the Vision.

"Oh," I say, seeing now the reason for her sunglasses, the way she touched my hand and how she told Karen the time. "Oh," I repeat, wondering at it all.

"Do you still want to go?" she asks.

This is a tough question. I mean 10 seconds ago I was drooling at the possibility. Now, all of a sudden, my feet are freeze-dried. So is my brain. What is the matter with me? I mean, big deal, so she's blind. Which means she doesn't realize I'm really a 14-year-old geek whose panting she can probably hear. Which also really means all she wants

What clues were given that Cynthia was blind? ✗

to do is go for a boat ride. If I say yes, she'll think I'm being nice. If I say no, she'll think I'm prejudiced.

"Of course I want to go," I hear my nice self say. But as the words leave my lips, I realize I'm not so sure.

We're out on the middle of the lake, boogying along flat out in Dad's boat. Cynthia is grinning from ear to beautiful ear. Her dark hair is blowing in the wind. And she's *hanging on to my arm* as I drive. I'm feeling happy and sad at the same time.

On the beach, I can see that they've set up the commercial shoot. There's a camera and some guys holding big reflector things trying to catch the sun. There's also a crowd of girls. I wonder if Karen is among them. They're too far away to make out their faces. I decide to get closer. We can watch from the water—I can watch from the water—I'll describe it to Cynthia. This is my plan.

But Cynthia has other ideas.

"Have you got water skis?" she asks.

"What?" I mean I heard her, I just don't believe the question. I throttle the boat down.

"Water skis, you know, for skiing on the water."

"That's what I thought you said," I say. "Yeah. We have water skis."

"Do you mind if I go?"

"Water skiing?"

"Yes, water skiing. Would it be all right?" asks the Beautiful Blind Cynthia.

No. No, of course it wouldn't be all right! What's a blind person going to do water skiing? She'll fall down, fall in the water and drown, and I will be responsible. I'll be responsible for taking out the boat without permission from my dad and causing a blind person, a beautiful blind person, to drown in the lake. No, absolutely not. No water skiing.

"Please?" she asks, reading my mind. She tightens her grip on my arm.

"What happens if you fall in the water?" I ask.

"I can swim," says Cynthia. "I can probably swim better than you."

This is true. I'm lousy at it. But that's not the point.

"How will you know which direction to swim in?" I ask. "I mean, you might swim out into the middle of the lake, and then what?" I think I got her.

"I assume you'll make some sort of noise, Ken. I may be blind, but I'm not deaf."

I look into her sunglasses and see my reflection, a skinny, pointy-nosed geek with a bump on his head. "Sure," I say, "Why not." Line up the firing squad. Shoot me now.

Ten minutes later, we're ready to go. Cynthia's in the water, holding onto the tow rope, skis pointed skyward. I know what's going to happen. I'll ease the throttle up, and she'll collapse. This'll go on for three or four tries, then, that's it. She'll quit. And I'll be able to get the boat back, say goodbye, refill the gas tank, and pray that Karen doesn't find out and tell Dad. I'm sure this is what's going to happen.

Not thinking about what I'm doing, I ease the throttle up at normal pace, like I've done a hundred times before. I look back and realize a terrible thing! I don't have a spotter, someone to check and make sure things are all right! And just as this thought is going through my mind, Cynthia rises out of the water and onto the skis, the first time! It took me 10 tries to get up the first time. How can this blind person do it? She's incredible!

So now I'm trying to spot and drive the boat at the same time. Anybody who has ever done this knows that it is not only really dangerous, it is really stupid. But the truth is, Cynthia looks great. She's a natural and she is grinning like there's no tomorrow. Maybe there isn't. Because when I look toward where I'm heading with the boat, I see the beach full of wanna-be-stars, the camera guys, the two dudes with sunglasses, all looming up in front of me. *I've got to turn, fast!*

This I know is going to dump Cynthia in the worst possible place, i.e., in front of everybody on the beach. So be it. Life has to end sometime. I turn.

What happens next is this: Cynthia feels the direction change on the tow rope. She leans into the turn and cuts a spray two metres high, and whip-cracks across the wake like a pro. I can't believe it. She doesn't go down. But it's enough for me. I head back to the dock a shaken man, well, *boy.*

"Wow, you're really good," I say as I'm putting stuff away.

"I know," she says. "I've been skiing since I was five."

"You didn't tell me that."

"You didn't ask. It's something I can do that's safe for me. I love it," says Cynthia, shaking her black hair. "Do I look okay?"

"You look fine," I say. She really does.

"My dad's meeting me at the Stones Throw. Would you walk me back?"

"Sure." The truth is I'll do anything for her, walk on hot coals, jump through fire, face the wrath of my dad....

When we get there, Cynthia's father is waiting. He seems like a pretty good guy, for a father, and before I know it, she's in his car saying goodbye. I'm half-surprised that she's not driving.

"Will I see you again?" I ask, leaning into the car window.

"I hope so. I should be back in a week or two. You've been really sweet," she says and draws my head toward her and kisses me on the cheek. "Bye," she says. I bump my head taking it out of the car window and stand there dazed as the blue car drives off.

Blue. And a vague bit of black exhaust. Usually I can tell you the make, model, and year. But not today. All I notice is that the car is blue, driving away with Cynthia.

I make it home and I'm calmly sweating, waiting to see if Dad's going to find out I took the boat today. He's out in the back, barbecuing steaks. Mom's getting a salad together. The only problem is Karen hasn't arrived.

"What happened to your head?" Mom asks.

"My knee gave out. I banged it."

"I told you to be careful," she says.

"Mom, it just goes whenever it feels like it. Being careful doesn't make any difference," I say. However, I *was* careful putting the boat away, and refilling the gas tank. So far, so good.

"Steaks will be ready in about five," says Dad, entering the cabin wiping his hands on his I'm-the-Cook apron. "So what did you do today?"

"Nothing. I met a girl."

"A *girl*," he says, his eyes opening wide.

"Well he's getting to that age," says Mom.

"What was her name?" asks Dad, always interested in the details.

"Cynthia," I say, realizing with a pang that I didn't even know her last name.

"Cynthia," says Mom. "That's an unusual name these days."

"She's really nice," I say. "Except she's blind."

"Blind?" They harmonize this, like a pair of backup singers. →Explain

"Yeah, you know, as in cannot see."

"That's …" Mom was probably going to say "interesting," but Karen slams through the door like a fullback, changing the direction of the ball game. "What happened to you?" asks Mom.

Karen plumps herself down on the big wicker chair, practically knocking the stuffing out of the cushion, adjusts her glasses, and makes a sound like a whinnying horse. She knows how to get your attention. Karen's neat that way.

"I spend all day getting ready for this stupid audition. I go for the audition, I get chosen to be one of the girls on the beach. I rehearse this stupid scene where we have to run up and down the beach about a million times and I can't see anything because I'm not wearing my glasses, so I keep bumping into people and missing the place where we're supposed to stop."

Karen says all this in one breath. She gulps air and continues.

"So finally I'm embarrassed to death because the director takes me aside and explains things to me like I'm stupid, which maybe I am, because now we're doing takes with the camera rolling and I'm still screwing up."

Here she stops again, but this time it's more for emphasis.

"And finally after about 14 takes, when I'm finally getting it right, some jerk comes roaring by in his boat with a water skier!" And she looks right at me.

"It wasn't me," I say.

"I know it wasn't you. You were with Cynthia," she says, then adds for Mom and Dad's sake, "She's blind."

"We heard," says Mom.

Yes! Yes! I was with Cynthia, and everybody knows that blind people can't ski. The perfect alibi! Thank you, Karen my beautiful sister. Thank you for not wearing your glasses. I want to kiss her, but I don't. That would be acting suspicious.

"Anyway," Karen continues. "The jerk goes by with the water skier, and the director and camera person and all the people who are in charge stop everything and have this huddle on the beach like this was a *football* game or something."

Karen hates football.

"Then they break up and tell us all thank you very much but we can go home." Karen is rolling her eyes in disbelief.

"That's it?" asks Dad.

"Yeah! That's it! Except we have to go back to the motel, get our stuff, then wait around for an hour and a half to sign these papers for some release or something. What a wasted day."

Wasted for Karen maybe, but I'm off the hook. I had a great day.

Everybody has sympathized with Karen and is now in the middle of trying to cut into Dad's burnt steak when a black van pulls into the yard. It's got Sunrise Films Inc. written on the side. Two people climb out. It's them, with the sunglasses and long hair. One of them still needs a shave. He has a videocassette in his hand. We're all wondering what's going on, especially me.

Dad answers the door.

"Is there a Kenny Martin living here?" asks Needs-a-Shave.

"Yes," says Dad. "He's right here."

Suddenly, I'm front and centre, chewing on a particularly tough piece of steak.

"We were shooting some footage for a commercial today and we just happened to get something that we're told you had a lot to do with." The steak is growing in my mouth. It is doubling in size and very dry.

"It's a shot of you on a boat and you're pulling a skier," says Doesn't-Need-a-Shave. I just about choke. Mom, Dad, and Karen all stop, mid-chew. They look at me.

"We'd like to use it," says Needs-a-Shave, waving the cassette. "If we can get your permission."

"Can we see it?" asks Dad, all innocently. "I'm sure we'd all like to see it first."

"Surely," says Needs-a-Shave.

A few seconds later, there, on our TV, in livid colour, is me. There's no mistake about it. I'm wild-eyed, I crank the steering wheel. The camera pulls back, and there is Cynthia, shooting up a two-metre spray. She is smiling.

It really is a great shot, but I'm dead meat.

To make a long story short, I make some money being in a commercial but can't really spend it because I've been grounded for a month. Grounding means no boat, a two-kilometre fence, and a nine o'clock curfew. It's really not that bad, no worse than last summer when I broke my knee, and especially now that I've got my guitar back. The only thing is, I can't turn up my amp.

So I spend a lot of time hanging out at the beach, when it's not raining, or at the Stones Throw with my buds, Snake and Jodie. Except they seem like such kids now. I mean they don't understand how I feel when I go there. All I can think of when I'm in the Stones Throw is Cynthia. It's like the place is haunted by her. Every time I walk in, I see her and it turns out to be someone else. Every time someone enters, I look up, hoping it's her. It's got to the point I don't want to go anymore, but don't dare not because it's the only place I'm likely to see her again. She said two weeks. About two weeks, and two weeks are up.

Lovestruck

Mom and Dad are getting concerned. "How come you're not eating?" they ask. I don't know. I'm just not hungry. "Go do something with Jodie and Snake," they say. But Jodie and Snake are fed up with me, which is fine because I'm fed up with them too. I don't even feel like playing guitar.

I'm practically living at the Stones Throw now. I've started going alone and drinking coffee, with lots of milk and sugar. It lasts longer than coke and you can drink more because they give you refills, so you can spend more time there without getting kicked out. The waitresses look at me funny. It's two days over two weeks.

On the third day after two weeks, I'm at the beach skipping stones. It's a beautiful day. I hate beautiful days. The same two kids are on the beach building another sandcastle. For some reason they're really noisy about it. They're having a ball. I want to tell them to shut up, that they've got no business having fun. They're just trying to bug me. I get half an urge to wring their scrawny necks. I see the headline, CRAZED YOUTH STRANGLES NOISY KIDS. I go up to the road instead.

A blue car passes, billowing black smoke. My heart leaps. Even though it's a cliché, my heart leaps when any blue car passes. My heart doesn't recognize clichés. It recognizes blue cars. This one pulls into the Stones Throw, a football field away. The black smoke settles. A man gets out. He crosses to the passenger side and opens the door. She gets out. It's Cynthia!

About 20 seconds later, I'm there. I would have been quicker but my knee gave out. My palms are scraped, my jeans are torn, and I'm covered in dust. But I don't care. Cynthia's here.

She's sitting at a table with her father. She's beautiful. She's even more beautiful than I remember. It's a funny thing about memory. It doesn't work the way you expect it to. I push back my hair and approach. "Hi," I say.

"Hello?" she says with a question mark, looking up. I know she can't see me.

"It's Ken," I say. Maybe she can't remember who I am. Maybe she couldn't remember who I was even if she could see me.

"Oh hi, how are you," she says, holding out her hand. "Dad, remember Ken. He took me water skiing. He's the one in the commercial."

"Yes, of course I remember. How are you, Ken?" He holds out his hand too. I take it. I'm standing there holding hands with two different people. I suppose I should shake them and let go. I do. "Would you care to join us?" asks Cynthia's father.

"Sure," I say. Is he kidding?

"In fact," he adds getting up, "why don't you join Cynthia while I go get the carburetor looked at? Let me know if you decide to do something."

"Okay Dad," says Cynthia.

He leaves and my mouth is full of swollen tongue. Or maybe it's heart. I swallow to try to get things back in place. But Cynthia speaks first.

"I've thought about you lots," she says.

"Me too," I say. "About you."

"That was fun we had, water skiing."

"Yeah, it was fun."

And here there's a pause where we try to figure out what to say next. I want to say I'm wildly and passionately in love with her, but I don't. Instead I finger-paint with some sugar that's spilled on the table.

"What are you doing?" she asks.

"I'm playing with some sugar."

She puts her hand on the table and sort of reaches across toward me. "Can I play too?"

"Sure," I pour sugar from the container, making a little cone on the back of her hand.

"It feels cool," she says.

I smooth the sugar out, spreading it evenly over the golden brown of her skin, part way up her wrist.

"That feels nice," she says.

I wet my finger with my tongue and touch the sugar, then put it back to my tongue. I do this fairly slowly, on different places, making little clear spots of skin surrounded by sugar.

"What are you doing now?"

"Making little islands of skin," I say. "Butterfly wings."

Cynthia smiles.

a) What did I like best?

b) What was your favourite part?

THE JADE PEONY

by Wayson Choy

WHEN GRANDMAMA DIED at 83 our whole household held its breath. She had promised us a sign of her leaving, final proof that her present life had ended well. My parents knew that without any clear sign, our own family fortunes could be altered, threatened. My stepmother looked endlessly into the small cluttered room the ancient lady had occupied. Nothing was touched; nothing changed. My father, thinking that a sign should appear in Grandmama's garden, looked at the frost-killed shoots and cringed: *no, that could not be it.*

My two older teenage brothers and my sister, Liang, age 14, were embarrassed by my parents' behaviour. What would all the white people in Vancouver think of us? We were Canadians now, *Chinese-Canadians,* a hyphenated reality that my parents could never accept. So it seemed, for different reasons, we all held our breath waiting for *something.*

I was eight when she died. For days she had resisted going into the hospital … *a cold, just a cold* … and instead gave constant instruction to my stepmother and sister on the boiling of ginseng roots mixed with bitter extract. At night, between wracking coughs and deadly silences, Grandmama had her back and chest rubbed with heated camphor oil and sipped a bluish decoction of an herb called Peacock's Tail. When all these failed to abate her fever, she began to arrange the details of her will. This she did with my father, confessing finally: "I am too stubborn. The only cure for old age is to die."

My father wept to hear this. I stood beside her bed; she turned to me. Her round face looked darker, and the gentleness of her eyes, the thin, arching eyebrows, seemed weary. I brushed the few strands of grey, brittle hair from her face; she managed to smile at me. Being the youngest, I had spent nearly all my time with her and could not imagine that we would ever be parted. Yet when she spoke, and her voice hesitated, cracked, the sombre shadows of her room chilled me.

Her wrinkled brow grew wet with fever, and her small body seemed even more diminutive.

"I—I am going to the hospital, Grandson." Her hand reached out for mine. "You know, Little Son, whatever happens I will never leave you." Her palm felt plush and warm, the slender, old fingers boney and firm, so magically strong was her grip that I could not imagine how she could ever part from me. Ever.

Her hands *were* magical. My most vivid memories are of her hands: long, elegant fingers, with impeccable nails, a skein of fine, barely seen veins, and wrinkled skin like light pine. Those hands were quick when she taught me, at six, simple tricks of juggling, learnt when she was a village girl in Southern Canton; a troupe of actors had stayed on her father's farm. One of them, "tall and pale as the whiteness of petals," fell in love with her, promising to return. In her last years his image came back like a third being in our two lives. He had been a magician, acrobat, juggler, and some of the things he taught her she had absorbed and passed on to me through her stories and games. But above all, without realizing it then, her hands conveyed to me the quality of their love.

Most marvellous for me was the quick-witted skill her hands revealed in making wind chimes for our birthdays: wind chimes in the likeness of her lost friend's only present to her, made of bits of string and scraps, in the centre of which once hung a precious jade peony. This wondrous gift to her broke apart years ago, in China, but Grandmama kept the jade pendant in a tiny red silk envelope, and kept it always in her pocket, until her death.

These were not ordinary, carelessly made chimes, such as those you now find in our Chinatown stores, whose rattling noises drive you mad. But making her special ones caused dissension in our family, and some shame. Each one that she made was created from a treasure trove of glass fragments and castaway costume jewellery, in the same way that her first wind chime had been made. The problem for the rest of the family was in the fact that Grandmama looked for these treasures wandering the back alleys of Keefer and Pender Streets, peering into our neighbours' garbage cans, chasing away hungry, nervous cats and shouting curses at them.

"All our friends are laughing at us!" Older Brother Jung said at last to my father, when Grandmama was away having tea at Mrs. Lim's.

"We are not poor," Oldest Brother Kiam declared, "yet she and Sek-Lung poke through those awful things as if—" he shoved me in frustration and I stumbled against my sister, "—they were beggars!"

"She will make Little Brother crazy!" Sister Liang said. Without warning, she punched me sharply in the back; I jumped. "You see, look how *nervous* he is!"

I lifted my foot slightly, enough to swing it back and kick Liang in the shin. She yelled and pulled back her fist to punch me again. Jung made a menacing move toward me.

"Stop this, all of you!" My father shook his head in exasperation. How could he dare tell the Grand Old One, his aging mother, that what was somehow appropriate in a poor village in China, was an abomination here? How could he prevent me, his youngest, from accompanying her? If she went walking into those alleyways alone she could well be attacked by hoodlums. "She is not a beggar looking for food. She is searching for—for …"

My stepmother attempted to speak, then fell silent. She, too, seemed perplexed and somewhat ashamed. They all loved Grandmama, but she was *inconvenient*, unsettling.

As for our neighbours, most understood Grandmama to be harmlessly crazy, others that she did indeed make lovely toys but for what purpose? *Why?* they asked, and the stories she told me, of the juggler who smiled at her, flashed in my head.

Finally, by their cutting remarks, the family did exert enough pressure so that Grandmama and I no longer openly announced our expeditions. Instead, she took me with her on "shopping trips," ostensibly for clothes or groceries, while in fact we spent most of our time exploring stranger and more distant neighbourhoods, searching for splendid junk: jangling pieces of a vase, cranberry glass fragments embossed with leaves, discarded glass beads from Woolworth necklaces.... We would sneak them all home in brown rice sacks, folded into small parcels, and put them under her bed. During the day when the family was away at school or work, we brought them out and washed every item in a large black pot of boiling lye and water, dried them quickly, carefully, and returned them, sparkling, under her bed.

Our greatest excitement occurred when a fire gutted the large Chinese Presbyterian Church, three blocks from our house. Over the still-smoking ruins the next day, Grandmama and I rushed precariously over the blackened beams to pick out the stained glass that glittered in the sunlight. Small figure bent over, wrapped against the autumn cold in a dark blue quilted coat, happily gathering each piece like gold, she became my spiritual playmate: "There's a good one! *There!*"

Hours later, soot-covered and smelling of smoke, we came home with a carton full of delicate fragments, still early enough to steal them all into the house and put the small box under her bed. "These are special pieces," she said, giving the box a last push, "because they come from a sacred place." She slowly got up and I saw, for the first time, her hand begin to shake. But then, in her joy, she embraced me. Both of our hearts were racing, as if we were two dreamers. I buried my face in her blue quilt, and for a moment, the whole world seemed silent.

"My juggler," she said, "he never came back to me from Honan ... perhaps the famine ..." Her voice began to quake. "But I shall have my sacred wind chime ... I shall have it again."

One evening, when the family was gathered in their usual places in the parlour, Grandmama gave me her secret nod: a slight wink of her eye and a flaring of her nostrils. There was *trouble* in the air. Supper had gone badly, school examinations were due. Father had failed to meet an editorial deadline at the *Vancouver Chinese Times*. A huge sigh came from Sister Liang.

"But it is useless this Chinese they teach you!" she lamented, turning to Stepmother for support. Silence. Liang frowned, dejected, and went back to her Chinese book, bending the covers back.

"Father," Oldest Brother Kiam began, waving his bamboo brush in the air, "you must realize that this Mandarin only confuses us. We are Cantonese speakers...."

"And you do not complain about Latin, French, or German in your English school?" Father rattled his newspaper, a signal that his patience was ending.

"But, Father, those languages are *scientific.*" Kiam jabbed his brush in the air. "We are now in a scientific, logical world."

Father was silent. We could all hear Grandmama's rocker.

"What about Sek-Lung?" Older Brother Jung pointed angrily at me. "He was sick last year, but this year he should have at least started Chinese school, instead of picking over garbage cans!"

"He starts next year," Father said, in a hard tone that immediately warned everyone to be silent. Liang slammed her book.

Grandmama went on rocking quietly in her chair. She complimented my mother on her knitting, made a remark about the "strong beauty" of Kiam's brushstrokes which, in spite of himself, immensely pleased him. All this babbling noise was her family torn and confused in a strange land: everything here was so very foreign and scientific.

The truth was, I was sorry not to have started school the year before. In my innocence I had imagined going to school meant certain privileges worthy of all my brothers' and sister's complaints. The fact that my lung infection in my fifth and sixth years, mistakenly diagnosed as TB, earned me some reprieve, only made me long for school the more. Each member of the family took turns on Sunday, teaching me or annoying me. But it was the countless hours I spent with Grandmama that were my real education. Tapping me on my head she would say, "Come, Sek-Lung, we have *our* work," and we would walk up the stairs to her small crowded room. There, in the midst of her antique shawls, the old ancestral calligraphy and multicoloured embroidered hangings, beneath the mysterious shelves of sweet herbs and bitter potions, we would continue doing what we had started that morning: the elaborate wind chime for her death.

"I can't last forever," she declared, when she let me in on the secret of this one. "It will sing and dance and glitter," her long fingers stretched into the air, pantomiming the waving motion of her ghost chimes: "My spirit will hear its sounds and see its light and return to this house and say goodbye to you."

Deftly she reached into the carton she had placed on the chair beside me. She picked out a fish-shaped amber piece, and with a long needle-like tool and a steel ruler, she scored it. Pressing the blade of a cleaver against the line, with the fingers of her other hand, she lifted up the glass until it cleanly *snapped* into the exact shape she required. Her hand began to tremble, the tips of her fingers to shiver, like rippling water.

"You see that, Little One?" She held her hand up. "That is my body fighting with Death. He is in this room now."

My eyes darted in panic, but Grandmama remained calm, undisturbed, and went on with her work. Then I remembered the glue and uncorked the jar for her. Soon the graceful ritual movements of her hand returned to her, and I became lost in the magic of her task: she dabbed a cabalistic mixture of glue on one end and skillfully dropped the braided end of a silk thread into it. This part always amazed me: the braiding would slowly, *very* slowly, *unknot*, fanning out like a prized fishtail. In a few seconds the clear, homemade glue began to harden as I blew lightly over it, welding to itself each separate silk strand.

Each jam-sized pot of glue was precious: each large cork had been wrapped with a fragment of pink silk. I remember this part vividly, because each cork was treated to a special rite. First we went shopping in the best silk stores in Chinatown for the perfect square of silk she required. It had to be a deep pink, a shade of colour blushing toward red. And the tone had to match—as closely as possible—her precious jade carving, the small peony of white and light-red jade, her most lucky possession. In the centre of this semitranslucent carving, no more than a few centimetres wide, was a pool of pink light, its veins swirling out into the petals of the flower.

"This colour is the colour of my spirit," she said, holding it up to the window so I could see the delicate pastel against the broad strokes of sunlight. She dropped her voice, and I held my breath at the wonder of the colour. "This was given to me by the young actor who taught me how to juggle. He had four of them, and each one had a centre of this rare colour, the colour of Good Fortune." The pendant seemed to pulse as she turned it: "Oh, Sek-Lung! He had white hair and white skin *to his toes! It's true.* I saw him bathing." She laughed and blushed, her eyes softened at the memory. The silk had to match the pink heart of her pendant: the colour was magical for her, to hold the unravelling strands of her memory …

It was just six months before she died that we really began to work on her last wind chime. Three thin bamboo sticks were steamed and bent into circlets: 30 exact lengths of silk thread, the strongest kind, were cut and braided at both ends and glued to stained glass. Her hands worked on their own command, each hand racing with a life of its own: cutting, snapping, braiding, knotting.… Sometimes she breathed heavily and her small body, growing thinner, sagged against me. *Death,* I thought. *He is in this room,* and I would work harder alongside her. For months Grandmama and I did this every other evening, a half dozen pieces each time. The shaking in her hand grew worse, but we said nothing. Finally, after discarding hundreds, she told me she had the necessary 30 pieces. But this time, because it was a sacred chime, I would not be permitted to help her tie it up or have the joy of raising it. "Once tied," she said, holding me against my disappointment, "not even I can raise it. Not a sound must it make until I have died."

"What will happen?"

"Your father will then take the centre braided strand and raise it. He will hang it against my bedroom window so that my ghost may see it, and hear it, and return. I must say goodbye to this world properly or wander in this foreign land forever."

"You can take the streetcar!" I blurted, suddenly shocked that she actually meant to leave me. I thought I could hear the clear chromatic chimes, see the shimmering colours on the wall: I fell against her and cried, and there in my crying I knew that she would die. I can still remember the touch of her hand on my head, and the smell of her thick woollen sweater pressed against my face. "I will always be with you, Little Sek-Lung, but in a different way … you'll see."

Months went by, and nothing happened. Then one late September evening, when I had just come home from Chinese School, Grandmama was preparing supper when she looked out our kitchen window and saw a cat—a long, lean white cat—jump into our garbage pail and knock it over. She ran out to chase it away, shouting curses at it. She did not have her thick sweater on and when she came back into the house, a chill gripped her. She leaned against the door: "That was not a cat," she said, and the odd tone of her voice caused my father to look with alarm at her. "I can not take back my curses. It is too late." She took hold of my father's arm: "It was all white and had pink eyes like sacred fire."

My father started at this, and they both looked pale. My brothers and sister, clearing the table, froze in their gestures.

"The fog has confused you," Stepmother said. "It was just a cat."

But Grandmama shook her head, for she knew it was a sign. "I will not live forever," she said. "I am prepared."

The next morning she was confined to her bed with a severe cold. Sitting by her, playing with some of my toys, I asked her about the cat: "Why did Father jump at the cat with the pink eyes? He didn't see it, you did."

"But he and your mother know what it means."

"What?"

"My friend, the juggler, the magician, was as pale as white jade, and he had pink eyes." I thought she would begin to tell one of her stories, a tale of enchantment or of a wondrous adventure, but she only paused to swallow; her eyes glittered, lost in memory. She took my hand, gently opening and closing her fingers over it. "Sek-Lung," she sighed, "*he* has come back to me."

Then Grandmama sank back into her pillow and the embroidered flowers lifted to frame her wrinkled face. I saw her hand over my own, and my own began to tremble. I fell fitfully asleep by her side. When I woke up it was dark and her bed was empty. She had been taken to the hospital and I was not permitted to visit.

A few days after that she died of the complications of pneumonia. Immediately after her death my father came home and said nothing to us, but walked up the stairs to her room, pulled aside the drawn lace curtains of her window and lifted the wind chimes to the sky.

I began to cry and quickly put my hand in my pocket for a handkerchief. Instead, caught between my fingers, was the small, round firmness of the jade peony. In my mind's eye I saw Grandmama smile and heard, softly, the pink centre beat like a beautiful, cramped heart.

THUNDER AND LIGHTNING

retold by Kathleen Arnott

A LONG TIME AGO, both thunder and lightning lived on this earth, among all the people. Thunder was an old mother sheep and Lightning was her son, a handsome ram, but neither animal was very popular.

When anybody offended the ram, Lightning, he would fly into a furious rage and begin burning down huts and corn bins, and even knock down large trees. Sometimes he damaged crops on the farms with his fire and occasionally he killed people who got in his way.

As soon as his mother, Thunder, knew he was behaving in this evil way, she would raise her voice and shout as loudly as she could, and that was very loud indeed.

Naturally the neighbours were very upset, first at the damage caused by Lightning and then by the unbearable noise that always followed his outbursts. The villagers complained to the king on many occasions, until at last he sent the two of them to live at the very edge of the village, and said that they must not come and mix with people anymore.

However, this did no good, since Lightning could still see people as they walked about the village streets and so found it only too easy to continue picking quarrels with them. At last the king sent for them again.

"I have given you many chances to live a better life," he said, "but I can see that it is useless. From now on, you must go right away from our village and live in the wild bush. We do not want to see your faces here again."

Thunder and Lightning had to obey the king and left the village, angrily cursing its inhabitants.

Alas, there was still plenty of trouble in store for the villagers, since Lightning was so angry at being banished that he now set fire to the whole bush, and during the dry season this was extremely unfortunate. The flames spread to the little farms which the people had planted, and sometimes to their houses as well, so that they were in despair again. They often heard the mother sheep's mighty voice calling her son to order, but it made very little difference to his evil actions.

The king called all his councillors together and asked them to advise him, and at last they hit on a plan. One white-headed elder said:

"Why don't we banish Thunder and Lightning right away from the earth? Wherever they live there will be trouble, but if we send them up into the sky, we should be rid of them."

So Thunder and Lightning were sent away into the sky, where the people hoped they would not be able to do any more damage.

Things did not work out quite as well as they had hoped, however, for Lightning still loses his temper from time to time and cannot resist sending fire down to the earth when he is angry. Then you can hear his mother rebuking him in her loud rumbling voice.

Occasionally even his mother cannot bear to stay with him and goes away for a little while. You will know when this happens, for Lightning still flashes his fire on the earth, but his mother is so far away that she does not see, and her voice is silent.

ATHENA

retold by Ingri and Edgar Parin d'Aulaire

ATHENA, THE GODDESS OF WISDOM, was the favourite child of Zeus. She had sprung fully grown out of her father's head.

Her mother was Metis, goddess of prudence, the first wife of Zeus. He depended on her, for he needed her wise counsel, but Mother Earth warned him that, were Metis to bear him a son, this son would dethrone him as Zeus had dethroned Cronus, his father who had dethroned his own father, Uranus. This must not happen, thought Zeus, but he could not do without her advice, so he decided to swallow her. Slyly, he proposed that they play a game of changing shapes, and Metis, forgetting her prudence, playfully turned herself into all kinds of animals, big and small. Just as she had taken on the shape of a little fly, Zeus opened wide his mouth, took a deep breath, and zip! he swallowed the fly. Ever after, Metis sat in his head and guided him from there.

Now it happened that Metis was going to have a daughter, and she sat inside Zeus's head hammering out a helmet and weaving a splendid robe for the coming child. Soon Zeus began to suffer from pounding headaches and cried out in agony. All the gods came running to help him, and skilled Hephaestus grasped his tools and split open his father's skull. Out sprang Athena, wearing the robe and the helmet, her grey eyes flashing. Thunder roared and the gods stood in awe.

Athena's constant companion was Nike, the spirit of victory. With Nike at her side, Athena led armies, but only those that fought for just causes. In time of peace she stood behind the artists of Greece and taught them the fine and useful arts. She had great pride in her own skills at the loom and the potter's wheel, but was happy to see her pupils excel as long as they showed her proper respect.

One of her pupils was Arachne, a simple country girl, who was wonderfully skilled at the loom. People came from far and wide to admire her weavings. Stupidly she boasted that she had learned nothing from Athena; indeed, that she was better than the goddess!

That hurt Athena's pride. Disguised as an old woman, she went to the girl and tried to talk sense into her.

"Your work is beautiful," she said, "but why compare yourself with the gods? Why not be contented to be the best among mortals?"

"Let the goddess Athena herself come and measure her skill against mine," Arachne answered haughtily.

Angrily Athena threw off her disguise and stood before the girl in all her glory.

"Vain girl," she said, "you may have your wish. Sit down at your loom and let us compete."

Athena wove the most beautiful tapestry ever seen, every thread and knot was perfect and the colours sparkled. It pictured the Olympian gods in all their glory and majesty.

Arachne's tapestry was also beautifully woven; Athena herself had to admit that the girl's craftsmanship was flawless. But what kind of picture had she woven? An irreverent scene making fun of Zeus and his wives!

In a wrath the goddess tore the tapestry to shreds and struck the girl with the shuttle. Immediately Arachne felt her head shrink almost to nothing, her nimble fingers change into long, spindly legs. Athena had turned her into a spider.

"Vainglorious girl, go on and spin your thread and weave your empty net forever," said Athena to Arachne, the spider. Athena was a just goddess and she could be very stern. She knew that the gods were great only as long as they were properly worshipped by mortals.

Athena was very fond of a certain city in Greece, and so was her uncle, Poseidon. Both of them claimed the city, and after a long quarrel they decided that the one who could give it the finest gift should have it.

Leading a procession of citizens, the two gods mounted the Acropolis, the flat-topped rock that crowned the city. Poseidon struck the cliff with his trident, and a spring welled up. The people marvelled, but the water was as salty as the sea that Poseidon ruled, and not very useful. Then Athena gave the city her gift. She planted an olive tree in a crevice on the rock. It was the first olive tree the people had ever seen. Athena's gift was judged the better of the two, for it gave food, oil, and wood, and the city was hers. From her beautiful temple on top of the Acropolis, Athena watched over Athens, her city, with the wise owl, her bird, on her shoulder, and under her leadership the Athenians grew famous for their arts and crafts.

THE STORY OF THE TOTEM POLE

retold by Norman Tait

"THE STORY OF THE POLE STARTS off when Man was alone on this earth. He was alone for a long while. And you can see Man right at the very bottom of the pole. He wandered the earth and was being taken care of by the spirits.

"Then one day he wondered, 'Why am I alone?' So he went into the forest and spoke to the spirit of the forest and said, 'Why am I alone? Isn't there anyone in this forest who could help me?' And the spirit of the forest said, 'I'll give you Black Bear. And if you learn to live in harmony with him, I will send you more of my children.' He did. And Man learned how to live with the forest people.

"Then he went on. In his travels, he noticed that there was nobody in the water. So he went to the spirit of the water and said, 'Why am I alone on the water?' The spirit of the water came forward and said, 'I will give you one of my children.' And he sent the Blackfish. He said, 'If you learn how to live with the Blackfish, I will send you more.' And Man learned how to live with the Blackfish and the people of the water.

"Then as time went on, Man noticed that there was nothing in the sky. So he said to the sky spirit, 'Send me one of your children. I've already proven that I could live with other than myself and my people.' And the sky spirit sent him the Raven. Man proved again that he could live with them.

"The proof that Man could live with the spirit children of the forest, the water, and the sky is everywhere around you. You look in the forest, and you find abundant animals. You look up in the sky, and you will see birds of all sorts. You look into the water, and you will see creatures of all kinds. Man learned how to live with them.

"That was one of the first stories that was passed on. If you want your children to go on living with you, learn how to live with them. If you can live with them, you can live with each other and you can live with yourself. That's the story of the pole."

THE FLASH

by Italo Calvino

IT HAPPENED ONE DAY, at a crossroads, in the middle of a crowd, people coming and going.

I stopped, blinked: I understood nothing. Nothing, nothing about anything: I didn't understand the reasons for things or for people, it was all senseless, absurd. And I started to laugh.

What I found strange at the time was that I'd never realized before. That up until then I had accepted everything: traffic lights, cars, posters, uniforms, monuments, things completely detached from any sense of the world, accepted them as if there were some necessity, some chain of cause and effect that bound them together.

Then the laugh died in my throat, I blushed, ashamed. I waved to get people's attention and "Stop a second!" I shouted, "there's something wrong! Everything's wrong! We're doing the absurdest things! This can't be the right way! Where will it end?"

People stopped around me, sized me up, curious. I stood there in the middle of them, waving my arms, desperate to explain myself, to have them share the flash of insight that had suddenly enlightened me: and I said nothing. I said nothing because the moment I'd raised my arms and opened my mouth, my great revelation had been as it were swallowed up again and the words had come out any old how, on impulse.

"So?" people asked, "what do you mean? Everything's in its place. All is as it should be. Everything is a result of something else. Everything fits in with everything else. We can't see anything absurd or wrong!"

And I stood there, lost, because as I saw it now everything had fallen into place again and everything seemed natural, traffic lights, monuments, uniforms, towerblocks, tramlines, beggars, processions; yet this didn't calm me down, it tormented me.

"I'm sorry," I answered. "Perhaps it was me that was wrong. It seemed that way. But everything's fine. I'm sorry," and I made off amid their angry glares.

Yet, even now, every time (often) that I find I don't understand something, then, instinctively, I'm filled with the hope that perhaps this will be my moment again, perhaps once again I shall understand nothing. I shall grasp that other knowledge, found and lost in an instant.

THE VISITATION

by Fernando Sorrentino

IN 1965, WHEN I WAS 23, I was training as a teacher of Spanish language and literature. Very early one morning at the beginning of spring I was studying in my room in our fifth-floor flat in the only apartment building on the block.

Feeling just a bit lazy, every now and again I let my eyes stray beyond the window. I could see the street and, on the opposite side, old don Cesáreo's well-kept garden. His house stood on the corner of a site that formed an irregular pentagon.

Next to don Cesáreo's was a beautiful house belonging to the Bernasconis, a wonderful family who were always doing good and kindly things. They had three daughters, and I was in love with Adriana, the eldest. That was why from time to time I glanced at the opposite side of the street—more out of a sentimental habit than because I expected to see her at such an early hour.

As usual, don Cesáreo was tending and watering his beloved garden, which was divided from the street by a low iron fence and three stone steps.

The street was so deserted that my attention was forcibly drawn to a man who appeared on the next block, heading our way on the same side as the houses of don Cesáreo and the Bernasconis. How could I help but notice this man? He was a beggar or a tramp, a scarecrow draped in shreds and patches.

Bearded and thin, he wore a battered yellowish straw hat and, despite the heat, was wrapped in a bedraggled greyish overcoat. He was carrying a huge, filthy bag, and I assumed it held the small coins and scraps of food he managed to beg.

I couldn't take my eyes off him. The tramp stopped in front of don Cesáreo's house and asked him something over the fence. Don Cesáreo was a bad-tempered old codger. Without replying, he waved the beggar away. But the beggar, in a voice too low for me to hear, seemed insistent. Then I distinctly heard don Cesáreo shout out, "Clear off once and for all and stop bothering me."

The tramp, however, kept on, and even went up the three steps and pushed open the iron gate a few centimetres. At this point, losing the last shred of his small supply of patience, don Cesáreo gave the man a shove. Slipping, the beggar grabbed at the fence but missed it and fell to the ground. In that instant, his legs flew up in the air, and I heard the sharp crack of his skull striking the wet step.

Don Cesáreo ran onto the pavement, leaned over the beggar, and felt his chest. Then, in a fright, he took the body by the feet and dragged it to the curb. After that he went into his house and closed the door, convinced there had been no witnesses to his accidental crime.

Only I had seen it. Soon a man came along and stopped by the dead beggar. Then more and more people gathered, and at last the police came. Putting the tramp in an ambulance, they took him away.

That was it; the matter was never spoken of again.

For my part, I took care not to say a word. Maybe I was wrong, but why should I tell on an old man who had never done me any harm? After all, he hadn't intended to kill the tramp, and it didn't seem right to me that a court case should embitter the last years of don Cesáreo's life. The best thing, I thought, was to leave him alone with his conscience.

Little by little I began to forget the episode, but every time I saw don Cesáreo it felt strange to realize that he was unaware that I was the only person in the world who knew his terrible secret. From then on, for some reason I avoided him and never dared speak to him again.

In 1969, when I was 26, I was working as a teacher of Spanish language and literature. Adriana Bernasconi had married not me but someone else who may not have loved and deserved her as much as I.

At the time, Adriana, who was pregnant, was very nearly due. She still lived in the same house, and every day she grew more beautiful. Very early one oppressive summer morning I found myself teaching a special class in grammar to some secondary-school children who were preparing for their exams and, as usual, from time to time I cast a rather melancholy glance across the road.

All at once my heart literally did a flip-flop, and I thought I was seeing things.

From exactly the same direction as four years before came the tramp don Cesáreo had killed—the same ragged clothes, the greyish overcoat, the battered straw hat, the filthy bag.

Forgetting my pupils, I rushed to the window. The tramp had begun to slow his step, as if he had reached his destination.

He's come back to life, I thought, and he's going to take revenge on don Cesáreo.

But the beggar passed the old man's gate and walked on. Stopping at Adriana Bernasconi's front door, he turned the knob and went inside.

"I'll be back in a moment," I told my students, and half out of my mind with anxiety, I went down in the lift, dashed across the street, and burst into Adriana's house.

"Hello!" her mother said, standing by the door as if about to go out. "What a surprise to see you here!"

She had never looked on me in anything but a kindly way. She embraced and kissed me, and I did not quite understand what was going on. Then it dawned on me that Adriana had just become a mother and that they were all beside themselves with excitement. What else could I do but shake hands with my victorious rival?

I did not know how to put it to him, and I wondered whether it might not be better to keep quiet. Then I hit on a compromise. Casually I said, "As a matter of fact, I let myself in without ringing the bell because I thought I saw a tramp come in with a big dirty bag and I was afraid he meant to rob you."

They all gaped at me. What tramp? What bag? Robbery? They had been in the living room the whole time and had no idea what I was talking about.

"I must have made a mistake," I said.

Then they invited me into the room where Adriana and her baby were. I never know what to say on these occasions. I congratulated her, I kissed her, I admired the baby, and I asked what they were going to name him. Gustavo, I was told, after his father; I would have preferred Fernando but I said nothing.

Back home I thought, That was the tramp old don Cesáreo killed, I'm sure of it. It's not revenge he's come back for but to be reborn as Adriana's son.

Two or three days later, however, this hypothesis struck me as ridiculous, and I put it out of my mind.

And would have forgotten it forever had something not come up in 1979 that brought it all back.

Having grown older and feeling less and less in control of things, I tried to focus my attention on a book I was reading beside the window, while letting my glance stray.

Gustavo, Adriana's son, was playing on the roof terrace of their house. Surely, at his age, the game he was playing was rather infantile, and I felt that the boy had inherited his father's scant intelligence and that, had he been my son, he would certainly have found a less foolish way of amusing himself.

He had placed a line of empty tin cans on the parapet and was trying to knock them off by throwing stones at them from a distance of several metres. Of course, nearly all the pebbles were falling down into don Cesáreo's garden next door. I could see that the old man, who wasn't there just then, would work himself into a fit the moment he found that some of his flowers had been damaged.

At that very instant, don Cesáreo came out into the garden. He was, in point of fact, extremely old and he shuffled along putting one foot very carefully in front of the other. Slowly, timidly, he made his way to the garden gate and prepared to go down the three steps to the pavement.

At the same time, Gustavo—who couldn't see the old man—at last managed to hit one of the tin cans, which, bouncing off two or three ledges as it went, fell with a clatter into don Cesáreo's garden. Startled, don Cesáreo, who was halfway down the steps, made a sudden movement, slipped head over heels, and cracked his skull against the lowest step.

I took all this in, but the boy had not seen the old man nor had the old man seen the boy. For some reason, at that point Gustavo left the terrace. In a matter of seconds, a crowd of people surrounded don Cesáreo's body; an accidental fall, obviously, had been the cause of his death.

The next day I got up very early and immediately stationed myself at the window. In the pentagonal house, don Cesáreo's wake was in full swing. On the pavement out in front, a small knot of people stood smoking and talking.

A moment later, in disgust and dismay, they drew aside when a beggar came out of Adriana Bernasconi's house, again dressed in rags, overcoat, straw hat, and carrying a bag. He made his way through the circle of bystanders and slowly vanished into the distance the same way he had come from twice before.

At midday, sadly but with no surprise, I learned that Gustavo's bed had been found empty that morning. The whole Bernasconi family launched a forlorn search, which, to this day, they continue in obstinate hope. I never had the courage to tell them to call it off.

LYSANDRA'S POEM

by Budge Wilson

WHEN I WAS A CHILD, my family lived beside the sea. But not precisely so. Not right on the edge of the Atlantic Ocean, with the horizon sliding away flat all the way to Spain. No. We lived in a little harbour town in Nova Scotia, more than a kilometre from any point of land where you could view the open sea. But apart from the fact that you couldn't see the ocean (except insofar as the harbour was a part of it), the sea might just as well have been smack dab in the middle of our town. A day without fog was a time for rejoicing. Most days, tourists crept through our streets in their shiny American cars, fresh off the Bar Harbour ferry from sunny New England, headlights on and honking. The winters were windy and damp and dispiriting, the springs endless and fluky—promising summer one day and sprinkling snow on the stunted tulips the next. In summertime, all expeditions were planned tentatively; sentences ended with the phrase "if it doesn't rain." Packed linens were attacked by mildew; wire coat hangers rusted; envelopes stuck together if they weren't stored in airtight plastic bags.

The fact is that we can't cope with too much fine weather in Nova Scotia. We're chicken-hearted about the heat, and are beaten down by it, plowed right under. And a brisk sunny day—a perfect day—undoes us. People with indoor jobs are irritable, tense; spirit and body are in active resistance to any activity that takes place inside a building. Those who are free to go outside—housewives, the unemployed, mothers trailing children, people on vacation—spill out of their houses onto the water, the beaches, the parks, or their own backyards. On such a day, not all those smiling people strolling along our Main Streets are tourists. Most of them are native Nova Scotians, agape at a miracle. People call in sick, sleep through the alarm, quit jobs. If there are six or seven of these days in a row, the whole economy is at peril: editors miss deadlines; back orders are ignored; laundry accumulates;

cupboards are bare. The sighting of a fog bank or the first rainy day is almost a relief.

One way or another, a climate like this is bound to rub off on people. One person may become surly and fixed, grey and dank of spirit, long-lived and persistent, and a trial to his family. Another can end up hopeful—the fruit of these spectacular sunny days when the light is clearer, more pungent than most other Canadians could ever imagine; if one dwells on and in those days, an optimist is bred, living for and believing in the arrival of such rare and golden times. Or you can be the way I was, stubborn and opportunistic, snatching what I could out of a resistant environment. Or like Lysandra Cochrane, at first tentative and careful, and then with no softness in her, bitter and barbed, with a heart as hard and as cutting as diamonds.

Lysandra! you may exclaim. What a name to issue forth from such a small and simple town in one of the back places of our land. No town is simple, let me say, but that does not explain Lysandra's name. Nova Scotians—especially those in coastal areas—have a way of leafing through literature (by which I mean anything from old school texts to the Bible and the obituary columns) to find names for their babies. The Cochranes fished around in heaven knows what sources, and pulled up Lysandra. Rumour had it that Mr. Cochrane—addicted to libraries, in any case—spent the day his wife was in labour in the reference library in Halifax, looking for names. He was a smart man, a sky-high scholarship student in his day. His Dalhousie bursary had covered tuition only, and he had lacked sufficient cash to puff out the sum enough to accept it. He was one of those ones who are "grey and dank of spirit." His ambition had been snuffed out before it had had a chance to warm up, and he lived his whole adult life as a minor clerk in a law office, watching other people cash in on the benefits of a university education. He drank a large percentage of his earnings, snapped at his pale wife (once a beauty according to my mother, but my imagination failed to grasp such an improbability), and sired four thin children.

Lysandra was my best friend. She was as dark as her mother was fair, a skinny kid, all angles and elbows and bony knees. Her skin was smooth and sallow, her hair long and limp. She was tall for her age when we were kids, and shy. She looked at strangers—and at teachers and fathers—out of enormous black eyes, head bent forward and down. She walked with an awkward jerky gait, as though she were not at home on her own legs, and as she passed by, the other kids would whisper, "Pigeon-Toed Cochrane!"

But when we were alone together, Lysandra was full of amazing thoughts, large ambitions, bizarre projects. Without being instructed, she thought in metaphors, and her speech was full of exotic images and odd rhythms. She invented a whole mini-language so that she and I could talk to one another without being understood by others. She intended to be a writer—an *author*, she said—famous and rich, and this thought permeated most of her other plans and inventions. Like her father, she haunted the library, but equipped with a hope he had long ago relinquished. She read all the good poets before she was 12, and a lot of the bad ones, too. She was gobbling up Shakespeare while I was stretched out on the floor on my stomach with *Crime Comics*. It was to her books that she retreated when her father went on his rampages, escaping his noise and the sight of her frowsy mother's stricken face—losing herself in whatever volume she had in her room, finding her place at a neatly inserted bookmark. If I were in the house at the time, we would race upstairs at the first hint of conflict, and I would watch this withdrawal. She wouldn't say a word to me, but would just sit up straight on a little yellow chair she had, her book held close to her face, not moving except to turn the pages. I both hated and relished these occasions. We didn't have high drama like this in my house, and I listened, breath held, to Mr. Cochrane's fierce catalogue of oaths—words to make me shudder all the while I was straining to keep from missing any of them. I was single-mindedly troubled by the sounds that came from Mrs. Cochrane, but this was part of the performance and had to be endured if I were to benefit from the rest of it. Besides, there was no escape for me. I could hardly march downstairs and walk through that battlefield and out the back door. I sat on the bed hunched under an afghan while Lysandra read on, her lips in a thin, tight smile.

In March of the year when we were in grade 7, the principal announced a poetry contest. He told us about it during Monday morning assembly, just before the national anthem. The entries to the contest would be due on May 27th. There would be three judges, headed by Miss Alexander, the vice-principal. The other two would be Mr. Knickle, the town mayor, and Mr. Reuben, the editor of the local newspaper, the *South Shore Standard.* Thus were prestige, professionalism, and masculinity added to the team of judges.

I was standing beside Lysandra in assembly when the competition was announced. Her bent head shot up, and she stared into space with eyes so wide open that they almost frightened me. Then she looked at me with oh such a gaze of wonder, such a look of peace and triumph. When she walked out of the auditorium, her step was smooth and sure, her shoulders high. No one whispered "Pigeon-Toed Cochrane" as she passed. No one would have considered mocking such a display of calm self-confidence.

Not everyone entered the poetry contest, but our English teachers urged us to write something for it, and many of us did. However, Lysandra was the only one to devote her entire life to it, filling a whole shoe box with poetry, long before May 27th. You could see her scribbling in her loose-leaf at recess time on the school swing set, or high on the jungle gym after the little kids had gone home from school in the afternoon. On Saturdays she would do her writing out on the granite bluff overlooking the harbour, or seated at the lunch counter at the Seaway Restaurant, making her Coke last for an hour and 45 minutes. I played with other kids during this period, because Lysandra was of no use at all to me.

The poem I entered in the contest was about a shipwreck, and it had 18 stanzas. The rhythm went jig-a jig-a jig, and there was a rhyme at the ends of lines one and two and again at three and four. Like slope, dope; eat, feet. It wasn't a forced kind of rhythm or anything. The beat went along easefully without any little words tacked on to make the right number of feet. I wrote it in March, during the week after the contest was announced, so that I would have the ordeal over and done with. It was a little like getting your Christmas shopping done all in one day on the first of November.

That spring was one that most Nova Scotians will always remember. The snows melted by the end of March, and April came sailing in with sunshine and a kind of sheltering softness that was foreign to all of us. We were playing softball and kick-the-can one month ahead of time, and by mid-May people were ignoring all warnings and planting their gardens in the warm moist earth. Even Mr. Cochrane looked cheerful as he walked to and from the law office, and Lysandra floated around town, notebook held close to her chest, looking as though she were in touch with a vision; and I suppose she was. On one of the rare occasions when she had time for me, she told me that her poem was already 22 pages long. I asked what it was about, and she said, "Life."

"Oh," I replied. She wouldn't let me read it, but one afternoon, I looked at the manuscript upside down when she spread the pages out on the bed so that I might admire its magnitude. The poetry wandered all over the sheets, with short lines and long ones, sometimes with whole sections dribbling down the centre of the page. After this unsatisfactory demonstration, she took the papers, folded them tenderly, and put them carefully back into the shoebox, stroking the top page with the flat of her hand. She closed her eyes and lifted her head as though in prayer. "I'll die if the house burns down," she said, her teeth clenched. At first I didn't understand, but then I did. I remember thinking, I hope I never love or want anything that hard. Just thinking about it exhausted me.

"You should make a copy," I said.

"Oh, well," she sighed.

Of course I was a shoo-in to win that contest. Miss Alexander, the vice-principal, was about 200 years old, and had no truck with any kind of verse that didn't rhyme and wasn't of the jig-a jig-a variety. I had often heard her speak scathingly of "free verse": "the lazy poet's way of avoiding a lot of hard work," she'd say, lips pulled down at the corners, eyebrows drawn together behind her thick glasses. What's more, her father had been a fisherman on the Banks, and had been shipwrecked way back in 1920, when she'd been old enough to take in all the details. Those same details she liked to dole out to anyone who presented a willing ear. I liberally stacked my poem with material that was not so much lifted from her as it was spiced with the flavour of her own tale.

But there were two men on the jury. Could they not have taken Miss Alexander's prejudices and swung them around? No, they could not. Mayors do not by definition necessarily know a great deal about poetry. Mr. Knickle knew next to nothing. The principal had put him on the jury to give it status. Mr. Knickle had agreed to serve because of political visibility. He had no intention of rocking any boats, poetic or otherwise.

Mr. Reuben, the editor of the *South Shore Standard*, knew a lot about local politics and the economic problems of the Atlantic seaboard; from time to time he wrote flat-footed editorials about these matters. He was familiar with the inequalities of freight rates and the need for federal subsidies. Poetry was not his territory. Moreover, both Mr. Knickle and Mr. Reuben had been taught by Miss Alexander when they were in grade 4. Mr. Reuben remembered what she had done when he cracked his knuckles once too often during Silent Prayer. During the meetings of the poetry jury, Mr. Knickle had to stifle an impulse to raise his hand every time he wanted to speak.

Besides, consider my poem. Where could you find a subject better designed to please two men? A shipwreck. Men doing traditionally male things—heroic and beset by danger. I won by acclamation.

On the afternoon when the contest results were announced, we were handed back our poems. I received a wristwatch and a return ticket to Halifax; best of all, the 18 verses of my poem were to be published in the next week's issue of the *South Shore Standard*—heady matters for a 13-year-old. I wound my watch noisily and put it on, arranging my face into an expression of humility.

Lysandra ran out of the schoolyard ahead of me, tripping over a discarded hockey stick and almost falling. The many pages of her poem went flying, and she had to chase around after them, rescuing them from the wind. Her face was ashen and without expression of any kind. She walked home alone, chin up, legs unsteady once again. A disembodied voice from somewhere behind me called out, "Pigeon-Toed Cochrane!"

That evening Mr. Cochrane took Lysandra's shoebox and threw its contents into the kitchen stove. Then, I was told by a neighbour, he stormed out of the house, swinging a bottle in each hand. He stayed away for three days, blind drunk in the middle of his grandfather's old woodlot.

The days, the months that followed, were difficult for me. Lysandra withdrew into a secret self and refused to speak to me. She arrived at school late, never calling for me, and left the minute the bell rang, walk-running home with her huge eyes staring straight ahead. Twice I called for her at her house. The first time, her thin, sad mother answered the door, looked at me, and sighed. "She's not feeling well today, Elaine," she said. The other time, her father greeted me. "You!" he growled, and slammed the door. I didn't try again.

The long summer vacation passed, and I found other friends. Sometimes I would see Lysandra off in the distance, walking alone on the beach, or sitting on Rocky Point hugging her knees, eyes fixed on the water. But never writing. The weather, tired after a halcyon spring, turned rainy and chilly, but Lysandra still paced the shore, her hair blowing in the wet wind. Nor fair, I thought. Twenty-three kids had entered that contest. It wasn't my fault that I won. Was it? Once I met her on the blueberry barrens. I had come up to get enough berries for Mom to make a pie. Lysandra was just sitting there on a granite boulder, hands limp in her lap.

"Lysandra," I pleaded. "It wasn't my fault."

"Wasn't it?" she said, eyes distant.

I looked hard at her, and noticed that she was pretty now, with a kind of wild gypsy beauty that didn't need fancy clothes or a trendy haircut.

"Lysandra. Please. Be nice again. I don't want our friendship to be wrecked."

"But it is," she said quietly.

"How can you do this to me for such a small thing?" I begged, not letting go.

"Small," she whispered. It was neither a question nor a statement. Then she got down clumsily from the rock and walked out of the woods without looking back, picking her way carefully through the bushes and over the hummocks and outcroppings of stone.

I went home and cried for a while in my room. Then I picked up my wrinkled copy of the *South Shore Standard* and reread my poem. A part of me wanted to tear it into little pieces, press it all into a hard damp ball, and throw it at the wall. The other part folded it carefully and put it in my desk drawer. Then I grabbed my swimsuit off a hook and went down to the beach to go swimming with my other friends.

Four years passed, and I was in grade 11. Grade 7 was long years behind me, and I scarcely noticed Lysandra as she came and went. Besides, my whole consciousness was absorbed by my feelings for Brett Houston. He had arrived fresh from the city of Toronto on the first day of school that year, and I had spent 24 weeks wanting him. As the year progressed, he had moved from pretty girl to pretty girl—in and out of our class—and I took courage from this fact. An early solid attachment, for instance, to the beauteous Sally Cornwall of grade 10, would have spelled permanence and hopelessness for me. But obviously he was still searching. Any minute it might be my turn.

And suddenly, miraculously, it was. Coming up behind me one day as I pulled books from my locker, he grabbed my arm and swung me around to face him. "Hi, cute stuff," he said in his wonderful flat Toronto voice. I looked at his size, his blond good looks, his casual grin, and my chest was alive with thundering heartbeats, tight with constricted breathing.

"Tonight," he said, moving his gum over to the other side of his mouth. "The movies. At eight. Time for a little ride first."

"Okay," I said, my hands shaking as they once again reached for my books, my eyes only marginally in focus.

"I'll walk you home," he said, slamming my locker door with a masterful bang.

Holy toledo, I thought.

As the weeks went by, as March moved into April and then into May, I marvelled that this beautiful person was in my possession. Gone were the months of moving from girl to girl. We were going steady. It had lasted seven whole weeks. I waited on him, packed picnic lunches, wrote essays for him, massaged his shoulders after baseball practice, watched sports programs on TV all Saturday afternoon, mended his socks, walked his dog. Even I could see that I looked different, my skin aglow, my eyes eager, my smile at the ready. I adored him. I watched his coming and his going with undisguised worship.

I had a part-time job at a local variety store, and on the night of the Spring Dance, I had to work the evening shift. I told Brett I'd meet him at the school after the store closed at nine o'clock. He had to get there early to attach the balloons to the ceiling. When I entered the darkened gymnasium by the side door, I almost bumped into him. Him and Lysandra. They were facing one another, standing sideways to me. She had cut her hair in low bangs, and the rest of it hung almost to her waist, black as night. She had on large loop earrings and a low-cut black peasant blouse. There was a lot of chest to see, and her chest was a good one. That's all I remember about what she was wearing. I was too busy taking note of the way she was running a slender finger up and down his forearm, saying, "C'mon, Brett. Let's dance just a little bit while you're waiting. No point just standing around. She won't mind."

As they came together to dance a slow number, I watched that same finger move slowly up his spine and then come to rest on the back of his neck. She lifted her lovely face to his, enormous eyes mocking, ready. As she and Brett moved off in the darkness they looked like one person. They were dancing that close.

He came back and collected me. I'll say that for him. That evening we danced like mechanical dolls—arms and legs moving, but no life in us or between us. I could see Lysandra over by the springboards and the parallel bars, watching us, smiling. Brett waited until the next day to abandon me—without a word of explanation or farewell.

I thought I would die of heartbreak or wished I could, but of course I did nothing of the sort. Brett followed Lysandra around like a panting puppy all spring, servile, pliant, and sent her an orchid for the graduation formal. I went to that dance with Horace MacNab, who danced like a tractor, lumbering along, squashing my feet. I laughed loudly and frequently, tossing my hair over my shoulders. Brett and Lysandra glided around the gym with their eyes closed, slow-dancing to everything, their bodies pressed hard together.

The day after the formal, Lysandra told Brett she was tired of him and gave him back his baseball crest. Then she could be seen once again in the town library, reading, reading, and writing page after page of poetry. She had lost her stunned, vapid look. She moved once more with measured coordination, with grace. She even spoke to me from time to time—a neutral unadorned hello in passing.

Brett moved away with his family in the fall of that year. His father said he couldn't hack the climate. He said he wanted to live someplace where he could depend on owning a dry pair of shoes. I met Brett 20 years later at a high-school reunion. He was 38 years old, balding, stout, boring, a petulant wife in tow. Lysandra did not attend the reunion.

By now I've read a lot of Lysandra's poetry. It appears in academic journals and in the better popular magazines. She has published seven volumes and has won two national awards. She often turns up on the literary pages of newspapers, and I'm as likely to see her name in *The Globe and Mail* as in *The Halifax Mail-Star*. The CBC loves to interview her. I don't understand many of her poems. They seem to be speaking a language that I never learned, and are plugged into a source of power that is a puzzle to me. But I can tell you this: her poetry contains such bitterness that the mind reels as it reads, dizzy from such savage images, such black revelations. The words claw out from the pages like so many birds of prey. And all of them seem to be moving in my direction.

A Mad Tea Party

an excerpt from Alice's Adventures in Wonderland *by Lewis Carroll*

THERE WAS A TABLE set out under a tree in front of the house, and the March Hare and the Hatter were having tea at it: a Dormouse was sitting between them, fast asleep, and the other two were using it as a cushion, resting their elbows on it, and talking over its head. "Very uncomfortable for the Dormouse," thought Alice; "only as it's asleep, I suppose it doesn't mind."

The table was a large one, but the three were all crowded together at one corner of it. "No room! No room!" they cried out when they saw Alice coming. "There's *plenty* of room!" said Alice indignantly, and she sat down in a large armchair at one end of the table.

"Have some wine," the March Hare said in an encouraging tone.

Alice looked all round the table, but there was nothing on it but tea. "I don't see any wine," she remarked.

"There isn't any," said the March Hare.

"Then it wasn't very civil of you to offer it," said Alice angrily.

"It wasn't very civil of you to sit down without being invited," said the March Hare.

"I didn't know it was *your* table," said Alice: "it's laid for a great many more than three."

"Your hair wants cutting," said the Hatter. He had been looking at Alice for some time with great curiosity, and this was his first speech.

"You should learn not to make personal remarks," Alice said with some severity: "it's very rude."

The Hatter opened his eyes very wide on hearing this; but all he *said* was "Why is a raven like a writing desk?"

"Come, we shall have some fun now!" thought Alice. "I'm glad they've begun asking riddles—I believe I can guess that," she added aloud.

"Do you mean that you think you can find out the answer to it?" said the March Hare.

"Exactly so," said Alice.

"Then you should say what you mean," the March Hare went on.

"I do," Alice hastily replied; "at least—at least I mean what I say—that's the same thing, you know."

"Not the same thing a bit!" said the Hatter. "Why, you might just as well say that 'I see what I eat' is the same thing as 'I eat what I see'!"

"You might just as well say," added the March Hare, "that 'I like what I get' is the same thing as 'I get what I like'!"

"You might just as well say," added the Dormouse, which seemed to be talking in its sleep, "that 'I breathe when I sleep' is the same thing as 'I sleep when I breathe'!"

"It *is* the same thing with you," said the Hatter, and here the conversation dropped, and the party sat silent for a minute, while Alice thought over all she could remember about ravens and writing desks, which wasn't much.

The Hatter was the first to break the silence. "What day of the month is it?" he said, turning to Alice: he had taken his watch out of his pocket, and was looking at it uneasily, shaking it every now and then, and holding it to his ear.

Alice considered a little, and then said "The fourth."

"Two days wrong!" sighed the Hatter. "I told you butter wouldn't suit the works!" he added, looking angrily at the March Hare.

"It was the *best* butter," the March Hare meekly replied.

"Yes, but some crumbs must have got in as well," the Hatter grumbled: "you shouldn't have put it in with the breadknife."

The March Hare took the watch and looked at it gloomily: then he dipped it into his cup of tea, and looked at it again: but he could think of nothing better to say than his first remark, "It was the *best* butter, you know."

Alice had been looking over his shoulder with some curiosity. "What a funny watch!" she remarked. "It tells the day of the month, and doesn't tell what o'clock it is!"

"Why should it?" muttered the Hatter. "Does *your* watch tell you what year it is?"

"Of course not," Alice replied very readily: "but that's because it stays the same year for such a long time together."

"Which is just the case with *mine*," said the Hatter.

Alice felt dreadfully puzzled. The Hatter's remark seemed to her to have no sort of meaning in it, and yet it was certainly English. "I don't quite understand you," she said, as politely as she could.

"The Dormouse is asleep again," said the Hatter, and he poured a little hot tea upon its nose.

The Dormouse shook its head impatiently, and said, without opening its eyes, "Of course, of course: just what I was going to remark myself."

"Have you guessed the riddle yet?" the Hatter said, turning to Alice again.

"No, I give it up," Alice replied. "What's the answer?"

"I haven't the slightest idea," said the Hatter.

"Nor I," said the March Hare.

Alice sighed wearily. "I think you might do something better with the time," she said, "than wasting it in asking riddles that have no answers."

"If you knew Time as well as I do," said the Hatter, "you wouldn't talk about wasting *it*. It's *him*."

"I don't know what you mean," said Alice.

"Of course you don't!" the Hatter said, tossing his head contemptuously. "I dare say you never even spoke to Time!"

"Perhaps not," Alice cautiously replied; "but I know I have to beat time when I learn music."

"Ah! That accounts for it," said the Hatter. "He won't stand beating. Now, if you only kept on good terms with him, he'd do almost anything you liked with the clock. For instance, suppose it were nine o'clock in the morning, just time to begin lessons: you'd only have to whisper a hint to Time, and round goes the clock in a twinkling! Half-past one, time for dinner!"

("I only wish it was," the March Hare said to itself in a whisper.)

"That would be grand, certainly," said Alice thoughtfully; "but then—I shouldn't be hungry for it, you know."

"Not at first, perhaps," said the Hatter: "but you could keep it to half-past one as long as you liked."

"Is that the way *you* manage?" Alice asked.

The Hatter shook his head mournfully. "Not I!" he replied. "We quarrelled last March—just before *he* went mad, you know—" (pointing with his teaspoon at the March Hare,) "—it was at the great concert given by the Queen of Hearts, and I had to sing

'Twinkle, twinkle, little bat!
How I wonder what you're at!'

You know the song, perhaps?"

"I've heard something like it," said Alice.

"It goes on, you know," the Hatter continued, "in this way—

'Up above the world you fly
Like a tea tray in the sky.
Twinkle, twinkle—' "

Here the Dormouse shook itself, and began singing in its sleep *"Twinkle, twinkle, twinkle—"* and went on so long that they had to pinch it to make it stop.

"Well, I'd hardly finished the first verse," said the Hatter, "when the Queen bawled out 'He's murdering the time! Off with his head!'"

"How dreadfully savage!" exclaimed Alice.

"And ever since that," the Hatter went on in a mournful tone, "he won't do a thing I ask! It's always six o'clock now."

A bright idea came into Alice's head. "Is that the reason so many tea-things are put out here?" she asked.

"Yes, that's it," said the Hatter with a sigh: "it's always teatime, and we've no time to wash the things between whiles."

"Then you keep moving round, I suppose?" said Alice.

"Exactly so," said the Hatter: "as the things get used up."

"But what happens when you come to the beginning again?" Alice ventured to ask.

"Suppose we change the subject," the March Hare interrupted, yawning. "I'm getting tired of this. I vote the young lady tells us a story."

"I'm afraid I don't know one," said Alice, rather alarmed at the proposal.

"Then the Dormouse shall!" they both cried. "Wake up, Dormouse!" And they pinched it on both sides at once.

The Dormouse slowly opened its eyes. "I wasn't asleep," it said in a hoarse, feeble voice, "I heard every word you fellows were saying."

"Tell us a story!" said the March Hare.

"Yes, please do!" pleaded Alice.

"And be quick about it," added the Hatter, "or you'll be asleep again before it's done."

"Once upon a time there were three little sisters," the Dormouse began in a great hurry; "and their names were Elsie, Lacie, and Tillie; and they lived at the bottom of a well—"

"What did they live on?" said Alice, who always took a great interest in questions of eating and drinking.

"They lived on treacle," said the Dormouse, after thinking a minute or two.

"They couldn't have done that, you know," Alice gently remarked. "They'd have been ill."

"So they were," said the Dormouse; "*very* ill."

Alice tried a little to fancy to herself what such an extraordinary way of living would be like, but it puzzled her too much: so she went on: "But why did they live at the bottom of a well?"

"Take some more tea," the March Hare said to Alice, very earnestly.

"I've had nothing yet," Alice replied in an offended tone: "so I can't take more."

"You mean you can't take *less*," said the Hatter: "it's very easy to take *more* than nothing."

"Nobody asked *your* opinion," said Alice.

"Who's making personal remarks now?" the Hatter asked triumphantly.

Alice did not quite know what to say to this: so she helped herself to some tea and bread-and-butter, and then turned to the Dormouse, and repeated her question. "Why did they live at the bottom of a well?"

The Dormouse again took a minute or two to think about it, and then said "It was a treacle-well."

"There's no such thing!" Alice was beginning very angrily, but the Hatter and the March Hare went "Sh! Sh!" and the Dormouse sulkily remarked "If you can't be civil, you'd better finish the story for yourself."

"No, please go on!" Alice said very humbly. "I won't interrupt you again. I dare say there may be *one*."

"One, indeed!" said the Dormouse indignantly. However, he consented to go on. "And so these three little sisters—they were learning to draw, you know—"

"What did they draw?" said Alice, quite forgetting her promise.

"Treacle," said the Dormouse, without considering at all, this time.

"I want a clean cup," interrupted the Hatter: "let's all move one place on."

He moved on as he spoke, and the Dormouse followed him: the March Hare moved into the Dormouse's place, and Alice rather unwillingly took the place of the March Hare. The Hatter was the only one who got any advantage from the change; and Alice was a good deal worse off than before, as the March Hare had just upset the milk-jug into his plate.

Alice did not wish to offend the Dormouse again, so she began very cautiously: "But I don't understand. Where did they draw the treacle from?"

"You can draw water out of a water-well," said the Hatter; "so I should think you could draw treacle out of a treacle-well—eh, stupid?"

"But they were *in* the well," Alice said to the Dormouse, not choosing to notice this last remark.

"Of course they were," said the Dormouse: "well in."

This answer so confused poor Alice, that she let the Dormouse go on for some time without interrupting it.

"They were learning to draw," the Dormouse went on, yawning and rubbing its eyes, for it was getting very sleepy; "and they drew all manner of things—everything that begins with an M—"

"Why with an M?" said Alice.

"Why not?" said the March Hare.

Alice was silent.

The Dormouse had closed its eyes by this time, and was going off into a doze; but, on being pinched by the Hatter, it woke up again with a little shriek, and went on: "—that begins with an M, such as mouse-traps, and the moon, and memory, and muchness—you know you say things are "much of a muchness"—did you ever see such a thing as a drawing of a muchness!"

"Really, now you ask me," said Alice, very much confused, "I don't think—"

"Then you shouldn't talk," said the Hatter.

This piece of rudeness was more than Alice could bear: she got up in great disgust, and walked off: the Dormouse fell asleep instantly, and neither of the others took the least notice of her going, though she looked back once or twice, half hoping that they would call after her: the last time she saw them, they were trying to put the Dormouse into the teapot.

"At any rate I'll never go *there* again!" said Alice, as she picked her way through the wood. "It's the stupidest tea party I ever was at in all my life!"

SAVE THE MOON FOR KERDY DICKUS

by Tim Wynne-Jones

THIS IS KY'S STORY. It happened to her. It happened at her place in the country. I wasn't there when it happened, but I know what her place in the country looks like, and that's important. In this story, the way things look is really important.

There's more than one version of this story. If Ky's younger brothers, Brad or Tony, told you the story, it would come out different. But not as different as the way the Stranger tells it. We know his name now, but we still call him the Stranger. Perhaps you know his version of the story. It was in the newspapers. Well, the *National Enquirer*, anyway.

Describe Tan Mori's house.

Ky's father, Tan Mori, built their house in the country. It's a dome. It looks like a glass igloo, but it's actually made of a web of light metal tubing and a special clear plastic. From the outside you can see right into the house, which Ky didn't like one bit at first, because it wasn't very private. But the house is at the end of a long driveway surrounded by woods, so the only things that can look at you are blue-jays, raccoons, the occasional deer and, from way up high on a hot day, turkey vultures circling the sky.

It wasn't a hot day when this story happened. It was two days before Christmas and there was a bad freezing rain. But let me tell you more about the house, because you have to be able to see the house in order to understand what happened. You have to imagine it the way the Stranger saw it.

For one thing there's all this high-tech office stuff. Ky's parents are both computer software designers, which means that just about everything they do can be done on a computer. Word processing, video monitors, a modem, a fax machine—they're always popping on and off. Their lights blink in the dark.

You also have to know something about Ky's family if you want to see what the Stranger saw when he arrived at their door. You especially have to know that they have family traditions. They make them up all the time. For instance, for the past three years it's been a tradition that I go up from the city for Ky's birthday in the summer, and we go horseback riding. I'm not sure if that's what tradition really means, but it's nice.

It's also a tradition with Ky's family to watch the movie *It's a Wonderful Life* every Christmas. And so, two nights before Christmas, that's what they were doing. They were wearing their traditional Christmastime nightclothes. They were all in red: red flannel pyjamas, even red slippers. Ky had her hair tied back in a red scrunchie. That's what the Stranger saw: this family in red.

They had just stopped the movie for a break. They were going to have okonomiyaki, which is kind of like a Japanese pizza and pancake all mixed up together with shredded cabbage and crabmeat and this chewy wheat glutten stuff called seitan. This is a tradition, too. Ky's father, Tan, likes to cook. So they watch *It's a Wonderful Life* and they have this mid-movie snack served with kinpara gobo, which is spicy, and other pickly things that only Tan and Barbara, Ky's mother, bother to eat. But the kids like okonomiyaki.

Tan Mori is Japanese. Here's how he looks. He wears clear-rimmed glasses. He's short and trim and has long black hair that he wears pulled tightly back in a ponytail.

Ky doesn't think the Stranger had ever seen a Japanese person up close before. He probably hadn't ever seen someone who looked like Barbara Mori, either. She isn't Japanese. She has silvery blonde hair but it's cut very, very short so that you can see the shape of her head. She's very slim, bony, and she has one of the nicest smiles you could imagine. She has two dark spots beside her mouth. Ky calls them beauty marks; Barbara laughs and calls them moles.

It was Barbara who first noticed the Stranger while Tan was cooking the okonomiyaki and the boys were getting bowls of shrimp chips and Coke and Ky was boiling water for green tea.

The freezing rain was pouring down on the dome, but inside it was warm, and there were little islands of light. A single light on a post lit up the driveway a bit.

"There's someone out there," said Barbara. "The poor man." She went to the door and called to him. The kids left what they were doing to go and look.

He was big and shadowy where he was standing. He was also stoop-shouldered, trying to hide his head from the icy downpour.

Barbara waved at him. "Come!" she called as loudly as she could. "Come." Her teeth were chattering because she was standing at the open door in her pyjamas and cold wind was pouring in.

The Stranger paused. He seemed uncertain. Then a gust of wind made him lose his balance and he slipped on the ice and fell. When he got up he made his way toward the house slowly, sliding and slipping the whole long way. He was soaked clear through all over. He only had a jean jacket on. No gloves or hat. As he approached the house, Ky could see that, although he was big, he was young, a teenager. Then Barbara sent her to the bathroom for a big towel.

By the time she got back with the towel, the boy was in the house, standing there dripping in the hall. Barbara wrapped the towel around his shoulders. She had to stand on her toes; he was big. He had black hair and he reminded Ky of a bear she had seen at the zoo after it had been swimming. He smelled terrible. His wet clothes smelled of alcohol and cigarette smoke. The kids all stepped away from him. Tony crinkled up his nose, but Barbara didn't seem to care.

"Come in and get warm," she said, leading him toward the kitchen.

I haven't told you about the kitchen yet. Well, there is a kind of island shaped like a kidney with a built-in stove and sink. Since the walls of the dome are curved, all the cupboards and drawers and stuff are built into the island. Lights recessed into the ceiling above bathe

the island in a warm glow so that the maple countertop looks like a beach.

Tan was already pouring the Stranger some tea when Barbara brought him over and tried to set him down near the stove where it was warmest. But he wouldn't sit. Tan handed him a tiny cup of steaming tea. The cup had no handle. The Stranger didn't seem to know what to do, but the warmth alone was enough to make him take it. His hands were huge and strong and rough. The tiny cup looked like it would break if he closed his fist.

He took a sip of the tea. His eyes cleared a bit.

"Dad's in the truck," he said.

"Oh, my God," said Barbara. "Where? We should get him. Tan?"

The Stranger nodded his big bear head in the direction that the truck was but, of course, you couldn't see it from the house. Ky looked down the driveway, but there is a bend in it so she couldn't see the road.

Tan had turned off the gas under the frying pans and was heading toward the closet for his coat.

"I'll bring him back," he said.

"No!" said the Stranger. His voice cracked a little. "He's okay. He's sleepin'. Truck's warm."

Nobody in the Mori family knew what to do. Tony looked about ready to laugh. Ky glared at him. Tan shrugged and looked at Barbara. "It's not too cold as long as he's sheltered." She nodded and Tan turned the stove back on. The okonomiyaki were ready to flip. He flipped them. The Stranger stared at them. Maybe he thought they were the weirdest pancakes he'd ever seen. It's hard to know what he was thinking. Then he looked around.

"Where am I?" he asked.

"The fifth line," said Barbara, filling his cup. The Mori house is on the fifth concession line of Leopold County.

"The fifth?" he asked. He stared around again. He looked as if he didn't believe it. "The fifth?" He stared at Barbara, who nodded. He stared at Tan. Tan nodded, too. The Stranger kept staring at Tan, at his red pyjamas, his long ponytail, his bright dark eyes behind clear-rimmed glasses. "Where am I?"

That's when the fax machine started beeping and the Stranger spilled his tea. Brad got him a tea towel but he didn't seem hurt. He stared into the dark where the computer stuff is. There are hardly any walls in the dome.

The fax machine beeps when a transmission is coming through. Then it makes a whirring sound and paper starts rolling out with a message on it.

The boy watched the fax machine blinking in the shadows, because the lights were not on in the office part of the dome.

"It's just what my parents do," said little Tony. The machinery was still a mystery to him, too.

The Stranger looked at Tan again—all around at the dome. There's a second floor loft but it's not big, so the Stranger could see clear up to the curving roof and out at the rain pelting down. If there had been stars out he could have seen them. He seemed to get a little dizzy from looking up.

"Sit," said Barbara, and this time she made him sit on a stool next to the kitchen island. He steadied himself. To Ky he looked like someone who had just woken up and had no idea what was going on.

By now the fax machine was spewing out a great long roll of paper which curled to the floor. The Stranger watched it for a minute.

"I think we should get your father," said Barbara in a very gentle voice.

"No," said the boy firmly. "He's asleep, eh. We was at Bernie's. You know Bernie?"

But none of the Moris know Bernie. "Cards," he said. "Having a few drinks … Christmas …" He looked back at the fax. "What is this place?"

Tan laughed. He flipped two okonomiyaki onto a warm plate and handed them to the boy. "Here. You look like you could do with something warm to eat."

"More to read?" asked the boy. He thought Tan had said more to read.

Tan handed him the pancakes. "Try it," he said.

Ky went and got the spicy sauce. She poured a bit on the pancake and sprinkled some nori, toasted seaweed, on top. The Stranger looked at Ky and at the food steaming under his nose. It must have smelled funny to him. He looked around again. He was having trouble putting all this together. These strange sweet salty smells, these people all in red.

"You never heard of Bernie?" he asked.

"No," said Ky.

"Bernie Nystrom?"

"Never heard of him."

"Over on the …" he was going to say where it was that Bernie Nystrom lived, but he seemed to forget. "Dad's out in the car," he said. "We got lost."

"Not a great night for driving," said Tan filling the Stranger's cup with more steaming tea.

"Saw your light there," he said, squinting hard as if the light had just shone in his eyes. "Slid right out." He made a sliding gesture with his hand.

"It's pretty icy," said Tan.

"Never seen such a bright light," said the Stranger.

Ky remembers him saying this. It rankled her. He made it sound as if their light had been responsible for his accident. Her mother winked at her.

Tony looked like he was going to say something. Brad put his hand over his brother's mouth. Tony struggled but the Stranger didn't notice. The fax stopped.

"You sure you ain't never heard of Bernie?" he asked one more time. It seemed to matter a great deal, as if he couldn't imagine someone not knowing good ol' Bernie Nystrom.

"Is there someone we could phone for you?" Barbara asked. "Do you need a tow or something?"

The Stranger was staring at the okonomiyaki. "Anita who?" he asked. At that, both Brad and Tony started giggling until Ky shushed them up.

"A *tow* truck," said Barbara, very carefully. "To get you out of the ditch."

The boy put the plate down without touching the food. He rubbed his hands on his wet pants. He was shivering. Barbara sent Brad to get a blanket.

"Could I use your phone?" the boy asked. Ky ran to get the cordless phone from the office area. There was a phone closer, but Ky always uses the cordless.

You have to see this phone to imagine the Stranger's surprise. It's clear plastic. You can see the electronic stuff inside it, the speakers and amplifiers and switches and everything.

The Stranger stared at it, held it up closer to his eyes. That was when Ky thought of all the time travel books she'd read and wondered if this guy was from some other century. Then she remembered that he had come by truck. That's what he'd said anyway. She wondered if he had been telling the truth. He sure didn't want anyone going to look for his father. Maybe he had been planning on robbing them? But looking at him again, she realized that he was in no condition to rob anyone. She showed him how the phone worked.

"What's your number?" she asked.

"Don't got no number," he said. But he took the phone and slowly punched some numbers anyway. He belched, and a sour smell came from his mouth. Ky stepped back quickly, afraid that he was going to throw up.

The phone rang and rang and no one answered it. Ky watched the Stranger's face. He seemed to fall asleep between each ring and wake up again, not knowing where he was.

"Neighbours," he said, hanging up after about 30 rings. He looked suspiciously at the phone, as if to say, How could I reach anyone I know on a phone like that?

Then he looked at Ky and her family. "Where am I *really*?" he asked.

Brad came back with a comforter and Barbara suggested to the Stranger that he wear it while she put his wet things in the dryer. He didn't like that idea. But as nice as Barbara is, as small as she is, she can be pretty pushy, and she was afraid he was going to catch pneumonia. So the Stranger found himself without his clothes in a very strange house.

Maybe it was then, to take his mind off wearing only a comforter, that he tried the okonomiyaki. He was very hungry. He wolfed down two helpings, then a third. It was the first time he smiled.

"Hey," said Ky. "It's almost Christmas. You'd better save some room for turkey dinner."

"What?" said the Stranger.

"You'd better save some room for turkey dinner."

The Stranger stopped eating. He stared at the food on his plate. Ky wanted to tell him she was just kidding. She couldn't believe he had taken it so seriously. She was going to say something, but then he asked if he could phone his neighbour again. He still didn't have any luck. But now he seemed real edgy.

Then the telephone answering machine in the office took a long message. It was a computer expert phoning Tan, and he talked all in computerese, even though it was nighttime and two days before Christmas.

The Stranger must have heard that voice coming from the dark side of the dome where the lights flashed. Maybe that was what threw him. Or maybe it was when the VCR, which had been on Pause, came back on by itself. Suddenly there were voices from up in the loft. Ky can't remember what part of the movie it was when it came back on. Maybe it was when the angel jumped off the top of the bridge to save the life of the hero. Maybe it was a part like that with dramatic music and lots of shouting and splashing. Maybe the Stranger didn't know it was just a movie on TV. Who knows what he thought was going on there? Maybe in his house there was no TV.

He got edgier and edgier. He started pacing. Then, suddenly, he remembered his neighbour, Lloydy Rintoul.

"You know Lloydy," he said.

Nobody did.

"Sure," he said. "Lloydy Rintoul." He pointed first north and then east and then north again as he tried to get his bearings in this round house with its invisible walls.

"You don't know Lloydy?"

The Stranger, despite his size, suddenly looked like a little lost boy. But then he shook his head and jumped to his feet.

"Lloydy, he's got a tractor," he said. "He'll pull the truck out." He started to leave. "I'll just get him, eh." He forgot he did not have any clothes on. Tan led him back to his stool. Barbara told him she'd check on the wash. Tan said they should maybe phone Lloydy first. But Lloydy didn't have a phone either. The people Ky knows in the country all have phones and televisions. But there are people around Leopold County who have lived there longer than anyone and lived poor, scraping out a living on the rocky soil just like their forefathers and foremothers did.

Maybe the kids were looking at the Stranger strangely then, because suddenly he got impatient. Ky said that he looked like a wild bear in a downy comforter cornered by a pack of little people in red pyjamas.

"I'm gonna get Lloydy," he said loudly. It sounded like a threat. It scared the Moris a bit. Barbara decided to get him his clothes even though they were still damp.

And so the Stranger prepared to go. They didn't try to stop him but they insisted that he borrow a big yellow poncho because it was still raining hard.

Now that he had his clothes back on and his escape was imminent, the Stranger calmed down a bit.

"I'll bring it back," he said.

"I'm sure you will," said Tan, as he helped him into the poncho.

Ky went and got him a flashlight, too. It was a silver pencil flashlight she had gotten for her birthday. She had to show him how it worked.

"I'll bring this back," he said to her.

"Okay," she said. "Thanks."

And then he was gone. He slid on the driveway and ended up with a thud on his backside.

"He'll have some awful bruises in the morning," said Barbara.

She called to him to come back. She told him she would call for help. He turned halfway down the driveway and seemed to listen, but his hearing wasn't very good even up close, so who knows what he thought she said. She did mention getting the police. Maybe he heard that. Whatever, he turned and ran away, slipping and sliding all the way. Tan considered driving him, but the ice was too treacherous.

"What are the bets," said Brad, "that we never see that stuff again?"

They never did. The Stranger never did return the poncho or the flashlight. In the morning the family all went out to the road. There was no truck there. Somehow, in his drunken haze, the Stranger must have found Lloydy Rintoul or somebody found him or his dad woke up and got the truck out. It was a mystery.

Ky tried to find Bernie Nystrom's name in the phone book. There was no listing. The boy had never said the name of his neighbour and they already knew that Lloydy Rintoul had no phone, so there was no way of tracking him down. The Moris didn't really care much about getting their stuff back, though. It was Christmas, after all.

I saw the story in the *National Enquirer* in January. I was in line at the grocery store with my mother, reading the headlines of the tabloids. I enjoy doing that. There are great stories about tribes in Brazil who look like Elvis Presley, or some 75-year-old woman who gives birth to twin dolphins, or families of eight who live in an abandoned filing cabinet. But this headline jumped off the page at me.

TEEN ABDUCTED BY MARTIANS!
Country boy undergoes torturous experiments
while constrained in an alien flying saucer!
Experts wonder: Who or what is Kerdy Dickus
and what does he want with our moon!

I don't know why I flipped open to page 26 to read the story. I don't know why I paid good money to actually buy the rag. Somehow I knew. And when I showed the picture on page 26 to Ky, she gasped.

It was him. There was the Stranger showing the huge bruises inflicted by the aliens on his arms and ribs and thighs. He told of how he had seen a blinding light and the truck had been pulled right off the road by the saucer's powerful tractor beam. He told of how the aliens had hypnotized him and brought him to their saucer. He told of the drugs they had made him drink; how they tried to get his father, too, but he had stopped them. He told of the weird food they had made him eat and how it had made him throw up all the next day. His mother could attest to his ill health. "I've never seen him so green," she said. "And he's normally such a healthy lad."

It was his mother who had contacted the *National Enquirer*. She read it all the time and she knew it was a story that would interest them.

His father, too, although he had managed somehow to stay out of the clutches of the aliens' hypnotic powers, could attest to the attack on the car. And then—blackness. There were two hours missing out of his recollection of the night. The aliens had obviously zapped him.

"Something ought to be done about this kind of menace!" said the father.

According to the newspaper, the boy underwent several sessions with a psychiatric investigator after the incident. The investigator specialized in AATT: Alien Abduction Trauma Therapy. He put the boy in a deep trance and interviewed him at length. "Truth drugs" were administered, and all the results concurred: the boy had obviously undergone a close encounter with alien beings. Under the trance the boy revealed some overheard conversation that might, the investigator believed, partially explain the purpose of the aliens' trip to earth.

"This might be a recognizance mission." Other experts in the field agreed. "But their long-term goal has to do with our moon and the saving of it. From what? *For* what? It is hard to tell."

One line had become imprinted on the boy's mind. The only spoken part he recalled vividly from his close encounter.

"Save the moon for Kerdy Dickus."

"Perhaps," said the psychiatric investigator, "there is some alien purpose for the boy remembering this one line."

The article went on to give a pretty good account of the aliens, what they looked like, what their flying saucer looked like. But you already know all that.

I had heard about the Stranger from Ky. That's how I somehow recognized the story in the *Enquirer*. The next time I saw the Moris, I showed them the paper. But after they all laughed themselves silly, we talked about it a lot.

Should they try to find the Stranger, now that they knew his name? Even without a phone, they could easily track him down. Should the paper be contacted, so that the truth could be known? What about the psychiatrist who specialized in AATT? The experts?

"I wouldn't mind getting my flashlight back," Ky admitted, but she wasn't really serious.

And so they have never followed up on the story. Ky always imagines she'll run into the Stranger one day in the nearby town. I hope I'm with her. Maybe I'll be up there for her birthday. Maybe it will be raining. Maybe we'll be coming out of a store and he'll be coming in wearing the big yellow poncho. He'll walk right by us, and Ky and I will turn just as he passes and whisper the magic words.

"Save the moon for Kerdy Dickus."

Then we'll hop in our saucer and slip off back to our own world.

GREEN GRASS, RUNNING WATER

an excerpt from the novel by Thomas King

LIONEL HAD ONLY MADE THREE MISTAKES in his entire life, the kind of mistakes that seem small enough at the time, but somehow get out of hand. The kind that stay with you for a long time. And he could name each one.

The first mistake Lionel made was wanting to have his tonsils out. It had happened when he was eight, and, in many ways, it was more a simple error in judgment. Several of the kids at school developed sore throats, and Lois James wound up having her tonsils out. What Lionel noticed most about Lois's tonsils was that she got to stay home from school for over two weeks and you couldn't even tell she had had an operation. Then, too, the teachers treated her like she was royalty or something. Mrs. Pratt brought Lois a sucker, the kind with a hard candy shell and a chewy fudge centre. Green, Lionel's favourite. So when Lionel developed a sore throat, he began thinking about Lois and her tonsils. When his throat didn't improve, his mother took him to the band office to see Dr. Loomis.

Dr. Loomis was a skinny old man with a huge pile of white hair and eyes that looked as though they would pop out of his head. His tongue was inordinately long, and, as he talked, he would run it around his face, catching the sides of his mouth and the bottom of his chin. Once a week, he came out to the reserve to doctor the sick. There was no formal clinic, and he seldom had any patients. Most of the people on the reserve went to see Martha Old Crow or Jesse Many Guns, who were the doctors of choice. Dr. Loomis generally spent his time in the cafeteria, drinking coffee, and talking about the hospital in Toronto where he had trained just after the turn of the century.

Lionel's mother had taken Lionel to see Martha first, and, after Martha was done feeling his ears and shoulders and looking in his eyes, she said, "Simple thing, this. Maybe take this boy to see the Frog doctor. No one comes to see him last week. Maybe his feelings are hurt, that one."

So, on Wednesday, Lionel's mother arrived at the band office with Lionel in tow. Dr. Loomis shook Lionel's mother's hand and touched his nose with his tongue, and told her that her boy was in the best of hands. "I studied in Toronto, you know," he said.

Lionel told him that his throat hurt something awful, that it was hard to swallow or move his head, and that he kept making mistakes on his math homework. Dr. Loomis pursed his lips and nodded gravely. He squeezed Lionel's neck and face and shoulders and had Lionel suck in air in quick, noisy gulps.

Lilly Morris, who worked behind the snack bar, got on the phone, and, by the time Dr. Loomis got around to thumping Lionel on the chest and feeling under his armpits, there were about 20 people in the cafeteria.

"Does it hurt here?"

"Something awful."

"There, too."

"Does it hurt here?"

"Ohhhhh ..."

Charlie Looking Bear who was two years older than Lionel and related through a second marriage, grabbed his crotch and asked in a high voice, "Does it hurt here?" But Dr. Loomis ignored Charlie and continued to prod Lionel with his bony fingers. Finally, he took a flat stick out of his jacket pocket and stuck it down Lionel's throat. "Say 'ahhhhh.' "

"Well," said Dr. Loomis, "the boy has a sore throat. Pretty bad one, too. Can't do much about it. Best thing is a little crushed aspirin mixed up with honey and lemon. Give him lots of fluids. Maybe keep him in bed for a couple of days."

"It hurts real bad!" said Lionel.

"Course, the tonsils are inflamed and they don't look all that healthy. Wouldn't hurt to get them out sometime. They can just keep getting inflamed. Always better to get them out when the child is young."

Lionel could see the distress in his mother's face. "Don't think we need a hospital," she said. "We should wait and see."

"I can't even eat!" said Lionel.

"It's an easy operation," said Dr. Loomis.

Lionel's mother shook her head. "He's not doing too well in school right now. If he had that operation, how much school would he miss?"

This is where, as Lionel remembered, the idea began to fall apart.

"Actually," said Dr. Loomis, "there's no need to miss any school at all. We could do it this summer."

"Summer?" said Lionel. "I don't want no operation during the summer."

Charlie was grinning. "What would John Wayne do?" he whispered, and he grabbed his hair and pulled his head off to one side and made cutting motions across his throat.

"We don't want you missing any more school, honey."

"I don't mind missing school. Lois had her tonsils out, and she missed school and she still gets good grades."

Dr. Loomis laughed, and his eyes bugged out of his head even more, and his tongue went looking for his chin. "Why don't you think about it and let me know. See how the throat does. He'd have to go to Calgary to have it done."

In the car, on the way home, Lionel sulked in the front seat and stared out the window. "I know I can't do any homework with my throat like this."

For the rest of the week and the next, Lionel shuffled around the house, coughing and complaining, until finally his mother called Dr. Loomis and asked him to arrange for an operation as soon as possible.

And so, in early February, Lionel and his mother drove the 210 kilometres to Calgary. One of Lionel's aunts lived in Calgary. "I'm going to stay with Jean," his mother told him, "so I can come and see you every day."

There were no beds available in the children's ward, and Lionel was given a bed in another wing. "It's just for the night," the nurse said. "After the operation, we'll move you in with the other children."

To his delight, Lionel discovered that the nurses were much too busy to bother with him, and he was free to roam the hospital. The cafeteria was his favourite stop. His mother had given him $3 in case of an emergency, which Lionel decided, after thinking about it, included the purchase of doughnuts. Later in the evening, a tall blonde woman came into the room.

"Hi," she said. "You must be the lucky young man who won the free plane ride."

Lionel liked playing these kinds of games. "That's me," he said. "When do we go?"

"Well," said the blonde woman, "We're almost ready. Have you ever been on a plane?"

"No!"

"Well, you certainly are lucky."

An hour later, a nurse came in with a wheelchair, and Lionel was put into a red and white ambulance, driven to the airport, and placed on a plane.

"Is my mother coming on the plane?"

"Don't worry, kid," said the ambulance driver. "Nurse said she's going to meet us in Toronto."

"Toronto!" said Lionel. "I've never been to Toronto!"

"Pretty exciting, huh?"

"It sure is."

When Lionel arrived at Sick Children's Hospital, everyone was so friendly. An older nurse who reminded him of his Auntie Louise took him to his room and told him all about the doctor who was going to perform the operation. This doctor had three children of her own, and heart operations, the nurse said, were a very common thing these days.

"Nothing wrong with my heart," said Lionel. "It's my tonsils that hurt."

"You don't have to worry," said the nurse. "A heart operation like yours is really very simple."

"My heart is just fine."

"And it'll be even better tomorrow."

Lionel thought the nurse was kidding and he laughed, and then he looked at her face. "Where's my mother?"

"She'll be here tomorrow, sweetheart. She'll be right here when you wake up. You better hop into bed, now, and get some sleep."

In that instant, Lionel knew that some horrible mistake had been made, that he was alone in Toronto, that his mother was in Calgary, that, in the morning, some doctor with three kids was going to cut his heart open. And he began to cry.

"My heart's good. There's nothing wrong with it. My tonsils are rotten, that's all."

The nurse tried to calm him down, told him she would see if the hospital could get in touch with his mother, and, in the meantime, why didn't he watch some television in the lounge which was just down the hall to the left. At the last moment, the nurse must have realized her mistake, because she called to him as he got to the door. "Wait a minute, honey," she said. "I'll go with you."

But it was too late. Lionel turned right and bolted down the hall. He found a set of stairs going down, crashed into the main lobby, and before anyone could do anything he was out the front door and into the night. He got as far as an arcade on Yonge Street and was trying to call home when the manager noticed that there was a barefoot Indian kid in what looked to be a hospital gown in his arcade and called the police.

By the time Lionel was dragged back to the hospital, insisting the entire way that his heart was just fine, the resident on call had had the good sense to phone Calgary and had discovered that the patient they had been expecting was a 10-year-old white child named Timothy and not an eight-year-old Indian boy named Lionel.

The next day, he was on a plane, his heart and tonsils intact, and, by the time they got back to the reserve, Lionel's throat felt fine.

But that wasn't the end of it. Fourteen years later, when he applied for an insurance policy, Lionel discovered that, while he had almost forgotten the incident, the original error had somehow worked its way into a computer file. The insurance company wanted him to have a physical with a separate evaluation of his heart condition.

THE OTHER FAMILY

by Himani Bannerji

WHEN THE LITTLE GIRL came home it was already getting dark. The winter twilight had transformed the sheer blue sky of the day into the colour of steel, on which were etched a few stars, the bare winter trees, and the dark wedges of the housetops. A few lit windows cast a faint glow on the snow outside. The mother stood at her window and watched the little hooded figure walking toward the house. The child looked like a shadow, her blue coat blended into the shadows of the evening. This child, her own, how small and insubstantial she seemed, and how alone, walking home through a pavement covered with ice and snow! It felt unreal. So different was this childhood from her own, so far away from the sun, the trees, and the peopled streets of her own country! What did I do, she thought, I took her away from her own people and her own language, and now here she comes walking alone, through an alien street in a country named Canada.

As she contemplated the solitary, moving figure, her own solitude rushed over her like a tide. She had drifted away from a world that she had lived in and understood, and now she stood here at the same distance from her home as from the homes which she glimpsed while walking past the sparkling clean windows of the sandblasted houses. And now the doorbell rang, and here was her daughter scraping the snow off her boots on the doormat.

Dinner time was a good time. A time of warmth, of putting hot, steaming food onto the table. A time to chat about the important things of the day, a time to show each other what they had acquired. Sometimes, however, she would be absent-minded, worried perhaps about work, unsettled perhaps by letters that had arrived from home, scraping her feelings into a state of rawness. This was such an evening. She had served herself and her child, started a conversation about their two cats and fallen into a silence after a few minutes.

"You aren't listening to me, Mother."

The complaining voice got through to her, and she looked at the indignant face demanding attention from the other side of the table. She gathered herself together.

"So what did he do, when you gave him dried food?"

"Oh, I don't remember, I think he scratched the ground near his bowl and left."

The child laughed.

"That was smart of him! So why don't we buy tinned food for them?"

"Maybe we should," she said, and tried to change the topic.

"So what did you do in your school today?"

"Oh, we drew pictures like we do every day. We never study anything—not like you said you did in your school. We drew a family—our family. Want to see it?"

"Sure, and let's go into the living room, OK? This is messy." Scraping of chairs and the lighting of the lamps in the other room. They both made a rush for the most comfortable chair, both reaching it at the same time and made a compromise.

"How about you sit in my lap? No? OK, sit next to me then and we will squeeze in somehow."

There was a remarkable resemblance between the two faces, except that the face of the child had a greater intensity, given by the wide, open eyes. She was fine boned, and had black hair framing her face. Right now she was struggling with the contents of her satchel, apparently trying to feel her way to the paintings.

"Here it is," she said, producing a piece of paper. "Here's the family!"

The mother looked at the picture for a long time. She was very still. Her face had set into an expression of anger and sadness. She was trying very hard not to cry. She didn't want to frighten the child, and yet what she saw made her feel distant from her daughter, as though she was looking at her through the reverse end of a telescope. She couldn't speak at all. The little girl too sat very still, a little recoiled from the body of her mother, as though expecting a blow. Her hands were clenched into fists, but finally it was she who broke the silence.

"What happened?" she said. "Don't you like it?"

"Listen," said the mother, "this is not your family. I, you, and your father are dark-skinned, dark-haired. I don't have a blond wig hidden in my closet, my eyes are black, not blue, and your father's beard is black, not red, and you, do you have a white skin, a button nose with freckles, blue eyes and blond hair tied into a ponytail? You said you drew our family. This is not it, is it?"

The child was now feeling distinctly cornered. At first she was startled and frightened by her mother's response, but now she was prepared to be defiant. She had the greatest authority behind her, and she now summoned it to help her.

"I drew it from a book," she said, "all our books have this same picture of the family. You can go and see it for yourself. And everybody else drew it too. You can ask our teacher tomorrow. She liked it, so there!"

The little girl was clutching at her last straw.

"But you? Where are you in this picture?" demanded her mother, by now thoroughly aroused. "Where are we? Is this the family you would like to have? Don't you want us anymore? You want to be a *mem-sahib*, a white girl?"

But even as she lashed out these questions the mother regretted them. She could see that she made no sense to the child. She could feel the unfairness of it all. She was sorry that she was putting such a heavy burden on such young shoulders.

"First I bring her here," she thought, "and then I try to make her feel guilty for wanting to be the same as the others." But something had taken hold of her this evening. Panic at the thought of losing her child, despair and guilt galvanized her into speech she regretted, and she looked with anger at her only child, who it seemed wanted to be white, who had rejected her dark mother. Someday this child would be ashamed of her, she thought, someday would move out into the world of those others. Someday they would be enemies. Confusing thoughts ran through her head like images on an uncontrollable television screen, in the chaos of which she heard her ultimate justification flung at her by her daughter—they wanted me to draw the family, didn't they? "They" wanted "her" to draw "the family." The way her daughter pronounced the words "they" or "the family" indicated that she knew what she was talking about. The simple pronoun "they" definitely stood for authority, for that uncontrollable yet organized world immediately outside, of which the school was the ultimate expression. It surrounded their own private space. "They" had power, "they" could crush little people like her anytime "they" wanted to, and in "their" world that was the picture of the family. Whether her mother liked it or not, whether she looked like the little girl in it or not, made not one jot of difference. That was, yes, that was the right picture. As these thoughts passed through her mind, her anger ebbed away. Abandoning her fury and distance, the mother bowed her head at the image of this family and burst into sobs.

"What will happen to you?" she said. "What did I do to you?"

She cried a great deal and said many incoherent things. The little girl was patient, quietly absorbing her mother's change of mood. She had a thoughtful look on her face, and bit her nails from time to time. She did not protest any more, but nor did she cry. After a while her mother took her to bed and tucked her in, and sat in the kitchen with the fearful vision of her daughter always outside of the window of the blond family, never the centre of her own life, always rejecting herself, and her life transformed into a gigantic peep show. She wept very bitterly because she had caused this destruction, and because she had hated her child in her own fear of rejection, and because she had sowed guilt into her mind.

When her mother went to bed and closed the door, the child, who had been waiting for a long time, left the bed. She crossed the corridor on her tiptoes, past the row of shoes, the silent gathering of the overcoats, and the mirror with the wavy surface, and went into the washroom. Behind the door was another mirror, of full length, and clear. Deliberately and slowly the child took off the top of her pyjamas and surveyed herself with grave scrutiny. She saw the brownness of her skin, the wide, staring, dark eyes, the black hair now tousled from the pillows, the scar on her nose, and the brownish pink of her mouth. She stood a while lost in this act of contemplation, until the sound of soft padded feet neared the door, and a whiskered face peeped in. She stooped and picked up the cat and walked back to her own room.

It was snowing again, and little elves with bright coloured coats and snow in their boots had reappeared in the classroom. When finally the coats were hung under pegs with names and boots neatly stowed away, the little girl approached her teacher. She had her painting from the day before in her hand.

"I have brought it back," she said.

"Why?" asked her teacher, "don't you like it any more?"

The little girl was looking around very intently.

"It's not finished yet," she said. "The books I looked at didn't have something. Can I finish it now?"

"Go ahead," said the teacher, moving on to get the colours from the cupboard.

The little girl was looking at the classroom. It was full of children of all colours, of all kinds of shapes of noses and of different colours of hair. She sat on the floor, placed the incomplete picture on a bit piece of newspaper and started to paint. She worked long at it—and with great concentration. Finally it was finished. She went back to her teacher.

"It's finished now," she said, "I drew the rest."

The teacher reached out for the picture and spread it neatly on a desk. There they were, the blond family arranged in a semicircle with a dip in the middle, but next to them, arranged alike, stood another group—a man, a woman, and a child, but they were dark-skinned, dark-haired, the woman wore clothes from her own country, and the little girl in the middle had a scar on her nose.

"Do you like it?"

"Who are they?" asked the teacher, though she should have known. But the little girl didn't mind answering this question one bit.

"It's the other family," she said.

THE TELL-TALE HEART

by Edgar Allan Poe

TRUE!—nervous—very, very dreadfully nervous I had been and am; but why *will* you say that I am mad? The disease had sharpened my senses—not destroyed—not dulled them. Above all was the sense of hearing acute. I heard all things in the heaven and in the earth. I heard many things in hell. How, then, am I mad? Hearken! and observe how healthily—how calmly I can tell you the whole story.

It is impossible to say how first the idea entered my brain; but once conceived, it haunted me day and night. Object there was none. Passion there was none. I loved the old man. He had never wronged me. He had never given me insult. For his gold I had no desire. I think it was his eye! yes, it was this! One of his eyes resembled that of a vulture—a pale blue eye, with a film over it. Whenever it fell upon me, my blood ran cold; and so by degrees—very gradually—I made up my mind to take the life of the old man, and thus rid myself of the eye forever.

Now this is the point. You fancy me mad. Madmen know nothing. But you should have seen *me*. You should have seen how wisely I proceeded—with what caution—with what foresight—with what dissimulation I went to work! I was never kinder to the old man than during the whole week before I killed him. And every night, about midnight, I turned the latch of his door and opened it—oh, so gently! And then, when I had made an opening sufficient for my head, I put in a dark lantern, all closed, closed, so that no light shone out, and then I thrust in my head. Oh, you would have laughed to see how cunningly I thrust it in! I moved it slowly—very, very slowly, so that I might not disturb the old man's sleep. It took me an hour to place my whole head within the opening so far that I could see him as he lay upon his bed. Ha!—would a madman have been so wise as this? And then, when my head was well in the room, I undid the lantern cautiously— oh, so cautiously—cautiously (for the hinges creaked)—I undid it just so much that a single thin ray fell upon the vulture eye. And this I did for seven long nights—every night just at midnight—but I found the eye always closed; and so it was impossible to do the work; for it was not the old man who vexed me, but his Evil Eye. And every morning, when the day broke, I went boldly into the chamber, and spoke courageously to him, calling him by name in a hearty tone, and inquiring how he had passed the night. So you see he would have been a very profound old man, indeed, to suspect that every night, just at twelve, I looked in upon him while he slept.

Upon the eighth night I was more than usually cautious in opening the door. A watch's minute hand moves more quickly than did mine. Never before that night had I *felt* the extent of my own powers—of my sagacity. I could scarcely contain my feelings of triumph. To think that there I was, opening the door, little by little, and he not even to dream of my secret deeds or thoughts. I fairly chuckled at the idea; and perhaps he heard me; for he moved on the bed suddenly, as if startled. Now you may think that I drew back—but no. His room was as black as pitch with the thick darkness (for the shutters were close fastened, through fear of robbers), and so I knew that he could not see the opening of the door, and I kept pushing it on steadily, steadily.

I had my head in, and was about to open the lantern, when my thumb slipped upon the tin fastening, and the old man sprang up in the bed, crying out—"Who's here?"

I kept quite still and said nothing. For a whole hour I did not move a muscle, and in the meantime I did not hear him lie down. He was still sitting up in the bed listening:—just as I have done, night after night, hearkening to the death watches in the wall.

Presently I heard a slight groan, and I knew it was the groan of mortal terror. It was not a groan of pain or of grief—oh, no!—it was the low stifled sound that arises from the bottom of the soul when overcharged with awe. I knew the sound well. Many a night, just at midnight, when all the world slept, it has welled up from my own bosom, deepening, with its dreadful echo, the terrors that distracted me. I say I knew it well. I knew what the old man felt, and pitied him, although I chuckled at heart. I knew that he had been lying awake ever since the first slight noise, when he had turned in the bed. His fears had been ever since growing upon him. He had been trying to fancy them causeless, but could not. He had been saying to himself—"It is nothing but the wind in the chimney—it is only a mouse crossing the floor," or "it is merely a cricket which has made a single chirp." Yes, he has been trying to comfort himself with these suppositions; but he had found all in vain. *All in vain*; because Death, in approaching him, had stalked with his black shadow before him, and enveloped the victim. And it was the mournful influence of the unperceived shadow that caused him to feel—although he neither saw nor heard—to *feel* the presence of my head within the room.

When I had waited a long time, very patiently, without hearing him lie down, I resolved to open a little—a very, very little crevice in the lantern. So I opened it—you cannot imagine how stealthily, stealthily—until, at length, a single dim ray, like the thread of a spider, shot from out the crevice and full upon the vulture eye.

It was open—wide, wide open—and I grew furious as I gazed upon it. I saw it with perfect distinctness—all a dull blue, with a hideous veil over it that chilled the very marrow in my bones; but I could see nothing else of the old man's face or person: for I had directed the ray as if by instinct, precisely upon the damned spot.

And now have I not told you that what you mistake for madness is but over-acuteness of the senses?—now, I say, there came to my ears a low, dull, quick sound, such as a watch makes when enveloped in cotton. I knew *that* sound well too. It was the beating of the old man's heart. It increased my fury, as the beating of a drum stimulates the soldier into courage.

But even yet I refrained and kept still. I scarcely breathed. I held the lantern motionless. I tried how steadily I could maintain the ray upon the eye. Meantime the hellish tattoo of the heart increased. It grew quicker and quicker, and louder and louder every instant. The old man's terror *must* have been extreme! It grew louder, I say, louder every moment!—do you mark me well? I have told you that I am nervous: so I am. And now at the dead hour of the night, amid the dreadful silence of that old house, so strange a noise as this excited me to uncontrollable terror. Yet, for some minutes longer I refrained and stood still. But the beating grew louder, louder! I thought the heart must burst. And now a new anxiety seized me—the sound would be heard by a neighbour! The old man's hour had come! With a loud yell, I threw open the lantern and leaped into the room. He shrieked once— once only. In an instant I dragged him to the floor, and pulled the heavy bed over him. I then smiled gaily, to find the deed so far done. But, for many minutes, the heart beat on with a muffled sound. This, however, did not vex me; it would not be heard through the wall. At length it ceased. The old man was dead. I removed the bed and examined the corpse. Yes, he was stone, stone dead. I placed my hand upon the heart and held it there many minutes. There was no pulsation. He was stone dead. His eye would trouble me no more.

It you still think me mad, you will think so no longer when I describe the wise precautions I took for the concealment of the body. The night waned, and I worked hastily, but in silence. First of all I dismembered the corpse. I cut off the head and the arms and the legs.

I then took up three planks from the flooring of the chamber, and deposited all between the scalings. I then replaced the boards so cleverly, so cunningly, that no human eye—not even *his*—could have detected any thing wrong. There was nothing to wash out—no stain of any kind—no bloodspot whatever. I had been too wary for that. A tub had caught all—ha! ha!

When I had made an end of these labours, it was four o'clock—still dark as midnight. As the bell sounded the hour, there came a knocking at the street door. I went down to open it with a light heart—for what had I *now* to fear? There entered three men, who introduced themselves, with perfect suavity, as officers of the police. A shriek had been heard by a neighbour during the night; suspicion of foul play had been aroused; information had been lodged at the police office, and they (the officers) had been deputed to search the premises.

I smiled—for *what* had I to fear? I bade the gentlemen welcome. The shriek, I said, was my own in a dream. The old man, I mentioned, was absent in the country. I took my visitors all over the house. I bade them search—search *well*. I led them, at length, to *his* chamber. I showed them his treasures, secure, undisturbed. In the enthusiasm of my confidence, I brought chairs into the room, and desired them *here* to rest from their fatigues, while I myself, in the wild audacity of my perfect triumph, placed my own seat upon the very spot beneath which reposed the corpse of the victim.

The officers were satisfied. My *manner* had convinced them. I was singularly at ease. They sat, and while I answered cheerily, they chatted familiar things. But, ere long, I felt myself getting pale and wished them gone. My head ached, and I fancied a ringing in my ears: but still they sat and still chatted. The ringing became more distinct— it continued and became more distinct. I talked more freely to get rid of the feeling: but it continued and gained definitiveness—until, at length, I found that the noise was *not* within my ears.

No doubt I now grew *very* pale—but I talked more fluently, and with a heightened voice. Yet the sound increased—and what could I do? It was *a low, dull, quick sound—much such a sound as a watch makes when enveloped in cotton.* I gasped for breath—and yet the officers heard it not. I talked more quickly—more vehemently; but the noise steadily increased. I arose and argued about trifles, in a high key and with violent gesticulations, but the noise steadily increased. Why *would* they not be gone? I paced the floor to and fro with heavy strides, as if excited to fury by the observation of the men—but the noise steadily increased. Oh God! what *could* I do? I foamed—I raved—I swore! I swung the chair upon which I had been sitting, and grated it upon the boards, but the noise arose over all and continually increased. It grew louder—louder—*louder!* And still the men chatted pleasantly, and smiled. Was it possible they heard not? Almighty God!—no, no! They heard!—they suspected!—they *knew!*—they were making a mockery of my horror!—this I thought, and this I think. But any thing was better than this agony! Any thing was more tolerable than this derision! I could bear those hypocritical smiles no longer! I felt that I must scream or die!—and now—again!—hark! louder! louder! louder! *louder!*—

"Villains!" I shrieked, "dissemble no more! I admit the deed!—tear up the planks!—here, here!—it is the beating of his hideous heart!"

Nonfiction

NONFICTION

Think of what you have read today, or what you are about to write in your classes. Chances are, much of this writing will be nonfiction, whether it comes in the form of a personal letter or an e-mail, a magazine article or a newspaper article, a movie review or an advice column, a chapter from a textbook or an encyclopedia entry.

Nonfiction writing informs us of aspects of our world—past and present, good and bad, simple and complex. The selections that were chosen for this unit reflect the range of styles found in nonfiction writing. In all of its forms, though, nonfiction has one dominant purpose—to inform readers about a particular person, place, event, or idea.

As you read the nonfiction selections in this anthology, notice how the main idea is stated near the beginning of the piece. Look closely at the overall organization of the details the author has included and how she or he puts them together to serve a purpose and appeal to an audience.

CHARACTERISTICS OF NONFICTION WRITING

A nonfiction selection
- presents facts to a specific audience
- usually states the main idea in the first or last sentence of the introductory paragraph
- can be organized in a variety of ways, for example, by time or comparison, or spatially
- usually restates the main idea in the concluding paragraph
- includes supporting details in intervening paragraphs
- may or may not contain personal opinions of the writer

On Love and a Lake

by Renée David

SEVERAL YEARS AGO, after my parents divorced, my dad started taking me and my three brothers to Otter Lake, Ont., where his parents used to own a cottage. We would only stay a week, but we loved every minute of it. We shoved as much fun as possible into our time there: bonfires at night, volleyball over fences, hours spent building towers in the sand. My hands would get stains on them from all the berries we picked and I never tired of being a dolphin or a stranded secret agent when we took a dip in the lake.

Now that we're older, the bonfires have been replaced by mudpout fishing and late-night card playing. The time we spend there is very special and as each year passes I start longing for the refreshing lake air sooner. This summer will be my seventh summer at the lake.

I'm 13 years old and I love these waters more than anyone, well almost anyone. I learned today that my dad has spent 46 summers on this lake, missing only three out of his life. His parents first brought him down when he was only three weeks old. He knows every creek and knows which ones lead to the best fishing spots in the lake "from years of paddling a canoe in it," he says. Well, today he took me out in the boat and we paddled around the lake. He showed me the shallows and the rock outcrops. He took me to the islands he played on when he was my age and showed me the lot he plans to buy someday. "You can drop your kids off with me and go out with your husband," he offers. He wants his ashes spread across the lake when he dies.

I've never known anyone to love something this much. And today when he took me around and pointed to "where the loons nest and where the otters used to slide," I know I'm being given the knowledge he has collected from summers spent falling in love with his lake. And I know someday he'll take my kids around and show them Snake Island, where he camped with his brothers, and that this precious knowledge will be passed down to them. Hopefully, they'll also learn the love for the lake he has passed down to me.

I believe that this wisdom, gathered from something that is so loved, is the most wonderful gift a person can be given. Thank you, Dad.

THE GOAL POST

by Edward Smith

MY PERSONAL SPORTS HISTORY is already legend.

I was always athletically minded. Unfortunately, I was never athletically bodied, a fact that took its toll on my performance.

At 12 I was almost 6 feet tall and weighed about 130 pounds fully clothed. Naturally, I wanted to play with the older boys and girls, both of which categories gave me problems. The boys finally let me into their group, starting me off in hockey as a goal post. The netting was held up on one side by a starrigan[1] frozen in the ice, and on the other by me.

Later, I graduated to water-nipper. When the puck went through the hole in the ice near the mouth of the brook, I had to roll up my sleeves, stick my arm down in the water, nip the puck between my fingers, and get puck, fingers, and arm back on dry ice before the whole thing sished over. When the ice failed to bear even my weight, the older boys would kindly haul me out of the brook before going on with their game. By the time I'd get home, my clothes would be like a suit of armour and they'd have to thaw me out behind the stove before the pants could be prised off.

Being named official puck-getter was a real thrill. We played our hockey on a long, narrow pond which in fall and early winter was one beautiful sheet of ice. When one of our stronger players took a shot on goal and missed, my job was to go after the puck and try to get it back before dark. Since we had only one puck, there was lots of incentive from the bigger fellows to get your butt back there in a hurry.

Finally, I made the team. Teachers will note that this is an excellent example of advancement as opposed to promotion.

Equipment in those days was modest: an Eaton's sale catalogue around each shin, your gun mitts, and nothing anywhere else. Unfortunately, and to our great discomfort, anywhere else was where we usually got hit. It wasn't uncommon at all to see some poor fellow hobbling home in the late afternoon, bent double at the waist and moaning something fierce. Few of us ever expected to beget.

Years later—and this is the truth—I was playing goal in some Halifax bush league when the coach discovered I wasn't wearing any protection there, and had several unkind things to say about it. Nobody told me it was dangerous, I just expected to take my lumps as always and not to faint. Actually, mainlanders are very fussy about that sort of thing. Nish.

My parents were always interested in my development as an athlete, although that development was somewhat slow. For years, they were the only parents who ever came to the pond to watch. Although as we got older and the games more competitive, others followed their example. In one game I actually got to touch the puck, or something equally heroic, and my father got so excited, jumping up and down, that his feet went out from under him and his whole 210 pounds landed on the back of his head. A player on the opposing team—New Perlican, I think—had the audacity to laugh hysterically at my prostrate father so I laid him out with my stick. It was most unsportsmanlike, and I'm ashamed of it to this day. But we were a close family, you know.

Many years later I actually scored a goal in a championship game in Gander Gardens. Smith senior got so overcome that he threw his cap on the ice. Then he grabbed the hat of the man next to him and threw that out, too. Very supportive was my father.

No one organized us back then. We did it all ourselves. We shovelled the snow off the pond, called sides, and went at it like maniacs until it was either too dark to see or everyone had gone home bent double at the waist and moaning something fierce.

Today, the young ones are organized and supervised and regulated from start to finish. In larger towns, that's the way it has to be, I suppose. But when I think of the dozens of volunteers it takes to make minor hockey possible in our town, I see once more my Mom and Dad, standing in the snow at the edge of the pond or sitting in the car at the side of the road, waiting for their pride and joy to get to his feet just long enough to get knocked sticks up again. In another time, in another place, they would have been volunteers of the finest order.

Because they cared.

---

1. starrigan: a dead evergreen tree or stump.

PAGES FROM A DIARY

by Sylvia Plath

This diary entry was written when the poet Sylvia Plath was 17.

November 13, 1949

AS OF TODAY I HAVE DECIDED to keep a diary again—just a place where I can write my thoughts and opinions when I have a moment. Somehow I have to keep and hold the rapture of being 17. Every day is so precious I feel infinitely sad at the thought of all this time melting farther and farther away from me as I grow older. *Now, now* is the perfect time of my life.

In reflecting back upon these last 16 years, I can see tragedies and happiness, all relative—all unimportant now—fit only to smile upon a bit mistily.

I still do not know myself. Perhaps I never will. But I feel free— unbound by responsibility, I still can come up to my own private room, with my drawings hanging on the walls … and pictures pinned up over my bureau. It is a room suited to me—tailored, uncluttered, and peaceful … I love the quiet lines of the furniture, the two book-cases filled with poetry books and fairy tales saved from childhood.

At the present moment I am very happy, sitting at my desk, looking out at the bare trees around the house across the street…. Always I want to be an observer. I want to be affected by life deeply, but never so blinded that I cannot see my share of existence in a wry, humorous light and mock myself as I mock others.

I am afraid of getting older. I am afraid of getting married. Spare me from cooking three meals a day—spare me from the relentless cage of routine and rote. I want to be free—free to know people and their backgrounds—free to move to different parts of the world, so I may learn that there are other morals and standards besides my own. I want, I think, to be omniscient…. I think I would like to call myself "The girl who wanted to be God." Yet if I were not in this body, where *would* I be? Perhaps I am *destined* to be classified and qualified. But, oh, I cry out against it. I am I—I am powerful—but to what extent? I am I.

Sometimes I try to put myself in another's place, and I am frightened when I find I am almost succeeding. How awful to be anyone but I. I have a terrible egotism. I love my flesh, my face, my limbs, with overwhelming devotion. I know that I am "too tall" and have a fat nose, and yet I pose and prink before the mirror, seeing more and more how lively I am.... I have erected in my mind an image of myself—idealistic and beautiful. Is not that image, free from blemish, the true self—the true perfection? Am I wrong when this image insinuates itself between me and the merciless mirror? (Oh, even now I glance back on what I have just written—how foolish it sounds, how over-dramatic.)

Never, never, never will I reach the perfection I long for with all my soul—my paintings, my poems, my stories—all poor, poor reflections ... for I have been too thoroughly conditioned to the conventional surroundings of this community ... my vanity desires luxuries which I can never have....

I am continually more aware of the power which change plays in my life.... There will come a time when I must face myself at last. Even now I dread the big choices which loom up in my life—what college? what career? I am afraid. I feel uncertain. What is best for me? What do I want? I do not know. I love freedom. I deplore constrictions and limitations.... I am not as wise as I have thought. I can see, as from a valley, the roads lying open for me, but I cannot see the end—the consequences....

Oh, I love *now,* with all my fears and forebodings, for now I still am not completely moulded. My life is still just beginning. I am strong. I long for a cause to devote my energies to....

EARLY DAYS

by Maria Campbell

Maria Campbell is a Métis from northern Saskatchewan. In this excerpt from her autobiography, she evokes the world of her childhood—a world of loving parents, a great-grandmother (named Cheechum) with magical abilities, a mischievous uncle, and felt-but-unseen spirits.

I WAS BORN during a spring blizzard in April of 1940. Grannie Campbell, who had come to help my mother, made Dad stay outside the tent, and he chopped wood until his arms ached. At last I arrived, a daughter, much to Dad's disappointment. However this didn't dampen his desire to raise the best trapper and hunter in Saskatchewan. As far as I can remember Daddy taught me to set traps, shoot a rifle, and fight like a boy. Mom did her best to turn me into a lady, showing me how to cook, sew, and knit, while Cheechum, my best friend and confidante, tried to teach me all she knew about living.

I should tell you about our home now before I go any further. We lived in a large two-roomed hewed log house that stood out from the others because it was too big to be called a shack. One room was used for sleeping and all of us children shared it with our parents. There were three big beds made from poles with rawhide interlacing. The mattresses were canvas bags filled with fresh hay twice a year. Over my parents' bed was a hammock where you could always find a baby. An air-tight heater warmed the room in winter. Our clothes hung from pegs or were folded and put on a row of shelves. There were braided rugs on the floor, and in one corner a special sleeping rug where Cheechum slept when she stayed with us, as she refused to sleep on a bed or eat off a table.

I loved that corner of the house and would find any excuse possible to sleep with her. There was a special smell that comforted me when I was hurt or afraid. Also, it was a great place to find all sorts of wonderful things that Cheechum had—little pouches, boxes, and cloth tied up containing pieces of bright cloth, beads, leather, jewellery, roots and herbs, candy, and whatever else a little girl's heart could desire....

My Cheechum believed with heart and soul in the little people. She said they were so tiny that unless you are really looking for them you will never find them; not that it matters, because you usually only see them when they want you to.

The little people live near the water and they travel mostly by leaf boats. They are a happy lot and also very shy. Cheechum saw them once when she was a young woman. She had gone to the river for water in the late afternoon and decided to sit and watch the sun go down. It was very quiet and even the birds were still. Then she heard a sound like many people laughing and talking at a party. The sounds kept coming closer and finally she saw a large leaf floating to shore with other leaves following behind. Standing on the leaves were tiny people dressed in beautiful colours.

They waved to her and smiled as they came ashore. They told her that they were going to rest for the evening, then leave early in the morning to go farther downstream. They sat with her until the sun had gone down and then said goodbye and disappeared into the forest. She never saw them again; but all her life she would leave small pieces of food and tobacco near the water's edge for them which were always gone by morning. Mom said it was only a fairy tale but I would lie by the waters for hours hoping to see the little people....

Sometimes in the evening when people were visiting, we children listened to them tell ghost stories, and because we lived beside the cemetery those stories would keep us awake long into the night. Daddy always seemed to run out of tobacco about eight o'clock in the evening and Jamie or I would have to go to the store. To get there we had to take a footpath down the hill, climb a barbed-wire fence into the graveyard, walk between rows of graves, climb over another fence, and go around the blacksmith shop to the store. We knew every single person buried in that graveyard for we had listened to so many stories about each one.

One grave in particular, right beside the fence, had a horrible story associated with it. Grannie Campbell used to tell us that the old man buried in it was called *Ke-qua-hawk-as,* which means "wolverine" in Cree. He was just as mean and as ugly as the animal and never allowed anyone near his house, not even relatives. They all died before he did and because there was no family left, people got together to build his coffin. They held a wake for him at Grannie's house. The men didn't finish digging his grave until quite late. Old Mrs. Vandal was outside, alone, when she heard someone talking. She listened and it was coming from the empty grave. The spirit of Wolverine was standing there complaining about the size of his grave and how useless those people were. So Mrs. Vandal got very angry and told him he should be happy that someone was kind enough to make him a grave after having always been so miserable. The men found her beside the hole shaking her fist. Grannie said every so often on certain nights you could still hear Wolverine complaining.

Whenever I had to go to the store in the evening I would jump the fence and run as fast as I could, feeling sure that Wolverine was behind me. I would jump the other fence and arrive at the store completely out of breath. And then going home through that graveyard again I would nearly die. It was worse climbing the hill as I couldn't see behind me. Daddy's youngest brother, Robert, was a terrible tease and was never afraid of ghosts. He would lie beside Wolverine's grave and when I came back from the store he would make scratching noises and talk in low gruff tones. I would be stiff with fright and would walk by the grave looking straight ahead. As I climbed over the fence he would groan louder and scratch harder. I would pee my pants from fear while running up the hill, and he would pound the ground to make a sound like footsteps right behind me. When I burst into the house babbling and screaming, Daddy would go out and see nothing. This happened several times and one night I couldn't stand any more. I came through the graveyard and heard those noises again, the groaning and scratching, and as I climbed the fence there was an awful scream and noises like someone falling and running towards me. I crumpled down and fainted.

I came to, at home, with Mom rubbing my wrists. Uncle Robert sat in a corner with a most terrified look on his face, all scratched up and bloody. He said that he was coming from the store behind me and Wolverine grabbed him and knocked him down, bawled him out for using his graveyard, and chased him away. He was too frightened to go home alone, so when Daddy came back he went with him. After Dad returned he laughed until he cried, then told us what had happened. He had followed Robert to the graveyard one night and watched him scare me, so this night he asked Mom to send me to the store again while he went ahead and hid in the bushes behind the grave. Then, when Robert came sneaking down, he waited until I had gone by. Robert was so absorbed in making his noises he heard nothing. Daddy had on an old fur coat and hat and he grabbed Robert's arm and groaned in his face. Poor Robert nearly died. He screamed and started to run, so Daddy grabbed his feet and when he fell, climbed on his back and berated him for sitting on his grave. He said he would haunt him forever if he came near again. Poor Uncle, he finally got away and raced to the hill, but forgot the barbed-wire fence and ran right into it. He picked himself up, and ran past me, racing to our house. Mom came and found me and carried me home. I had no more trouble with Wolverine after that, but I was still frightened of that graveyard. In a way I liked being afraid, and if Jamie had to go to the store instead of me I was disappointed.

EVERYTHING IT CARRIES AWAY

by Bill Richardson

A FEW WEEKS AGO, I flew from the West Coast to the prairies, and when I was nearly home, I looked down on the floods. Unaccustomed as I am to interpreting the mind of a river from more than 10 000 metres, I'm not sure I would have recognized the field-wrecking insurrection for what it was, were it not for prior knowledge acquired through news reports. From my lofty vantage point, it looked to me as though the normally placid Assiniboine was content to divide its liquid assets between two safe banks and keep its counsel.

My father picked me up at the airport. We are a little tentative with each other when we meet after a time apart. That's our way. By the time we'd reached the car (which, for some reason, he has started calling "the Vehicle"), we'd exhausted all our conversational set pieces. Luckily, there was the river to fall back on. True, it has heaped the bulk of its indignities on rural Manitoba and Saskatchewan. Nevertheless, it is this self-same river that runs right through the middle of Winnipeg, only a few blocks from the house where I grew up and where my parents still live. I felt sure there must be tales to tell of near misses, of washed-out sidewalks, and of knee-deep basements.

Flood stories were among the narrative staples of my childhood. In fact, my brothers and I learned from an early age about the close link between diluvian drama and the mythology of our own beginnings. How our parents were married in the midst of the great Winnipeg flood of May 1950, when the combined anger of the Red and the Assiniboine threatened to wash the whole city away, was an oft-told tale.

Even now, when I look at the pictures of that big day, I think of all the stories: of how my grandparents were late because they had to drive 30 kilometres out of the city to find a place to cross the river; of the last-minute change of venue because the church was submerged; of how my father was heaving sandbags against the advancing water only an hour or two before his own wedding. I look at the photo of them getting into the decorated car after the service, my mother in her fairy-tale dress, my father in his new suit, and think of them hurrying to board their plane for Minneapolis. The river is only hours away from cresting, but they, like all newlyweds, simply had to trust that everything would work out for the best. I think of them looking down from those unfamiliar heights on what they knew to be the flood, but seeing just the slow amble of the green-grey river following its own path south.

By the time they returned, the crisis was over. They bought a house for about the same price they paid for the Vehicle they now drive. My father hammered a nail into one of the beams in the basement and hung up his sandbagging hip-waders. They were still there, the last time I thought to check.

"Been down to look at the river?" I asked brightly, as the ignition turned over.

"River?" he asked, seemingly surprised that I would pull such a question randomly from out of the air. "No. Not recently."

"I just thought that with the flood and all…."

"Oh! The river," he said, as though he had suddenly remembered this as something we once shared. "The flood. No."

We settled into a silence that shifted, as it always does, from awkward to companionable. At home, he parked the Vehicle and carted one of my bags into the house, not even looking to the south where the dangerous river rolled and rumbled, challenging its margins. It made me sad to see how he turned his back on the flood; sadder still to see in his forsaking the foreshadowing of how I will one day do the same. Not now, though. For now, and for as long as I'm able and as long as I care, I will be the guardian of that boisterous roiling, and the keeper of what it means and meant. All that night, I lay in bed and imagined it. I could scarcely sleep for thinking of everything it was carrying away.

TOM LONGBOAT

by Jack Granatstein

TOM LONGBOAT AS THE GREATEST Canadian star? The idea will surprise those who have never heard of him, but once his name rang throughout the land. Runner and scholar Bruce Kidd remembers regularly meeting people "who volunteered, proudly, that they had seen Longboat run and he was the finest athlete they had ever seen."

So it seemed. Longboat was an Onondaga born on the Six Nations Reserve near Brantford, Ont., who began running competitively while still in his teens. In 1906, he won the Around the Bay marathon in Hamilton, and then with a shrewd eye for publicity and money he outran a horse over a 12-mile course. The next year he easily captured the Boston Marathon in the then-record time of two hours 25 minutes and was labelled the world's premier distance runner. The *Montreal Star* made Longboat its favourite and posted hour-by-hour mile-by-mile bulletins of his big races outside its offices.

But at the 1908 Olympics in London, both Longboat and his Italian rival, Dorando Pietri, collapsed before the finish, leading to speculation that performance-enhancing drugs or an overdose, however administered, might have been involved. That scandal could have finished Longboat's career, but instead the controversy renewed and heightened public interest in marathon racing. The ruckus Longboat precipitated with his managers by taking charge of his own training and buying out his contract did nothing to diminish his fame, though there were the inevitable suggestions that "the Indian" could not handle money or the intricacies of something as complicated as race training. The sneers faded when Longboat continued to do well, running after 1912 as a professional.

In 1912, he set the record for 15 miles—one hour 18 minutes 10 seconds, a full 7 minutes faster than his amateur record. And he engaged in an epic 10 races before sellout crowds against Alf Shrubb, a British-born immigrant to Canada who was widely recognized as the best middle-distance racer in the world. Shrubb always won if the race was between 10 and 16 miles long, but Longboat won if the distance was over 20 miles. His uncanny ability to keep enough in reserve for a finishing kick always left Shrubb—and everyone else—in the dust at the longer distances. He truly was the marquee star of marathon racing.

The coming of the First World War saw Longboat, only 27 years old, enlist in the Canadian Expeditionary Force. He served with distinction as a dispatch runner in France and Flanders, racing for the army whenever he could get the opportunity (and the army cooperated by posting him to seven different units to facilitate his racing and reaping the publicity he won). In 1917, Longboat and Olympic marathoner Joe Keeper combined to win the interallied cross-country championship for the Canadian Expeditionary Force.

At one point in the war, Longboat was reported to have been killed, and his wife remarried. After the war, Longboat lived and worked as a garbage collector in Toronto until, troubled by alcoholism and penniless, he retired back to the reserve. He was Canada's greatest Native athlete, Canada's greatest marathon runner, and arguably Canada's premier athlete of all time. And he had the courage and persistence to succeed in the face of racist attacks and slurs.

He was a star at a time when Canadians craved them. Victorian intellectual Goldwin Smith had complained in the 1880s when oarsman Ned Hanlan dominated the public prints that nothing was more offensive than the idea that Canada was indebted to an athlete for "redemption from obscurity and contempt." Athletes may claim that they are not role models, but they are, as Kidd wrote, "powerless to turn off the popular identification." Still, it was splendid that, if Canadians had to turn to a sports hero for gratification, or redemption, it should be the brilliant marathoner from the Six Nations who inspired them in the years before the First World War forced them to concentrate their national attention on more important events.

ANNA LANG

by John Melady

"LANA, I'LL BE BACK!"

Anna Lang of Nauwigewauk, New Brunswick, looks back at the events that led up to her winning of the Cross of Valour as if they were all part of a terrible dream, a nightmare that somehow came true, a time so horrible she is amazed she escaped it.

At noon on Tuesday, September 9, 1980, 32-year-old Lang and her friend, 31-year-old Lana Walsh, were returning from Saint John where they had been working out in a city gym. With them, in the rear seat of Anna's new red two-door Buick, was Walsh's four-year-old son Jaye. Anna was driving.

Because the day was warm, Lana had opened the passenger-side window. The two women chatted about the events of the morning, and about the dangerous situation some 10 kilometres ahead, at the Hammond River bridge.

The bridge is a 100-metre-long, two-lane reinforced concrete structure carrying provincial Highway 1 over the Hammond River, 30 kilometres northeast of Saint John. The traffic deck of the bridge is 9 metres above the water, and is supported by five massive, tapered pillars. At the overpass the river is about 80 metres wide and over 2 metres deep. The current is not strong.

Drivers approaching the bridge from either direction must first negotiate a series of hazardous downhill curves. But on this day the major hazard at the Hammond River was the bridge itself. For over a week the south lane had been closed.

"They were replacing the right guardrail of the thing," recalls Anna Lang. "Because one lane was closed, they had traffic lights set up at each end. The only trouble was, you could be halfway across and the lights would change and cars would start coming toward you. That happened to me one night, and I had to crowd into the construction area to let them pass. That was why I hated the bridge, and why Lana and I were talking about it as we went along. Both of us said we knew somebody would be hurt there before long. It was just too dangerous."

As the two women travelled, neither knew that a gasoline truck was behind them, out of sight but rapidly drawing closer. The huge 20-wheel, 50-tonne Brunswick Petroleum transport was driven by 34-year-old Charles Steeves, a trucker with 14 years of accident-free experience behind him. The tanker carried 45 000 litres of gasoline.

In the meantime, on the bridge ahead, work was halted while the construction crew ate lunch. Several men had gone to their cars for sandwiches, or to the nearby Mandarin House restaurant for a hot meal. Only a handful of workers remained on the job. The time was 12:35 p.m.

As Anna eased her car around the long curve that leads down onto the western end of the bridge, she saw that the temporary traffic light facing her was green. At this point, though she didn't know it, Charles Steeves's gasoline tanker was less than 20 metres behind her. Then the light turned red.

"When the red came on, I automatically stopped the car," explains Lang with a shudder. "Then I looked in the rearview mirror. All I could see were two headlights and a grille. Perhaps I saw the body of the truck but I can't remember it. The grille seemed to fill my whole back window and his horn was blaring and I was screaming: 'Oh God, Lana he's not going to stop. He's not going to stop.' "

Up in the cab of his truck, Charles Steeves was terrified. He jammed on his brakes and sounded his horn. Yet he knew he could never stop in time. "My God," he thought to himself, "I'm going to kill them all."

The careening tanker smashed into the back of the Lang auto, demolishing the entire rear end and ramming the trunk against the front seat. In the same instant, the back window exploded inward and hundreds of jagged glass particles were driven into the interior of the car. Little Jaye Walsh was knocked flying into the front seat.

"When the back window popped, the glass made the inside of the car look like a cave with ice crystals hanging down," Lang recalls. "The ice kept coming until it covered the roof, the sides, and even the dash. I remember being pushed forward and then crawling back to the seat again. My head hit the steering wheel and my glasses were thrown off. Everything was so slow that it's still imprinted on my mind. It was as if you were watching a movie and all these things were happening at once—but they were barely moving. Lana was thrown around as much as I was."

Walsh was tossed screaming against the windshield, shattering it. At the same time, with a mother's instinct, she grabbed Jaye and held him to her. The possibility that he would be harmed bothered her far more than the thought of injury to herself.

The few remaining construction workers on the bridge froze at the sudden loud crash. However, a young man named Steve Hickey, who had been walking across with his three-year-old nephew Kevin, didn't even pause to see what was happening. He scooped the child off his feet and raced across the bridge and out of danger.

In desperation, Charles Steeves had tried to swing the huge truck to the left, into the narrow space between the Lang car and the side of the bridge. He had failed. As his truck telescoped the car, the two vehicles plowed through black and yellow traffic barriers and construction equipment, and finally rammed the cement forms and steel reinforcing rods from which the new guardrails would be built.

"The impact of the crash tore the tires from my car," explains Lang. "Then there was a loud, grating, grinding sound, like a teacher scratching her nails across a blackboard—only a hundred times as loud. Sparks were flying and everyone was screaming and by this time the truck had jackknifed and we were still moving forward."

Two seconds later, both vehicles reared to the right and plunged into space.

"I tried my best to keep my truck on the bridge," Steeves said later. "I never dreamed we would both end up in the river. There was no guardrail, and when I saw that my truck was headed for the edge, I thought, 'I have to get out, she's going to blow.' I jumped at the last minute, and I could feel her starting to go when I jumped. I don't remember hitting the ground."

Jumping from his moving truck, Steeves fell headlong into a series of steel reinforcing bars that were imbedded upright in cement. Despite the fact that his side was badly lacerated and one of the rods was driven into his leg, he got to his feet and scrambled to safety, shouting at the workers to get off the bridge. Blood was spurting from his leg all the while.

Then the first explosion came.

Bystanders watched in utter horror as gasoline, ignited by flying sparks from the collision, shredded the steel of the truck like the burst of a bomb. A waterfall of fire poured from the bridge as the compartmentalized fuel bays were torn open, one after the other. As each exploded, the sound ricocheted along the river, shook buildings a kilometre away, and sent a tower of flame higher than the trees. This was followed by a pall of smoke that was seen from as far away as Saint John.

In the dining room of the Mandarin House restaurant, which looks out on the Hammond River bridge, a waitress was taking orders. Both she and the dining room patrons heard the collision, but none of them was prepared for the pillar of fire that roared up from the river below. "The waitress screamed and came running from the dining room," recalls Lily Yee, one of the restaurant's owners. "I grabbed the phone and called the fire department. Then I yelled at my husband to get our papers and get out. I was afraid the whole place would burn. The customers left right away. They said they couldn't eat after what they had seen. We closed the place down for over an hour."

While all this was happening, Anna Lang's battered Buick hit the water, right side up.

"When we were being pushed along the bridge, there was so much racket," says Lang, "but when we went over the side my car seemed to spin around and I could see the restaurant. I knew it should have been behind me, though, and for a minute I had no idea where I was. I suppose the car was in the air at the time. Then I guess we went into the water. For a minute everything was silent and I can recall thinking, 'Oh God, it's all over.' Suddenly there was water in the car."

A moment later the transport tractor fell into the river on its roof, a metre away. Then the shattered tanker landed on its side, disgorging burning gasoline into the water in shimmering, scorching, deadly waves. Further explosions came, each adding more fuel to the wild inferno. The leaping, crackling, roaring flames obliterated all signs of life.

But there was life.

"My car sank right away," explains Lang, "and water started pouring in. I kept holding my breath until I thought my lungs would burst. The next thing I knew, Lana was holding Jaye and I was floating over them, out the right window. I remember hitting the surface and gasping for air, but the whole river was burning and I could hardly breathe. It was so hot.

"Because we had been to exercise class, both Lana and I had a lot more clothing on than we normally would have. I was wearing jeans and a couple of heavy sweaters over my tights and leotards. As soon as the jeans and sweaters got wet, they weighed a tonne so I knew I had to get rid of them if I was going to be any help to Lana and Jaye. By this time they had gone to the surface, so I started swimming for shore.

"As I was swimming I was saying, 'Lana, I'll be right back, I'll be back.' She never heard me say that and I never heard her say, 'Anna, please come back for me.' I guess we both thought these things but we never mouthed the words."

Now the fire was spreading farther and farther over the river. Rings of flame alternated with patches of clear water as Anna fought her way through the inferno toward shore, 40 metres away. "I tried to duck under each ring and then get my breath in the clear spaces," she says, "but that was not always possible. It was so hot on top, I felt better if I stayed under. Then I remember getting to shore and trying very hard to quickly take my outer clothes off. When I finally got rid of them, I went back in."

While Anna was struggling with her wet clothes, Lana Walsh and Jaye were having difficulties in the water.

"I was trying to hold Jaye up," Lana said later. "We had gone down several times and I was getting tired. So tired. And the heat was unbearable. Everything was burning. My big sweater was pulling me down and I was getting so tired that I was starting to give up. I wanted to save Jaye, but the heat was so bad. Everything was burning and I had to keep pushing his head under the water. Then I looked and he wasn't moving, and I thought he was dead. But then his eyelids moved. The water was burning and Jaye's hair was on fire."

Jaye floated on his back and his mother held onto him with her left hand, keeping herself afloat with her right. When his hair began to burn, she would push him under and put the flames out.

"Then I saw Anna on the shore," Walsh says, "but she seemed so far away. I saw blood pouring down her face. She was taking off her jeans and sneakers, and I can see her now splashing into the water. She came back for us. The water was burning but she really came back for us."

"As soon as I couldn't feel the bottom anymore, I started swimming," recalls Lang. "I decided to grab Jaye instead of his mother because I was afraid she might panic and drown us all. I knew if I got Jaye, she would hold on. That's what happened. He had taken swimming lessons the winter before and I think that's what saved him.

"I finally got to them," Lang adds, "and grabbed Jaye by the shoulder and started pulling both of them after me. Every so often my hair would go on fire and I had to keep ducking to put it out. I believe Lana was in too much shock to do that.

"As we got closer to the shore, everything seemed to be so quiet. Jaye was very quiet and so was Lana. I guess there were people up on the bridge watching, although I was not aware of it. I was just too busy."

But not everyone was on the bridge watching.

Two local teens, Eric Sparks and Jack Chaisson, both 18, had been in a car behind the gasoline tanker. They had witnessed the accident, but had been able to stop before becoming involved in it.

When they saw the vehicles plunge off the bridge, they left their car and made their way down the south embankment to the edge of the river. Almost without thinking, Sparks took off his pants and waded into the water to help with the rescue. By this time Anna was approaching the shore with Jaye and Lana in tow.

"There was still a lot of burning gas around us, but I could see those guys ahead of me," recalls Anna. "They were standing on the bank and one had no pants on. I remember thinking, Why is he in his underwear? When I saw him coming into the water, I kept saying, 'Please help me, God. I'm not going to make it.'

"Eric got to me just as my feet touched the bottom again. He grabbed Jaye and handed him to Jack and then he got Lana. They had to carry them because Lana wasn't able to walk. At this point, I didn't want to look at her, or at Jaye. I didn't know what they looked like, if they were cut, had broken arms or anything. I didn't know what I had done to them."

Finally Anna managed to pull herself up onto the rocky shore, her head, face, and neck now severely burned, her face bloody, and what was left of her clothes in tatters. She would not know until later that she had two cracked vertebrae in her back.

Even though they were now on shore, they were far from safe. Across the water the crackling flames engulfed more and more of the tanker, but still the flow of gasoline had not slowed.

"We've got to get out of here right away," Jack cried, "That thing is going to blow again."

He had no sooner said the words than the last of several explosions boomed across the water, spewing a geyser of steam, mud, flaming gasoline, and hunks of shattered steel into the air. The earth shook and little Jaye clasped Jack Chaisson in a terrified but silent bear-hug. Eric knelt on the ground beside Lana, placed his arms under her back and legs, and hoisted her into his arms. Anna, by now so exhausted she felt she would drop, wobbled unsteadily for a moment, then straggled along after the others, away from the flames. Steadily, painfully, doggedly, the group made its way along the rocky shore, crossed under the bridge and then, helped by several others including trucker Charles Steeves, managed to reach the top of the bank and safety.

The first ambulance arrived four minutes later.

Anna, Lana, and Jaye were all hospitalized as a result of their ordeal. Anna's injuries were the most serious and she was incapacitated for the longest time. Her back healed on its own, but the third-degree burns to her face and head required skin grafting, plastic surgery, and hair transplants. She was well enough, however, to fly to Ottawa two years later to receive her Cross of Valour—although she claims she did not deserve it.

Anna Lang and Lana Walsh are still friends. To this day neither feels safe crossing the Hammond River bridge.

What happened to the 3 of them?

Cudjoe and Nanny, Heroes of the Maroons

by Kat Mototsune

In 1875, a group of more than 500 men, women, and children arrived in Halifax, Nova Scotia. They were the Maroons. Deported from Jamaica, they were forced to leave the land where they had fought for freedom from English slavery for 150 years. After five long, cold years in Halifax, these refugees won their petition to be transferred to Sierra Leone in West Africa. In West Africa the Maroons were near the land of their ancestors, but far from Jamaica which had long been their home. They settled there among other freed slaves, passing on stories of their Jamaican homeland and of the leaders of their long struggle in that country. Names like Cudjoe and Nanny were invoked with pride and reverence.

JAMAICA WAS under Spanish rule from 1494, when Christopher Columbus reached the island, to 1655, when the British invaded. As they faced the British, the Spanish freed the black slaves they had brought from Africa. These freed slaves, and those who had previously escaped into the wild mountainous interior of Jamaica, formed a group that became known as the Maroons, probably from the Spanish word *cimarrón* which means "wild and untamed." The Spanish helped organize, train, and set the Maroons against the British. Although the Spanish were defeated in Jamaica in 1655, the Maroons remained a "thorn in the side of the English" until the end of the eighteenth century.

The English brought thousands of slaves from Africa to work on their large sugar plantations. The knowledge that free black people lived in the mountains encouraged many of these slaves to escape to join them. Four times in 20 years the slaves rebelled; some escaped and joined the rebels' towns. When a slave ship from Madagascar wrecked on the Jamaican coast, the survivors joined the Maroons. Although a small group of Maroons signed a treaty with the English in 1663, by the end of the seventeenth century there were about 2000 rebel

Maroons on the island, warring with the British to retain their independence.

The Maroons were divided into two groups. One group lived in the Blue Mountains in the northeast of Jamaica. They were known as the Windward Maroons, for the prevailing winds that blow on the northeast coast of the island. The other group of Maroons lived in the northwest section of the island: they were known as the Leeward Maroons, or the Trelawny Maroons. Their greatest hero was a military leader named Cudjoe.

Cudjoe was a Coromantee slave from what is now Ghana. The Coromantee people were known for being courageous and warlike and Cudjoe was fierce and shrewd. He united the Maroons from several African bands—from Ghana, Nigeria, Dahomey, Madagascar—and under his leadership they became excellent guerrilla warriors. They swooped down from the hills to raid plantations and then disappeared back into the difficult terrain. They became expert shots with muskets. The rough, mountainous country where they had been forced to retreat became their greatest advantage: they learned to move quickly and quietly over the rocky ground and became skilled in travelling through untracked forest. The British tried to rout Cudjoe's people with Indian trackers, dog handlers from Cuba, the militia, and finally two regiments of regular soldiers—all without success.

It wasn't until the 1730s that the British discovered it was difficult for Cudjoe and his people to get food. The Maroons cultivated hidden provision grounds to grow what they needed. The English governor's men were sent in greater and greater numbers to destroy the Maroon provision grounds and to cut off any other supplies of food and water.

Cudjoe led the Leeward Maroons westward into an area of Jamaica known as the Cockpit Country. A large plateau of limestone, where deep ravines and sinks separate saw-toothed ridges of rock and where the trees grow straight out of stone, the Cockpit Country provided Cudjoe and his people with a secure stronghold, which could only be reached through narrow, easily defended passes. Their *abengs*—shell or cow-horn trumpets—allowed the Maroons to send coded warning messages over long distances.

But the Cockpit Country was very dry and the English soon cut off the Maroons' sources of water and food. Cudjoe knew he had to change tactics to save his people. In 1739, the British finally offered to make a treaty with Cudjoe. Cudjoe met with an English officer, they exchanged hats as a sign of friendship and agreed to a treaty which gave Cudjoe's people liberty and large swaths of land. Cudjoe and his successors were empowered with complete jurisdiction over their people, except for the death penalty. For a time, it looked as though the Trelawny Maroons could live with what Cudjoe had won for them.

The other group of Jamaican Maroons, the Windwards, established themselves high in the Blue Mountains, and near a waterfall they built their centre—Nanny Town. The male leaders of these Maroons included Cuffee, Quao, and Adou, but it was Nanny who, as *obeah-*woman or high priestess, inspired spiritual power and unity. Many of the British records present Nanny as a legend or give brief mention of her as a Maroon religious woman, but her name entered the Jamaican language in several terms—Nanny Town, Nanny thatch, Nanny pot, Nanny Hill, Nanny River—giving us some idea of her importance to the Windward Maroons. Her story inspired many stories of her supernatural powers. There is a legend of the Nanny pot, or cauldron, which boiled without fire, and was said to attract and drown any English soldier who approached Nanny Town. It was also said that Nanny could catch enemy bullets and fling them back at the attackers to kill them.

The Windward Maroons were more self-sufficient than Cudjoe's people and cultivated the valleys where they lived. Like the Leeward Maroons, they used the high territory to their advantage, inhabiting natural fortresses. Without as much need to raid plantations for supplies, Nanny's Maroons held fast against the British as much through their united spirit and culture as through their battle strategy.

They managed to hold off the British troops until 1734, when the English dragged small swivel guns up the steep mountainsides and blasted Nanny Town to the earth. Nanny was among the few survivors.

As warlike as Cudjoe, Nanny led her people into battle with the English. She was even said to be able to spirit the best slaves out of their bondage. Nanny's people responded to her religious authority: their faith in her kept them united in battle and her bravery has been kept alive by the Maroon people, to whom she is as much a hero as Cudjoe.

Most survivors of Nanny Town continued their fight for independence under the leadership of Quao. Only three months after Cudjoe signed his treaty in 1739, Quao made a similar agreement with the British. Nanny's status as a political leader and her determination to retain independence are indicated by a separate treaty that the British agreed on with Nanny, a full year after those signed by Cudjoe and Quao. Nanny and her people received similar rights as the rest of the Maroons—freedom and land.

The Maroon treaties of 1739–1740 seemed to uphold an uneasy peace for about 50 years. But the Maroon people were neither as independent as they wished, nor as free as they had been. The land granted the Maroons was not expanding to keep up with the growing population and it was better suited for warfare than for agriculture. Maroon villages were supposedly self-ruled, but each was assigned a white superintendent. Worst of all, the British expected the Maroons to help in their hunt for runaway slaves, and this horrible activity was their only source of income. In 1795, the second Maroon War broke out as the Maroons demanded more rights from the English. But this time there were no heroes like Nanny and Cudjoe to lead them. By means of a trick truce and a broken promise that no Maroon would be forced to leave Jamaica, the English deported the last of the Maroons from their homeland to Halifax in 1875—never to see their beloved Jamaica again.

Hesquiaht—A People, a Place, and a Language

by Karen Charleson

THERE ARE NO ROADS that can take us here. Not even the network of overgrown logging roads will lead us to this pristine place. We travel by boat, across miles made long by open Pacific water, to tuck ourselves behind the reefs and swells into the safety of this Vancouver Island harbour. Where once again the name of the territories before us and the name of a people coincide. Where people, place, and language are all a single whole called Hesquiaht (*hesh'-kwi-aht*).

No longer needing to hurry, we move more slowly inside the harbour, savouring the thrill of being here. Though we have made this voyage many times, the excitement of reaching our destination—a place named Iusuk (*i-yu'-sook*) near the head of the harbour—is always fresh and new, as if we were arriving for the first time.

My husband's father was born here, beside the river. The same river that still meanders into the dark green of old forest cover and still teems with coho and chum salmon each fall. A house once stood where the salal grows thick and tangled now, on a spit of land wedged between ocean beach and river bank. The past is tangible enough to taste in the salt air, to blend inside our lungs with the present. Across the low-tide beach, long lines of barnacle-encrusted stakes poke out of the sand: the remains of fish fences that were embedded so deeply that generations of tides and children and storms have been unable to move them. In the forest, cedar trees from which former residents stripped bark and planks continue to grow taller and thicker.

We operate a rediscovery program here, a series of annual wilderness camps for youths and adults from Hesquiaht and around the world. Iusuk gives them an awareness of the natural world, the power of indigenous culture, and a renewed sense of themselves.

Such awareness comes easily here, in beauty that is obvious to the smallest child: towering snags, trees where eagles perch, a river gliding from its forest haven to meet the sea, a mountain looming behind the line of shore trees, a beach of sand and gravel with massive rocks at the points. Camping here in summer, we are bathed in shade until mid-morning, as the sun steadily climbs behind the mountain and curtain of trees. Bald eagles scan our campsite from the treetops then move around the nearest point for more privacy. Packs of harassing crows dive at single ravens, forcing them to hop from tree to tree. Marbled murrelets were here a few years ago; they have disappeared for the time being, but the sandpipers are back in greater numbers. When human activities quiet, they appear and feed from the tide-bared sand. In the evening, softened light caresses us until, across the expanse of harbour, the sun disappears beneath the flat lowland of Hesquiaht Peninsula.

In late winter, schools of herring boil off Iusuk's shore, waiting to spawn on the beds of kelp and eelgrass. Life is at its richest and most diverse: eagles, seagulls, and hosts of ducks arrive in such numbers that their bits of lost plumage dot the waters. Steller's sea lions patrol the bay. Grey whales feed for weeks, fattening themselves for their migration north.

Come spring, black bears traverse the beach and forest on regular routes. They amble by us campers slowly, undisturbed by our presence on their way to overturn rocks at the ocean's edge to search for small crabs. They move quickly only when startled by sudden noise or strange scents.

Iusuk was a designated Hesquiaht Indian Reserve until the 1960s. How it came to be taken away from the Hesquiaht and transferred to provincial control, placed within a logging licence and then within a provincial park, is a convoluted story. Convoluted enough that the Hesquiaht First Nation is currently in court, suing Canada for its return.

When we leave here, quiet descends. Not silence, but an absence of human noise. The bears and birds revert to routes and sites that they avoided in our presence. Iusuk has enriched and replenished us once again. As we pull out into the waters of the harbour, the place looks the same as when we arrived—serene and eternal.

THROUGH THE LOOKING GLASS

by Joanna Norland

A teen scene columnist for the *Ottawa Citizen* wonders how much time is too much time to spend on your appearance.

CONCERN ABOUT ONE'S APPEARANCE, a hallmark of youth, is being handled in a unique way by a good friend of mine. Her resolution this year is to check her face in the mirror only once a day, in the morning. For the balance of the day (within the limits of human fortitude) she abstains from thinking about her looks. When she told me about her intention I felt fortunate in my unbridled year-round licence to agonize over my split ends, ragged cuticles, height (or lack thereof), pimple count, skin moisture content, and pasty-facedness. Then yesterday I asked my friend how she was coping with her new, nonreflective existence.

"Oh, it's great," she gushed. "All of a sudden, I have so much extra time for everything else."

As teenagers, we do tend to invest an inordinate amount of energy in activities related to our appearance. The flourishing goods-and-services sector offers us a smorgasbord of opportunities for doing this. The Yellow Pages list scores of beauty salons ready and eager to perm our hair, dye it blond, add chestnut highlights and, finally, restore it to its original texture and shade. The mere research required to decide whether or not a bob is preferable to the layered look can occupy one's every spare moment from Labour Day to Victoria Day. Should we, nonetheless, find ourselves shackled with an occasional free afternoon (an unlikely occurrence), clothing boutiques provide Instant Protection from the embarrassment of being clad in last week's trends. In addition, there are the oh-so-important routines demanding continual attention. Unwanted body hair must be cauterized daily. The results of past diet plans need to be updated and then subjected to computer analysis. Skin-cell-conditioning-and-regenerating programs must be followed religiously. Should even these unquestionably worthy enterprises fail to hold our complete concentration (a still more unlikely occurrence), a steady stream of friends is always in urgent need of advice or aid with regard to THEIR clothes, nails, body hair, diets, and skin treatments.

It's no wonder we never seem to have time to devote to our subordinate interests. If every day I spent half an hour exercising, I might build up enough strength to do one full push-up by June. If I spent the time reading, I might complete *War and Peace* by Christmas. If I slept in, I'd be far more pleasant company in the morning. Instead, I awaken early to blow-dry my hair. Rationally, I know that my adherence to this ritual does little to improve my quality of life. I doubt that people respond to me more favourably because I'm modishly coifed. Still, on some level, I really do feel that my acceptability is dependent upon my spending X number of hours contemplating, discussing, improving upon (or at the very least writing about) the face I present to the world, the hair surrounding it, and the body supporting it.

A little perspective would be liberating. Maybe I might even benefit from adopting my friend's resolution. But then, the unflinching tenacity, the stony determination, and the relentless intra-psychic struggle involved in such an endeavour would probably leave me too exhausted to enjoy its rewards.

PADDLE TO THE AMAZON

by Don Starkell

Don Starkell had a dream: to paddle a canoe 20 000 kilometres from Winnipeg, Manitoba to Belem, Brazil. The route would take him down the Mississippi River, around the coast of Mexico, and through South America to the mouth of the mighty Amazon River.

After 10 years of planning, Don—a famous long-distance paddler—pushed his 6.4-metre fibreglass canoe into the Red River on June 1, 1980. But he wasn't going alone. With him were his two sons: Jeff, 18, and Dana, 19. Jeff would travel with them as far as Mexico before returning home; but Dana, despite his allergies and asthma attacks, would go the whole way. Two years later, two proud Canadians, father and son, had paddled nearly 20 million strokes and set a record for a thrilling voyage of discovery they would never forget.

Don kept a log of their adventures—a diary in which he wrote almost every night before crawling into the tent. When he made these entries, he and Dana were well over halfway to their goal.

February 28: Misión Nuevas Tribus, Tama Tama, Venezuela

TONIGHT, THANK GOD, we are safe in Tama Tama. I have made only the briefest notes over the past few days, and with very good reason: The evening after I last wrote, at Kirare, just past suppertime, my head started aching, I grew dizzy, and my muscles and stomach began to cramp. I began shivering. I lay down on the tarp in the sun and, even in the heat, had to ask Dana to cover me. To add to my miseries, a few bees got under the tarp and into my clothing, and I got a severe sting on the leg as I tried to roll onto my side.

Two hours later, Dana, too, began to complain of shivering and cramps, and then he was up and vomiting. As he staggered back to his bed on top of the canoe he moaned something about our having malaria.

"We haven't got malaria," I told him. "Don't get carried away." But there was nothing I could do to prevent him taking a couple of extra malaria pills, even though they're strictly a preventative measure and do no good after the fact. I have to admit that we hadn't been taking them as regularly as we should have; they tend to give us headaches and to weaken us. I laid off them, but, for the first time in many years, took aspirins to try to allay the terrible pain in my temples and skull.

Just after dark, it began to rain, but we were too weak to set up any sort of shelter, and simply lay there shivering and sweating, as our tarp soaked through.

The next eight or nine hours were an agonizing blur of half-sleep and fear. Our alarm went off as usual at 5:30, but Dana couldn't move. I was in no shape to get up either, but was too scared to lie there, convinced that, if we didn't get to Tama Tama for help, we'd die.

The pain and tremors and weakness were now more severe than anything I'd ever experienced. Although we couldn't be sure, we now suspected we'd picked up a case of water or food poisoning—maybe from a can of Venezuelan sausages we'd eaten at supper the night before, maybe from the river water, which we've been drinking liberally for weeks. The river bottom around our sand bar was slimy with what was probably crocodile waste.

I was determined to move, knowing that, if we didn't, our condition might worsen, so that we wouldn't be *able* to move. I knew the story of Captain Scott and his men, all of whom starved and froze to death while returning from the South Pole in 1912. They became storm-bound just 16 kilometres from a known food depot, and decided to wait until the storm improved before carrying on to their much-needed nourishment. The storm got worse, and they never moved.

We were 80 kilometres from Tama Tama—80 upstream kilometres.

I bullied and prodded Dana into getting up, and, soon after 6:00 a.m.—unable to eat, barely able to stay upright—we launched the canoe and angled into the current. It was the beginning of two days of torture, particularly for Dana, who, by this time, was far worse off than I was. I had actually begun to feel marginally better as I got up and moving.

All day, Dana lifted his paddle as if it were lead, constantly begging me to stop. All I could do was keep at him to do his best, to keep pulling, even though his weak stroke was of very little use; several times, he slumped in the bow, and I was afraid he might fall overboard. But I knew if I gave him any sympathy, he'd probably quit altogether and I'd have to paddle myself, a nearly impossible task into the stiff current. As it was, we were gaining less than 3 kilometres per hour. "We can't quit," I kept hectoring. "We have to keep paddling; we've gotta keep going—just a few more kilometres." Meanwhile, the sun burned down at equatorial strength. We were precisely three degrees north of the equator.

By about 2:30, we were all but unconscious. A flat rock island came into view in the middle of the river, and we dragged the canoe onto it, stretched out the tarp, and fell asleep. We had come 27 kilometres.

At suppertime, Dana was able to eat half a can of green peas, his first nourishment in 24 hours. I didn't feel like eating, but forced down a fair quantity of food, knowing that if I could keep it down, I'd be better off.

The night air soothed us, but the morning brought no noticeable improvement in our condition. If anything, Dana was weaker, and I had lost my appetite altogether. When we had each forced down a single platano, we headed off on a grim re-enactment of the previous day's travels. Our goal was to get past the mouth of the Río Cunucunuma, maybe 30 kilometres away, which would put us about 15 kilometres from Tama Tama. Again I was forced to harass Dana almost constantly to keep him functioning. We were eventually forced into our old last-ditch game, choosing a branch or rock upstream, fighting our way to it, choosing another branch or rock, and so on. By late morning, Dana's complexion was a pale but distinct green.

We passed the Río Cunucunuma during the mid-afternoon, and just when everything was at its lowest ebb a strange event lifted us briefly from our miseries. Suddenly, without speaking, Dana pointed to shore, leaving his arm extended for several seconds. "Look," he said softly. At first I saw nothing but a thick fallen tree angling from the river bank down into the water. But as we inched forward, a massive snake came into view, lying draped and twisted on the tree trunk, apparently sunning itself. I took it for a boa constrictor and frantically dug into our #4 equipment box, searching for my camera. In my excitement, all my cramps and weakness vanished.

We paddled until our bow was within 4 metres of it, and I snapped a picture, keeping Dana in the frame for size comparison. "Jump out on the log," I said. "I'll take your picture with it!" But he refused to budge.

We then paddled right up to the fallen tree and, when the snake showed no interest in us, I decided to get out onto the trunk for a better photo. This upset Dana, and he began scolding me for taking stupid risks. But I knew that a boa, being primarily a land snake, would shy away from water and that I'd be pretty safe with the water behind me.

As I stepped slowly up the log, Dana pulled the canoe ahead 3 or 4 metres. "What are you doing?" I demanded.

"I don't want to be anywhere near that thing," he said.

Despite my arguing, he wouldn't come back. I was determined to take another picture, a close-up, and continued up the log, amazed by the snake's great size. It was as big around as a man's waist and easily 6 metres long. I'd estimate its weight at over 140 kilograms. It had several long gashes on its skin, as if it had been fighting, and, as I got closer, I could see a heavy swelling in its midsection—undoubtedly the animal with which it had done battle. Perhaps the most incredible thing was the relatively small size of the snake's head—about as big as two closed fists. It seemed impossible to think that it had swallowed an animal that must have been as big as a medium-sized dog. Flies swarmed over the congealed blood of its cuts. "I think it's dead!" I called to Dana, and took a quick photo of it.

"No," he called back, "I can see it breathing!"

Part of the snake's body was draped over a small branch that angled toward me, which I now grabbed and jiggled, to no effect. "It's dead!" I called. But when I shook the branch harder, the massive creature slowly raised its head and swung it in my direction, throwing me into an adrenaline panic. For a few seconds, I stared at it from less than 2 metres away, and it stared back, occasionally flicking its forked tongue. I took another step toward it, feeling that I could bluff it back into the jungle. Again, I grabbed the branch, this time giving it a good tug. But instead of retreating, the snake started ever so slowly down the log toward me. It was then—too late—that I realized it was not a boa at all but a deadly anaconda: only an anaconda would move toward water with such confidence.

Dana was now hanging onto a branch some 6 metres upstream and in no position to rescue me. The only thing I could think of doing was to stand up on the log—I'd been crouching—and to make myself seem as big as possible by throwing my arms in the air. I did this and began roaring like a grizzly bear (in spite of my knowledge that snakes are deaf). The snake advanced about a metre. Then, when I repeated my grizzly act, it stopped half a metre in front of me and plunged into the water below. Its splash reached Dana 6 metres away. My camera and I were soaked, but I had my pictures. My legs shook as I climbed into the canoe, feigning calmness.

For a couple of hours during the late afternoon we searched for a camping spot, but could find nothing on the steep 2-metre river banks. By six o'clock, with darkness coming, we had no choice but to tie up alongshore, beneath overhanging vines, and prepare for a night in the canoe. Dana opened a can of tuna, saw some bubbles in it, and refused to eat it. "It's poison," he said, "just like the sausages." I tasted a bit which seemed fine; I told him he was paranoid. But when he persisted in his complaints, I, too, got suspicious and reluctantly threw the can in the river.

Dana ate half a cup of raisins. I wasn't hungry, but forced myself to eat. Then we moved some equipment from my end of the canoe to Dana's so that I had a little sleeping cocoon beneath the gunwales. Dana stretched out on top of the equipment boxes, and we prepared for a painful night.

This morning Dana looked awful—his face was flushed, his head ached, he couldn't bend his back. He was crankier than he's been for months. When we were about to leave, he refused to untie his end of the canoe, showering me with abuse as we sat there. When I went to untie it myself he threatened me with his paddle.

For the first kilometre or so, he refused to take a stroke, complaining that I'd exhausted him yesterday with 12 hours on the water. And I couldn't refute it; I *have* worn him out; he *is* exhausted; he *is* too sick to paddle. But how else could we have made it to where we are?

He eventually picked up his paddle. For four hours we crawled upcurrent and about 10:00 a.m. we saw what should have made us throw our arms in the air and shout for joy—or weep for it. But we were too tired for any display of emotion. On the far shore, amid the trees, the bank gradually fell away into a broad channel that signified the beginning of Casiquiare Canal. Our battles with the current were over.

The Misión Nuevas Tribus is located on the Orinoco a couple of kilometres beyond the opening to the canal, and we had reached it within an hour. We staggered up the banks and onto the parklike grounds, among well-built houses and meeting halls. What puzzled us was that there didn't seem to be any people around. Then we saw two young Native children, who disappeared behind a building when they saw us. We walked to the building and peeked through the screens, surprised to see several dozen Native children sitting around with a few adults. At this point Dana felt too weak to walk and returned to the canoe. A hundred metres away, in the trees, was a large hall, from which I could now hear singing. As I walked toward the hall, it dawned on me that it was Sunday morning; the mission was at church. I sat down in the shade waiting for the service to end, and was soon spotted from inside by Larry Fyock who had befriended us in Puerto Ayacucho. He rushed out to welcome me to Tama Tama.

As I write this evening, I can already feel the life and health returning to my body. Dana, too, is feeling better and *looks* better, as I'm sure I do, after a shave, shower, and shampoo. We're staying in the home of Fran and Laura Cochran, who divide their time between here and the mission office in Puerto Ayacucho, where we first met them. We're still pretty weak, but I don't think we're going to need any special medicines—just lots of shade and rest and plenty of the same healthy food we've had since arriving. What a relief it's been just to be out of the sun. We had dinner this evening with Elmer and Tina Barkman and their family. Elmer is a Canadian from Blumenort, Manitoba, about 65 kilometres from Winnipeg. So we are not only among friends but among neighbours.

LETTERS FROM VIETNAM

by Thomas Kingsley

What is it really like to be a soldier fighting overseas? These letters written home by a soldier in Vietnam give us a glimpse of the terrible reality.

The U.S. was secretly involved in Vietnam long before the American public became generally aware of the war in 1964. At that time, Vietnam was split into communist North Vietnam and U.S.-supported South Vietnam. A rebellion supported by the North was about to overthrow the unpopular regime in the South. Although many Americans disagreed, the U.S. government decided that the South Vietnamese government had to be defended, no matter what the cost.

The U.S. sent its bombers to attack North Vietnam and its soldiers to fight in South Vietnam. Eventually more than 57 000 young Americans (along with at least 2 million Vietnamese) died in a brutal and unpopular war which spread to the neighbouring countries of Laos and Cambodia. It was a war where the massive American firepower did not distinguish friends from enemies, or soldiers from civilians, and it was a war the U.S. couldn't win: the last American soldiers left in 1973, and South Vietnam finally collapsed and was taken over by the North in 1975.

Most of the American soldiers were young draftees, like the author of these letters.

In December 1970, Private Thomas Kingsley arrived in Vietnam and wrote the following three letters.

Dear Mom and Dad,

This country is so beautiful. I don't believe it! It reminds me of Canada. It's so calm, picturesque, and serene: Presently I'm at Cam Ranh Bay. It's like a small resort town.

Love,
Tom

Dear Mom and Dad,

It's hard to experience Christmas when it's 110 degrees (40°C) out. However, in between beers I managed to dream what it was like on

> **Glossary**
>
> ARVN: acronym for the South Vietnamese Army, America's ally
>
> GI: an ordinary American soldier
>
> lifer: someone who chose to join the army; a career soldier
>
> LZ: "landing zone," a base area supplied by helicopter
>
> "made contact": made contact with the enemy
>
> My Lai: a Vietnamese village where U.S. soldiers murdered hundreds of unarmed civilians
>
> TET: a major Vietnamese festival (the largest battles of the war began during TET in 1968)
>
> VC: "Viet Cong," one of the U.S. names for the enemy soldiers
>
> "Vietnamization": a policy brought in by the U.S. late in the war—as U.S. troops withdrew, South Vietnamese troops were supposed to take over the main share of the fighting

the morning of Christmas. We didn't have to work today—they gave us a special dinner and free beer—so if this letter sounds incoherent it's because I had more beer than dinner. Merry Christmas!

I bought myself a camera, so I should have a lot of good shots when I get back. As I said before, this place is really beautiful, and I was not surprised to find that many lifers bring their wives and families out here to live.

I spent Christmas with some close friends (you'd be surprised how fast you meet "friends"), listened to Bob Hope on the radio—he was about 50 km away—and went to a show they had on our firebase. I still haven't reached my final destination, so don't try to write yet. It will be another week before I find out what I'll be doing and where.

So far everything has been real quiet and everything is going fine. There are always rumours flying around though. The lifers say the war is over and everyone is pulling out. We were told we would be pulling out the 15th of January—that doesn't mean me, specifically—it means my division, the First Air Cavalry; no telling when they'll get to my company.

By the way, I enjoyed Christmas a day earlier than you did.

Merry Christmas and Love,

Tom

Dear Mom and Dad,

You'll have to excuse the handwriting again; I'm using a single cracked board as a backboard, and my hands are terribly dirty.

I have finally reached my end destination, a place called Mace Firebase. During the welcoming orientation it was stated only two men have been killed in the last six months from this battalion, which numbers about 600 men. So I guess I am in a fairly safe location.

The name Air Cavalry refers to air mobility. Wherever we go we are transported by helicopter. You know how I am afraid of heights; well, these people are scaring the hell out of me! I guess these helicopters are safe, though, but it seems to me they are held together with string and chewing gum; they rattle, shake, and lurch something terrible. All kidding aside, though, these helicopters are really efficient. They carry rockets, machine guns, small bombs, and other assorted weapons. They fly both daytime and nighttime missions, by means of a large searchlight on the latter. Transport helicopters carry about 10 men each and are flanked and protected by gunships (helicopters loaded with armament).

Before we go on a mission, artillery will clear out an area with heavy bombing. They will then shift their target to the perimeter of the area we are to land in, in case the enemy wishes to attack us. When we are dropped off, the gunships will hover in the area until our position is positively fortified; then it will make runs in the surrounding area to look for the enemy. Sounds pretty safe, doesn't it? I hope so!

Right now I am on guard duty. I sit in a bunker with three other guys and listen to what is happening on the other side of the barbed wire. The other side of the wire is off limits to everyone after six o'clock and you're supposed to shoot on sight. However, we never do—too many drunken GIs around. Just a while ago there were two kids playing about 100 m from the wire. Naturally we didn't shoot them, even though they could have been VC, but instead called headquarters, who in turn sent a party out to question them. All was legitimate and the kids were sent on their way.

By the way, have a good time on New Year's Eve, even though this letter is late.

Well, it's getting dark now so I have to concentrate on my work.

Love,
Tom

In late January 1971, Thomas Kingsley wrote two letters with differing perspectives on the same subject. The first was to his parents while the second was to a friend.

Dear Mom and Dad,

We've been at the LZ now for two days. The only duty we have to do for the five days is guard duty nightly—which lasts for one hour per person. When we first arrived back from the jungle, there sitting in front of our little caves was a truckload of beer and Coke. During the daytime we play football, softball, volleyball, and other games. The greatest joy is that we're served three hot meals a day.

I sent home three cartridges of film to be processed. Half of them probably won't come out—some were taken from helicopters, trees, mud holes, and all kinds of other hazards.

It's a shame I couldn't caption the pictures because you probably won't understand what they're about. But at least you'll see what we wear, our surroundings, and other insights. I couldn't get any good shots of how we sleep because it's always too dark; we always travel in triple canopy jungle (three levels of growth). Which is why the jungle is so safe—we have literally cut our way through and therefore have only one passageway to protect. We set up trip flares across the path (a wire across the path attached to a flare) and land mines. If the enemy attempts to come any other way we will hear them.

Our first mission was completely uneventful, which doesn't displease me in the least. Our leader explained that for TET we are going out into the jungle and hiding for 15 days. By the way, I've found the jungle is the safest place to be. No one knows where you're at, you can hear people coming a mile away, and it's very easy to protect yourself and hide. No one expects a large TET offensive this year. But enough of tactics.

Our LZ, which we have nicknamed Peggy, is about 40 km northeast of Bien Hoa. We never travel more than 15 km in any direction from Peggy.

If I'm not writing on the lines, take into consideration I'm writing this by candlelight. I also lost my pen in the darkness—that's why the change of colour.

I expect to hear from you shortly.

Love,

Tom

Dear Bob,

The first month has passed unceremoniously and uneventfully, which doesn't displease me in the least. There have been times, though, when I have been scared to death—a couple of times when I thought it was all over. I look back now and laugh because it wasn't even close.

It's really hell, man. I saw a medivac operation after a company had been hit by our own artillery. Four dead—everyone was injured, most just slightly. But it was sickening. They carry the dead by a rope hanging from a helicopter (the dead man is inside a plastic bag) and just lower him to the ground—then throw him on a truck!

The fourth one was still alive when he came in—he was in the 'copter—and died a while later. He had no right leg at all; and seeing it just turned me to jelly, man—and guys just sitting around crying—it really shakes you up. And for no reason at all!

The kids spit at you—there's a bitter hatred between us and the South Vietnam troops because they carry new weapons and we don't; and we do all the fighting while they sit on their asses all the time. Man, it makes you burn.

And I haven't seen any action yet—none of my friends have been hurt and no one in my company has been injured. But it will only be a matter of time. And how do you react—how do you blow off steam? A lot of guys grow a hatred for all the Vietnamese—that's why we have happenings like My Lai. Others take it out on the Army; in Nam they average two frags a week (fragging is where a man simply pulls the pin on a hand grenade and tosses it at a lifer).

It's bigger than that, though—it's the whole country—to allow such an atrocity to happen. I suppose because nobody really realizes what's happening here or can't imagine or picture it. I know I couldn't.

But I'll tell you, man, if I ever get back there and hear someone say Vietnam was worthwhile or it was our obligation—I'll hit him right in the face. Because this is nothing but a shame—such a big mistake at such a huge cost. You can't believe it till you see it.

Oh well, enough rambling. I'm writing this in the morning and last night I had a good cry—because I was thinking too much—that's why all the emotion. Don't tell Mom or Dad or Mary about this letter because they think everything is okay....

Tarzan

In late February Thomas Kingsley wrote to his friend Bob again.

Hi, old buddy,

I'm a little calmer today for no apparent reason. I guess I'm getting used to this. After I finished that last letter, we made contact three more times that day—I didn't sleep very well that night. Then we made contact once on each of the next two days. So I'm getting used to it. (That takes me right up to today.) A couple of guys got hurt and three enemy were killed, I think (no one knows for sure)—we found one. Although I was very teed off when I wrote the last letter, I still feel exactly the way I did then. When we get back to the LZ I'm sure one of the boys will do the commanding officer in. The two guys who got hurt were his fault—the guy is completely ignorant. Enough of the war stories, though.

Yes, I can receive packages, but just remember everything I receive I have to carry on my back—don't have a locker to store it in—so don't be sending me 18 hardbacks.

I found an article in *Playboy*, an advertisement put out by a group that opposes the war (Vietnam Veterans Against the War). My friend Bob and myself got the whole squad together and joined in each sending a contribution. We also signed a petition stating our feelings and gave it to the CO.

You asked about the jungle. Well, I was really scared at first—you run into spiders (huge ones), an occasional snake, and other animals, but they never bother you. You can be sleeping and they'll run right over you, but unless you sit on one, they don't bite. The biggest spider out here couldn't kill a person—but it could sure lay you up for a while—but then I could use a couple of weeks out of the bush. I sleep in a hammock that's killing my back—you know what they are, tie each end of a giant rag to a tree!

I just had a great idea—what I could really use which would remind me of civilization, would be a bottle of rum. They send out a couple of Cokes on log day, so I'd have a mix. I could mix it in my canteen cup. (March 6th is my birthday)—hint.

Well, I have to get a letter off to Mary.

Take it easy,
Tom

On March 6 Thomas Kingsley wrote a birthday letter to his parents.

(My Birthday)

Good morning,

It's about 10:00 and I'm just sitting around in my hammock—I don't know how much longer it's going to hold me. We're in the mountains and it's absolutely beautiful! We're right at the very top and the sights are something else—I can see the South China Sea from my hammock!

Another good thing, there are no Viet Cong here because there is no water. So, the next 10 days or so will be like a vacation. Rumour has it this will be our last jungle mission—after this we'll be pulling guard duty at Bien Hoa, which would please me greatly—I've been out here for three months now without a break. I guess the Army is trying to make the deadline of May 1, to extract all jungle forces out of combat positions. We would then be used as a backup force (while pulling guard) so for me it's very important that Vietnamization works— otherwise it won't be much of a break if we have to keep bailing the ARVNs out. The 10 000 GIs in Laos are backup forces, but little good that title is doing them! The First Air Cavalry Division will definitely not be sent to Cambodia or Laos because our obligations in this region are too demanding; plus we're located too far away. It will be interesting to see what effect this Laos thing will have on the whole war.

I'll be sending a tape home soon.

Love,
Tom

On March 22, 1971, Thomas Kingsley's parents received this message.

Mr. and Mrs. Frederick E. Kingsley:

The Secretary of the Army has asked me to express his deep regret that your son, Private First Class Thomas E. Kingsley, died in Vietnam on 20 March 1971. He was on a military mission when an automatic explosive device placed by a friendly force detonated. Please accept my deepest sympathy. This confirms personal notification made by a representative of the Secretary of the Army.

Kenneth G. Wickman
Major General USA
The Adjutant General
Department of the Army
Washington, D.C.

Mr. Preston (and Mr. Rawat) Go to New Delhi

by John Stackhouse

LEWIS T. PRESTON AND D. S. RAWAT came to New Delhi this month for the same reason: development.

Mr. Preston is president of the World Bank, the Washington-based juggernaut that has about $90 billion (U.S.) in loans outstanding to developing countries. He earns $285 000 a year, tax-free. And at 65, the career banker is getting his first taste of development.

Mr. Rawat scrapes by on a metal worker's income in a southern Indian city. He is infected with the AIDS-causing human immunodeficiency virus. And at 28, he too is getting his first taste of development.

This was Mr. Preston's first visit to southern Asia since assuming the president's job in 1991, and he was accorded all the privileges of a head of state. There were the armed escorts, the prime minister's lunch, the five-star hotels, and a visit to the Taj Mahal under a full moon. There was a private plane, too, arranged by the Indian government to avoid the pain that Indian Airlines inflicts on most other air travellers. And there were the carefully planned project visits: family planning in Rajasthan, irrigation in Haryana, slum upgrading in Bombay.

Mr. Rawat came to Delhi, second-class, on the punishing overnight train from his home in Pune, two hours outside Bombay. With 2000 other people arriving by plane, train, and automobile, he came for the Second International Congress on AIDS in Asia and the Pacific.

As one of the few Indians to admit publicly to being HIV-positive, Mr. Rawat thought the congress might be interested in his attendance. He thought delegates might want to know how HIV is slowly crippling India's work force. Or how some Indian doctors refuse HIV-infected persons medical treatment. Or how AIDS is such a taboo in India that he has not been able to tell his illiterate wife that he has the virus.

As founder of a new group, the Association for People with AIDS and HIV Infection, Mr. Rawat also figured he could learn something about AIDS. The Pune doctor who paid his train fare seemed to agree.

Until they saw what AIDS congresses held in five-star hotels are all about.

The New Delhi congress brimmed with pharmaceutical and medical-supply companies from around the world, offering products that few Indians could ever afford. There were nongovernmental organizations by the dozen, too, many with a vague understanding of AIDS but a crystal-clear understanding of the World Bank's $84-million soft loan to India to fight AIDS. Much of the money is to be disbursed to NGOs for public education.

During a break in the congress, Mr. Rawat sat by the hotel swimming pool and talked to a couple of security guards. He was waiting to see some European NGO representatives who had promised to teach him about "proposal writing" and building a mailing list, but first they had to make dinner plans.

So while Mr. Rawat waited, he agreed to recount his week in New Delhi. He arrived at the congress in time to see India's vice-president receive flowers from a few HIV-infected children (adults with HIV were kept off stage), and was promptly told he could not attend the meetings unless he paid a $300 registration fee.

Congress organizers eventually waived the fee, but told Mr. Rawat he would have to find his own accommodation. Since his nearest friend lives 70 kilometres outside New Delhi, that is where he would have to stay. And so, every morning and every evening, Mr. Rawat boarded a bus to travel two to three hours for the congress.

The next day, Mr. Preston was in Bombay, holding court with the local media at the sumptuous Taj Mahal Hotel. As he spoke, scores of protesters marched outside the hotel to voice their opposition to the bank-financed Sardar Sarovar dam on the Narmada River, a project that could displace 250 000 people.

In India, perhaps in all the world, no single project has caused more damage to the bank's claim to environmental friendliness than the

Sardar Sarovar dam. This year, an independent review committee—led by no less an authority than Bradford Morse, former head of the United Nations Development Program, and Canadian Thomas Berger—found the project to be riddled with environmental flaws. Yet after a brief study of the report, the bank's directors pushed these findings aside.

Months later in Bombay, the Narmada opponents—the very villagers about to lose their homes—thought they might get an audience with the World Bank president. Washington had finally come to them. But they, too, were pushed aside. At first, local officials told the demonstrators that Mr. Preston was ill. Then a bank official told them the president had "no time to spare."

Rumours began to fly that Mr. Preston was not tied up in meetings but, in fact, was watching a fashion show in the hotel. The rumours led to a melee. The melee led to a police charge with lathis (bamboo truncheons).

Back in New Delhi, on the penultimate day of the AIDS congress, someone found Mr. Rawat a room in a government guest house for $2 a night. He took it, for one night.

"I'm not sorry I came," he said, "but I thought this conference was about people like me with HIV."

COVERING THE SPORTS BEAT

by Catherine McKercher and Carman Cumming

SPORTSWRITERS ARE PRAISED as wordsmiths and dismissed as hacks. They are criticized as "homers" when they flatter the home team and attacked as traitors when they don't. The men who write sports—and today, still, most sportswriters are men—are admired by some as the last real men in the news business and derided by others as dinosaurs from a male-dominated past. Some critics like to claim, half-jokingly, that sports journalism is an oxymoron, like military intelligence or jumbo shrimp. In some newsrooms, the "real" reporters—those who specialize in the grimmer worlds of crime, politics, or business—look at sportswriters with envy. How nice it would be, they think, to work in "the toy department."

But behind the many myths of sports writing is the reality that sportswriters produce more copy—and more of it on deadline—than many other reporters. They cope with more than their share of the usual reporting pressures: demanding sources, critical readers, and second-guessing executives. And they're expected to *write*, not just to set down facts.

In his memoirs of a four-decade-long career as a sportswriter, Trent Frayne writes: "some people with nine-to-five jobs may regard the sportswriter's life as a ride on the gravy train.... The reality is that working sportswriters actually *work* in a competitive, repetitive field. Most times, meeting tight deadlines, they see about half the events they're attending, often stuffing conditional leads into their computers—if this team wins use this one and if that team wins use that one, occasionally glancing up from the machine to see how the game's progressing" (Frayne 1990, 308).

Adding pressure to the sportswriter's already intense job is the knowledge that the audience is extraordinarily keen. "We have the kind of reader every other part of the newspaper would die to have," says Lynn McAuley, who was a sports editor of the *Ottawa Citizen*.

"They are full of passion, they are knowledgeable, they are connected with what you are writing about, they are emotional about what you're writing about. They hunger for analysis and opinion, and they're very vocal. If every part of the paper had that kind of reader, I don't think circulation would be a problem."

The job of covering sports is far more complex and far more difficult than spending Saturday afternoons watching the home team beat the visitors. Game coverage, like council meeting coverage on the municipal beat, is a basic component of the job. But sportswriters are also called on to cover an enormous range of stories—from salary negotiations to land deals, from court proceedings to coaching changes, or from pharmacology to AIDS.

They are also expected to include more opinion and analysis in their copy than are news reporters. For the most part, news reporters are actively discouraged from assessing the performance of the people they cover. Sports reporters, on the other hand, are encouraged—indeed, even required—to analyze what they cover. A court reporter who writes like a sportswriter ("Judge Brown seemed tired and cranky as he took his place on the bench. He rubbed his shoulder, still sore from yesterday's six hours of notetaking....") risks contempt of court. A sports reporter who writes dry and cautious accounts, or who limits the story to exactly what the jury of fans saw, risks contempt of the reader.

Not surprisingly, the best sportswriters tend to be among the best writers in the newsroom—beat reporters who write so vividly the reader can feel the scratch of the artificial turf on bare knuckles, or columnists who can move readers to tears over their bacon and eggs. For new reporters, the sports department is hard to crack. Reporters on the city side of most newsrooms can often work fairly quickly into a beat such as education or courts and use that as a springboard to other beats. Since beat shuffles are fairly common, news reporters can move in and around the variety of reporting and editing jobs in a fairly short time. Sports departments, on the other hand, tend to be small, stable, and tightly knit. A sportswriter may end up covering junior hockey for years, moving up only when the reporter covering the National Hockey League moves on or becomes a full-time columnist. ("Or dies," says McAuley.)

Unlike city reporters who may arrive in the newsroom with little knowledge of who's who at the courthouse or in the city administration, novice sports reporters often know a lot about sports. They may have tried their hand at covering sports competitively themselves. In either case, the odds are they are sports fans, people who want to write sports because they love the game.

Being an avid fan is no ticket to a sports writing career. Wayne Parrish—a longtime sportswriter, columnist, and sports editor—says good fans make poor reporters. They are so thrilled to be talking to their idols that they have trouble asking the tough questions a reporter needs to ask. They have more trouble than the nonfan in maintaining the perspective and balance that are basic to good reporting.

Parrish says that when he was hiring new writers for the sports department, he looked first and foremost at reporting skills. "I'd prefer to hire a reporter who has an interest in sports and a knowledge of sports but whose primary interest is journalism," he says.

In the past, taking a first job as a sports reporter usually meant following a career as a sports reporter. In recent years, however, cross-overs—news reporters who move to the sports department for a while, or sports reporters who move to news or entertainment—are becoming more common.

In part this reflects growing professionalism in the news business. Most new reporters these days have some journalism training, which helps them move in and out of what were once distinctly specialized areas. Sports departments still prefer to choose their own reporters, though, and may go for people who freelance their way into a full-time job.

Regardless of how they are hired, new sports reporters must be willing to start at the bottom and be prepared to spend a long time there. They pay their dues by covering amateur sports, high school sports, and the occasional tournament, or by working on the desk, putting together the statistics pages. The move up requires skill, talent, and luck.

The sports beat crosses local, provincial, national, and international boundaries. Depending on the size of the sports department and the season, an individual writer may cover more than a dozen types of sports, and scores of types of stories that touch on sports in some way.

It is impossible to provide any comprehensive map of the sports-writer's terrain, since it varies from writer to writer, from employer to employer, and from season to season. What can be said safely, though, is that the job of sports writing is a good deal wider and more complex than most new reporters realize. Newcomers tend to focus on a narrow range of sports—their favourite pro team, perhaps—and on game coverage itself.

SNIGLETS

by Richard Hall and Friends

Words get into the English language in many interesting ways. Sometimes we just need to invent a word for a thing that is difficult to describe. This is what Rich Hall tries to do with sniglets. "Sniglets," he says, "are words that are not in the dictionary, but should be...."

Aquadextrous: (*ak wa deks' trus*) adj. Possessing the ability to turn a bathtub faucet on and off with your toes.

Babblogesture: (*bab blo jes' cher*) n. The classroom activity of not knowing the answer but raising one's hand anyway (after determining a sufficient number of other people have also raised their hands, thus reducing the likelihood of actually being called on).

Buckstacy: (*buk' stuh see*) n. The joy of finding money you forgot you had in your coat pocket.

Charp: (*charp*) n. The green mutant potato chip found in every bag.

Choconiverous: (*chahk o niv' ur us*) adj. The tendency when eating a chocolate Easter bunny to bite off the head first.

Elbonics: (*el bon' iks*) n. The actions of two people manoeuvring for one armrest in a movie theatre.

Examnesia: (*eks am nee' zia*) n. Loss of memory while writing an exam.

Flopcorn: (*flop' korn*) n. The unpopped kernels at the bottom of the cooker.

Frust: (*frust*) n. The small line of debris that refuses to be swept into the dust pan.

Holeymoley: (*ho lee mow' lee*) n. That tiny hole in your pocket that inevitably grows on a diet of coins and keys.

Musquirt: (*mus' kwirt*) n. Water that comes out of the first squirts after you squeeze a mustard bottle.

Mustgo: (*must'go*) n. Any item of food that has been sitting in the refrigerator so long it has become a science project.

Phonesia: (*fo nee' zhuh*) n. The affliction of dialing a phone number and forgetting whom you were calling just as they answer.

Pigslice: (*pig' slys*) n. The last unclaimed slice of pizza that everyone is secretly dying for.

Pupsqueak: (*puhp' skweek*) n. The sound a yawning dog emits when it opens its mouth too wide.

Rumphump: (*rump' hump*) n. The seat on the school bus directly over the rear wheel.

Scannicpanic: (*skan' ik pan' ik*) n. The act of tearing apart a living room in search of the television remote control instead of just walking over and *manually* turning on the TV.

Subnougate: (*sub new' get*) v. To eat the bottom caramels in a candy box and carefully replace the top level, hoping no one will notice.

Witlag: (*wit' lag*) n. The amount of time between delivery and comprehension of a joke.

Wondracide: (*wun' druh side*) n. The act of murdering a piece of bread with a knife and cold butter.

Zoomer: (*zum' er*) n. A day spent doing work due yesterday.

EXPOSURE TO SECONDHAND SMOKE

by Warren Clark

PUBLIC CONCERN about environmental tobacco smoke (ETS), also known as secondhand smoke, has grown considerably in the last decade. Communities across Canada have developed new laws and policies that ban or restrict smoking in many workplaces and public buildings.[1]

In the United States, the Centres for Disease Control reported that nearly 9 out of 10 nonsmoking Americans are exposed to ETS as measured by their blood levels of cotinine, a chemical the body metabolizes from nicotine.[2] In Canada, no similar national measures of exposure to ETS using blood tests exist. However, the 1995 General Social Survey (GSS) did investigate Canadians' exposure to secondhand smoke.

Nearly half of nonsmokers are exposed to secondhand smoke In 1995, 4.5 million nonsmoking Canadians aged 15 and over were exposed to cigarette smoke on a daily basis. Another 2.2 million were exposed to it at least once a week, while about 840 000 were exposed to it less frequently. In terms of percentages, about 28 per cent of nonsmokers aged 15 and over breathed secondhand smoke every day,

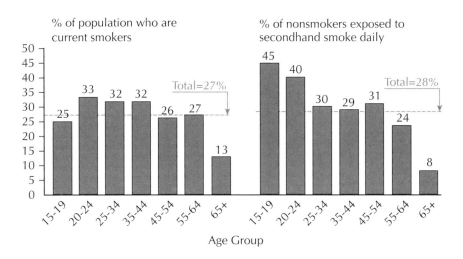

while about 19 per cent were exposed to it somewhat less often. Just over half of nonsmokers reported that they were not exposed to ETS.

Teenaged nonsmokers most likely to be exposed to secondhand smoke An age group's exposure to secondhand smoke and its members' smoking rates parallel each other, perhaps because social interactions are most common between people of similar age. Smoking rates and nonsmokers' exposure to ETS for those aged 20 and over are quite similar. However, nonsmoking teenagers aged 15 to 19 had much higher rates of daily contact with secondhand smoke (45 per cent) than their 25 per cent smoking rate. Teenaged nonsmokers are not only exposed to ETS by their peer group but also by their parents. In fact, the home is the most common source of secondhand smoke for nonsmoking teenagers.

Exposure most common at home In 1995, 20 per cent of adult nonsmokers lived with a smoker. However, only 11 per cent of nonsmokers (1.8 million) encountered daily secondhand smoke at home because not all smokers smoked in their presence every day. Children are even more likely to be living with a smoker. Some 22 per cent of nonsmoking teenagers aged 15 to 19 experienced daily exposure to secondhand smoke at home while 37 per cent of children under the age of 12 had at least one parent who smoked daily.[3]

The harmful consequences of smoking at home are wide-ranging. Children exposed to ETS are particularly susceptible to respiratory infections while parental smoking is a substantial influence on teenaged smoking behaviour.[4] In fact, the majority (84 per cent) of adults who had ever smoked picked up the habit before they reached age 20. Governments have tried to restrict the sale of cigarettes to children and teenagers, yet many children live in homes where smoking parents set an example for future behaviour of their children.

More men exposed to secondhand smoke On a daily basis, about one in three nonsmoking men age 15 and over were exposed to secondhand smoke compared with less than one in four nonsmoking women. The home is the most common place of ETS exposure for women who do not smoke. Thirteen per cent breathe secondhand smoke every day

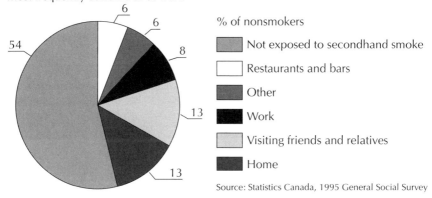

Nonsmokers' exposure to secondhand smoke occurs most frequently at home or at work

6
6
54
8
13
13

% of nonsmokers

Not exposed to secondhand smoke

Restaurants and bars

Other

Work

Visiting friends and relatives

Home

Source: Statistics Canada, 1995 General Social Survey

at home, which is double the proportion (6 per cent) who are most frequently exposed to ETS at work. For nonsmoking men, the pattern is the opposite: 15 per cent have daily ETS exposure at their workplace while 9 per cent breathe secondhand smoke daily at home. Women have higher ETS exposure at home in part because they spend more time at home than men, while men are employed for more hours than women and therefore experience greater exposure at work than women.

Half of nonsmoking households ban smoking in their homes About half of people living in nonsmoking households asked smokers to abstain from smoking in their home. Smoking restrictions in homes with a mix of smokers and nonsmokers were less common and less stringent: only one-third had limits, with total bans being most common. Not surprisingly, about 90 per cent of households comprised solely of smokers had no restrictions on cigarette smoking within the home.

Smoking parents are more likely to restrict smoking in their home if they have very young children; for example, asking smokers to abstain from smoking in the house, limiting smoking to certain rooms, or restricting smoking in the presence of young children. According to the 1995 GSS, nearly half (45 per cent) of smoking households with children under age 5 placed limits on smoking in the home. Those with older children, however, were less likely to do so: 34 per cent restricted smoking if the youngest child was age 5 to 14, 23 per cent if the youngest was age 15 or over, and 18 per cent if there were no children.

Secondhand smoke most frequent in manufacturing industries
Evidence of the health risks of secondhand smoke has been accompanied by the wave of social action to regulate tobacco smoking in the workplace and in public buildings to protect nonsmokers from exposure to smoke. In 1995, about 1.7 million nonsmokers (10 per cent), were exposed to secondhand smoke at work on a daily basis while another 374 000 encountered it at least once a week.

Exposure to secondhand smoke varies from industry to industry, influenced by the smoking behaviour of workers and smoking restrictions in each industry. In 1995, the lowest rate of nonsmokers' exposure to ETS occurred in industries with high proportions of white-collar workers: education and related industries (8 per cent); finance, insurance, and real estate industries (12 per cent); services to business management (12 per cent); and health and welfare community services (14 per cent).

In contrast, nonsmoking workers were more likely to be exposed to secondhand smoke in the manufacturing industries (36 per cent), nontraditional primary industries (32 per cent), transportation and storage industries (30 per cent), and product-differentiated manufacturing (29 per cent). The consumers' services industry—such as retail trade, personal and recreational services—lies somewhere in the middle with 21 per cent.

Three out of five nonsmokers bothered by ETS Secondhand smoke bothered the majority (61 per cent) of nonsmokers; in addition, 47 per cent of nonsmokers were physically irritated, reporting such symptoms as irritated eyes, breathing difficulties, or a sore throat. Nonsmokers exposed to smoke on a daily basis were less likely to indicate being annoyed (54 per cent) while those with less frequent exposure were more likely to feel that way—for example, 72 per cent of those exposed to ETS less than once a month were bothered by it. This may indicate that nonsmokers who are particularly troubled or irritated by smoke avoid situations where they are likely to encounter it. Alternatively, infrequent exposure may mean they are less habituated to ETS and therefore find it more irritating. Overall, women nonsmokers are more likely to object to ETS than men, regardless of the frequency of exposure. Not surprisingly, only 21 per cent of smokers felt bothered by smoke.

Beliefs about secondhand smoke The 1994–95 Survey on Smoking in Canada asked Canadians whether they felt cigarette smoking could cause health problems in a nonsmoker. The majority, 84 per cent, answered "yes." Young people and those who had never smoked were most likely to agree; older smokers were least likely to do so. The survey found that 96 per cent of 15- to 19-year-old nonsmokers believed there is a link between ETS and poor health among non-smokers, compared with only half of smoking seniors.

National data are not yet available to show the public's support for bans or restrictions on smoking in public places. However, according to an Ontario survey, the vast majority of adults—both smokers and nonsmokers—support smoking restrictions in public settings such as restaurants, workplaces, banks, and movie theatres.[5]

Summary In Canada over the past 20 years, the growth in our under-standing of the risk associated with secondhand smoke has been accompanied by changing attitudes on smoking and by the growing pressure of legislation, regulation, and voluntary action that addresses where smoking may occur in public. Many jurisdictions now have leg-islation to control or restrict smoking in various public settings, acting on the belief that smokers' rights end when their behaviour affects the health and well-being of others. Yet many nonsmokers continue to be exposed to secondhand smoke in their own homes and places of work.

1. Health Canada, *Smoking By-Laws in Canada 1995.* Ottawa: Office of Tobacco Control, 1995.

2. James L. Pirkle et al., "Exposure of the U.S. Population to Environmental Tobacco Smoke—The Third National Health and Nutrition Examination Survey, 1988 to 1991," *Journal of the American Medical Association* 275, no. 16 (24 April 1996): pp. 1233–1240.

3. Statistics Canada, *National Longitudinal Survey of Children and Youth,* 1994.

4. Warren Clark, "Youth Smoking in Canada," *Canadian Social Trends,* Winter 1996.

5. M. J. Ashley, S. B. Bull, and L. L. Pederson, "Restrictive Measures on Smoking in Ontario—Similarities and Differences between Smokers and Non-smokers in Knowledge Attitudes and Predicted Behaviour and Implications for Tobacco Programs and Policies," *The Ontario Tobacco Research Unit,* Working Paper, 1994.

A MOTHER'S HEART ACHES

by Carol Cayenne

I WRITE THIS LETTER to share my pain with all who would listen.

I know that there are other mothers like me, whose nights are filled with worry and fear. We never sleep until the front door closes behind our sons.

We sleep a very troubled sleep because the worry starts all over again the next day.

My heart aches as I watch my son head out the door every morning. I say goodbye and have a nice day.

I see him again in the evening as he bounces his basketball, throws a hoop, jogs around the block, or dashes across to the video store.

My heart aches. I am in a constant state of worry.

He is 17 years old, born at East York General Hospital, 183 centimetres tall, weighs approximately 66 kilograms. He dresses like most "hip hop" kids his age, oversized pants, hooded sweater, basketball or NFL cap on his head.

He fits the description of most young black men in Metro Toronto.

He is not the best student in his class; he can do much better but, like all kids, he thinks life is not only about school.

Like so many mothers, my heart aches, because like so many young black men he can be a target for any half-crazed person who believes that "all black kids (men) are big, tall, bad, and dangerous."

I speak as a mother to other mothers: black, white, Greek, Portuguese, Chinese, Aboriginal, or Latin American. I want my son to have a good life, free from violence.

None of us, including grandparents, aunts, and uncles, wants to witness the murders of our children nor do we want them to become murderers.

We want our children to be "somebody," as my mother used to say.

My heart aches.

Do I not weep when the bodies of young white women or Asian women are found raped and mutilated by the vicious hands of white men?

Yet, I do not look at all white males and see them as rapists, murderers, and child molesters.

When we confuse vicious and violent crime with race, we add fuel to the fire. We allow the hate to spill over and hurt innocent young children of that particular race.

I will continue to teach my son to respect others, have pride in who he is, a Canadian male of African descent, and I will teach him to love himself. But I will never teach him to bow his head, lower his eyes, or beg for respect from anyone—"massa" day is done forever.

I pray to God and hope, as I watch my son giggle on the phone with his friends, make plans for the day, talk about girls, that the racist and vengeful attitudes of a few will not hamper his zest for life because he is a young black male.

My heart aches.

DOGS AND BOOKS

by Christie Blatchford

AT SOME OF THE LOWEST moments of my life, in my times of worst despair, I have depended on two categories of friends to pull me through, and neither has ever let me down. One is books; the other is dogs.

This is not meant to disparage my human friends, some of whom I have relied on heavily, all of whom I love. But, as we all learn sooner or later, people can't always be with you when you need them. Sometimes, they mean to say the right thing, the comforting thing, but they say the wrong one. Other times, they have problems of their own and cannot be strong for you. Even when they are there, to hold your hand and kiss it better, they cannot take away the source of your unhappiness.

Books can. And so can dogs.

Books are the ultimate escape. When my heart has been broken, when I worry about my job or my writing, when I feel let down, betrayed, or unloved, I read a book. As a young woman in search of romance, I read, oddly enough, John D. MacDonald's Travis McGee books. When no one else was there to play the part, Travis was my white knight, a man both rough and tender, who loved both his friends and a woman who was loyal and sexy, fierce and faithful.

When my dad was in hospital and I was frantic he would never, ever get out, I could lose myself only when I read. I read everything, anytime—in the bathroom, on the subway, waiting for a bus, and every night before I fell asleep. And when my father went into hospital for the last time, and when he died, I cried and cried, and then remembered and remembered. The only thing that could stop the tears and the memories was reading. Much later, when I feared he was slipping away from my memory, I could bring him back, as sharp as daylight, by reading the book of Edna St. Vincent Millay's poetry he'd given me, or Kipling's *The Jungle Book* that he used to read to me as a child, or one of his favourite novels.

Not throughout my life, but for periods of it, the other source of comfort and love was my dog. As a pudgy young girl with all the usual insecurities, I came home from school every day to the whole-hearted adoration of Lucky, a big, ham-footed, foolish boxer. As a shy, easily embarrassed (and thus perfectly normal) teenager, it was sweet Mickey who welcomed me. As a reasonable young adult, I looked to wondrous, even-tempered, overtly affectionate Susie. And now, as a fairly well-adjusted, usually happy adult, I have Blux, the big, black half-Labrador with paws like hamburger buns and a heart the size of his geographic name.

It is trite to say that dogs love you no matter what; but they do, and there are times when the human being craves undemanding, uncritical, and wholly accepting love. If you're lucky, you get it as a child, from your parents; but as you become an adult you lose the right to remain uncriticized. They may love you anyway, but they are likely to explain that anyway at great and painful length. You can ignore a dog, leave him unattended and unwalked for far too long; yet the minute you walk through the door, he will be all over you like a cheap suit. You can be mean to a dog, and he will forgive you; what's more, he will never remember your meanness, let alone extract vengeance. When you want to play, so will he; when you need hugging, he will, too. When you crave quiet, pleasant company, that's just what he'll give you; when nothing and no one can make you laugh, he will reduce you to stupid, teary howling within seconds. When everyone you know is busy or in love or on vacation or booked up, it will be his distinct pleasure to be available.

Dogs are individuals as much as people are, but all dogs that are treated well share some delightful characteristics: loyalty, generosity, and a temperament that is warm and loving. And though it is silly to imbue them with human characteristics or understanding, they are none the less bright, inquisitive creatures who can immensely enrich your life. Also, they are worthy of love. Probably, there are some nice people around who happen not to like dogs, but I'll be damned if I can think of any.

I remember a friend whose three-year relationship abruptly ended. Suddenly, he was cut off from everything familiar—the woman he still loved, the house they had worked on together, the bed he knew, the street he was fond of, neighbours he knew, flowers he had planted. When he left, all he took were his clothes and a small knapsack of personal treasures.

He moved into a stark, modern apartment; he had virtually no furniture but cardboard boxes. David and I lived nearby, and saw him frequently in those days; and many times, when he thought no one would notice, I caught him looking with incredible love and gratitude at a large tan-and-white object on the floor beside him.

His dog was the one familiar, beloved face in his brave new world. He was properly appreciative, and respectful, and enamoured of her for simply being with him. And later, when his life straightened out, as it usually does for good people, and there was a new woman to share things with, he never forgot what his hound had meant to him in the dark days. You stick with them what brung you, my daddy always said. And 9 times out of 10, that's a hound.

Now, if only I could find a dog who'd read out loud to me: a jug of wine, a book to read, a dog beside me panting in the sun, tail wagging in slow motion in the heat. Well, that's heaven.

REVIEW: CANADIAN GEOGRAPHIC EXPLORER

You know you're in for a treat when a software program starts by telling you to "prepare to fly across Canada." *Canadian Geographic Explorer* starts with a 30-second coast-to-coast flight over a digitally simulated landscape model!

EXPLORER FEATURES four distinct sections. The Earth Observation section shows you what it's like to be looking down on Canada from Earth orbit. Take a simulated flight or look at the world's first 3-D satellite images (don't forget to put on the included 3-D glasses). See an image taken from a satellite over 800 kilometres above Earth showing metropolitan Toronto—there are over 3 million Canadians in this image! Hear what members of the Canadian Astronaut Team, such as Julie Payette and Chris Hadfield, say about space travel.

Want to make a map showing the distribution of national parks or the range of polar bears? Use the MapMaker section to create your own maps of Canada. You can mark points, measure distances, make your own labels, and draw in freehand using the pencil tool. The only downside is that you can't change your map layer by layer, instead you have to start all over again.

Test your knowledge of Canadian trivia with the smart-talking GeoRiddler. Beat your opponent to the buzzer (a.k.a. the keyboard) for a chance to earn big points. But if you get an answer wrong, you'll be left wondering because the Riddler doesn't provide the right answer.

In the Compareography section, you can choose from 10 categories of articles, video clips, and photos. Learn how Toronto got its name, see a video clip of western Alberta's wild horses, and look at a picture of Canada's speed skating team practising at the Olympic Oval in Calgary.

We had so much fun using this software, we almost forgot we were supposed to be reviewing it. If you like maps, exploration, and learning about Canada, *Explorer* is for you.

WE ARE CONCERNED ABOUT THE POOR ALL OVER THE WORLD

April 8, 1968

by Coretta Scott King

Four days after Martin Luther King's assassination, his widow gave this speech in Memphis City Hall.

TO MY DEAR FRIENDS in Memphis and throughout this nation:

I come here today because I was impelled to come. During my husband's lifetime I have always been at his side when I felt that he needed me, and needed me most. During the 12 years of our struggle for human rights and freedom for all people, I have been in complete accord with what he stood for.

I came because whenever it was impossible for my husband to be in a place where he wanted to be, and felt that he needed to be, he would occasionally send me to stand in for him. And so today, I felt that he would have wanted me to be here.

I need not say to you that he never thought in terms of his personal welfare, but always in terms of the Cause which he dedicated his life to, and that Cause we shared with him. I have always felt that anything I could do to free him to carry on his work, that I wanted to do this, and this would be the least that I could do.

Three of our four children are here today, and they came because they wanted to come. And I want you to know that in spite of the times that he had to be away from his family, his children knew that Daddy loved them, and the time that he spent with them was well spent. And I always said that it's not the quantity of time that is important but the quality of time.

I have been deeply gratified, and my spirit has been uplifted, because of the many thousands of persons and followers of my husband, like you, who have done so many wonderful things and said so many kind things to lift my spirit and that of our family. Your presence here today indicates your devotion, and I would say your dedication to those things which he believed in, and those things that he gave his life for.

My husband was a loving man, a man who was completely devoted to nonviolence, and I don't need to say that. And he, I think, somehow was able to instil much of this into his family. We want to carry on the best we can in the tradition in which we feel he would want us to carry on.

And this hour to me represents much more than just a time to talk about and to eulogize my husband, who I can say was a great man, a great father, and a great husband. We loved him dearly, the children loved him dearly. And we know that his spirit will never die.

And those of you who believe in what Martin Luther King, Jr., stood for, I would challenge you today to see that his spirit never dies and that we will go forward from this experience, which to me represents the Crucifixion, on towards the resurrection and the redemption of the spirit.

How many times I heard him say, that with every Good Friday there comes Easter. When Good Friday comes there are the moments in life when we feel that all is lost, and there is no hope. But then Easter comes as a time of resurrection, of rebirth, of hope and fulfilment.

We must carry on because this is the way he would have wanted it to have been. We are not going to get bogged down. I hope in this moment we are going to go forward; we are going to continue his work to make all people truly free and to make every person feel that he is a human being. His campaign for the poor must go on.

Twelve years ago in Montgomery, Alabama, we started out with the bus protest, trying to get a seat, the right to sit down on the bus in any seat that was available. We moved through that period on to the period of desegregating public accommodations and on through voting rights, so that we could have political power. And now we are at the point where we must have economic power.

He was concerned about the least of these, the garbage collectors, the sanitation workers here in Memphis. He was concerned that you have a decent income and protection that was due to you. And this was why he came back to Memphis to give his aid.

We are concerned about not only the Negro poor, but the poor all over America and all over the world. Every man deserves a right to a job or an income so that he can pursue liberty, life, and happiness. Our great nation, as he often said, has the resources, but his question was: Do we have the will? Somehow I hope in this resurrection experience the will will be created within the hearts, the minds, the souls, and the spirits of those who have the power to make these changes come about.

If this can be done, then I know that his death will be the redemptive force that he so often talked about in terms of one giving his life to a great cause and the things that he believed in.

He often said, unearned suffering is redemptive, and if you give your life to a cause in which you believe, and which is right and just—and it is—and if your life comes to an end as a result of this, then your life could not have been lived in a more redemptive way. And I think that this is what my husband has done.

But then I ask the question: How many men must die before we can really have a free and true peaceful society? How long will it take? If we can catch the spirit, and the true meaning of this experience, I believe that this nation can be transformed into a society of love, of justice, peace, and brotherhood where all men can really be brothers.

POETRY

Poems can make you laugh and cry, surprise you and comfort you. They can be short or long, or somewhere in between. Some rhyme; others are written in free-verse style. Whatever the form, well-written poems can inspire you to see the world in a new way and learn to appreciate the power of language. Poems are meant to be read and reread, silently and aloud, as you savour each image, word, and sound.

The poems in this unit, by long-established and recent writers, are short, as most poems usually are. Be sure, though, to take the advice of poet Ken Norris, who is featured on page 191 of this anthology.

> Slow down, for this is poetry
> and poetry works slowly.
> Unless you live with it a while
> the spirit will never descend.

CHARACTERISTICS OF POETRY

A poem
- may use similes and metaphors to create images
- may use symbols to convey meaning
- may use rhyme and alliteration to create rhythm
- can be structured, such as a sonnet or a haiku, or it may follow its own unique structure
- expresses a main theme, concept, emotion, or image

LINEAGE

by Margaret Walker

My grandmothers were strong.
They followed plows and bent to toil.
They moved through fields sowing seed.
They touched earth and grain grew.
They were full of sturdiness and singing.
My grandmothers were strong.

My grandmothers are full of memories
Smelling of soap and onions and wet clay
With veins rolling roughly over quick hands.

They have many clean words to say.
My grandmothers were strong.
Why am I not as they?

IDENTITY

by Julio Noboa

Let them be as flowers
always watered, fed, guarded, admired,
but harnessed to a pot of dirt.

I'd rather be a tall, ugly weed
clinging on cliffs, like an eagle
wind-wavering above high, jagged rocks.

To have broken through the surface of
stone, to live, to feel exposed to the
madness of the vast, eternal sky.
To be swayed by the breezes of an
ancient sea, carrying my soul, my seed,
beyond the mountains of time or into
the abyss of the bizarre.

I'd rather be unseen, and if then
shunned by everyone, than to be a
pleasant smelling flower, growing in
clusters in the fertile valley, where
they're praised, handled, and plucked
by greedy, human hands.

I'd rather smell of musty, green stench
than of sweet, fragrant lilac.
If I could stand alone, strong, and free,
I'd rather be a tall, ugly weed.

AN EARLY START IN MIDWINTER

by Robyn Sarah

The freeze is on. At six a scattering
of sickly lights shine pale in kitchen windows.
Thermostats are adjusted. Furnaces
blast on with a whoosh. And day
rumbles up out of cellars to the tune
of bacon spitting in a greasy pan.

Scrape your nail along the window-pane,
shave off a curl of frost. Or press your thumb
against the film of white to melt an eye
onto the fire escape. All night
pipes ticked and grumbled like sore bones.
The tap runs rust over your chapped hands.

Sweep last night's toast-crumbs off the tablecloth.
Puncture your egg-yolk with a prong of fork
so gold runs over the white. And sip
your coffee scalding hot. The radio
says you are out ahead, with time to spare.
Your clothes are waiting folded on the chair.

This is your hour to dream. The radio
says that the freeze is on, and may go on
weeks without end. You barely hear the warning.
Dreaming of orange and red, the hot-tongued flowers
that winter sunrise mimics, you go out
in the dark. And zero floats you into morning.

WHEN DAWN COMES TO THE CITY

by Claude McKay

The tired cars go grumbling by,
The moaning, groaning cars,
And the old milk carts go rumbling by
Under the same dull stars.
Out of the tenements, cold as stone,
Dark figures start for work;
I watch them sadly shuffle on,
'Tis dawn, dawn in New York.

But I would be on the island of the sea,
In the heart of the island of the sea,
Where the cocks are crowing, crowing, crowing,
And the hens are cackling in the rose-apple tree,
Where the old draft-horse is neighing, neighing, neighing
Out on the brown dew-silvered lawn,
And the tethered cow is lowing, lowing, lowing,
And dear old Ned is braying, braying, braying,
And the shaggy Nannie goat is calling, calling, calling
From her little trampled corner of the long wide lea
That stretches to the waters of the hill-stream falling
Sheer upon the flat rocks joyously!
There, oh there! on the island of the sea,
There I would be at dawn.

The tired cars go grumbling by,
The crazy, lazy cars,
And the same milk carts go rumbling by
Under the dying stars.
A lonely newsboy hurries by,
Humming a recent ditty;

Red streaks strike through the gray of the sky,
The dawn comes to the city.
But I would be on the island of the sea,
In the heart of the island of the sea,
Where the cocks are crowing, crowing, crowing,
And the hens are cackling in the rose-apple tree,
Where the old draft-horse is neighing, neighing, neighing
Out on the brown dew-silvered lawn,
And the tethered cow is lowing, lowing, lowing,
And dear old Ned is braying, braying, braying,
And the shaggy Nannie goat is calling, calling, calling
From her little trampled corner of the long wide lea
That stretches to the waters of the hill-stream falling
Sheer upon the flat rocks joyously!
There, oh there! on the island of the sea,
There I would be at dawn.

YOUR BUILDINGS

by Rita Joe

Your buildings, tall, alien,
Cover the land;
Unfeeling concrete smothers, windows glint
Like water to the sun.
No breezes blow
Through standing trees;
No scent of pine lightens my burden.

I see your buildings rising skyward, majestic,
Over the trails where once men walked,
Significant rulers of this land
Who still hold the aboriginal title
In their hearts
By traditions known
Through eons of time.

Relearning our culture is not difficult,
Because those trails I remember
And their meaning I understand.

While skyscrapers hide the heavens,
They can fall.

THE SHARK

by E. J. Pratt

He seemed to know the harbour,
So leisurely he swam;
His fin,
Like a piece of sheet-iron
Three-cornered,
And with knife-edge,
Stirred not a bubble
As it moved
With its base-line on the water.

His body was tubular
And tapered
And smoke-blue,
And as he passed the wharf
He turned,
And snapped at a flat-fish
That was dead and floating.
And I saw the flash of a white throat,
And a double row of white teeth,
And eyes of metallic grey,
Hard and narrow and slit.

Then out of the harbour,
With that three-cornered fin
Shearing without a bubble the water
Lithely,
Leisurely,
He swam—
That strange fish,
Tubular, tapered, smoke-blue,
Part vulture, part wolf,
Part neither—for his blood was cold.

FIREWORKS

by Amy Lowell

You hate me and I hate you,
And we are so polite, we two!

But whenever I see you, I burst apart
And scatter the sky with my blazing heart.
In spits and sparkles in stars and balls,
Buds into roses—and flares, and falls.

Scarlet buttons, and pale green disks,
Silver spirals and asterisks,
Shoot and tremble in a mist
Peppered with mauve and amethyst.

I shine in the windows and light up the trees,
And all because I hate you, if you please.

And when you meet me, you rend asunder
And go up in a flaming wonder
Of saffron cubes, and crimson moons,
And wheels all amaranths and maroons.

Golden lozenges and spades,
Arrows of malachites and jades,
Patens of copper, azure sheaves.
As you mount, you flash in the glossy leaves.

Such fireworks as we make, we two!
Because you hate me and I hate you.

LITTLE BOXES

by Malvina Reynolds

Little boxes on the hillside
Little boxes made of ticky-tacky
Little boxes on the hillside
Little boxes all the same,
There's a green one and a pink one,
And a blue one and a yellow one
And they're all made out of ticky-tacky,
And they all look just the same.

And the people in the houses
All went to the university
Where they were put in boxes
And they came out all the same
And there's doctors and lawyers
And business executives
And they're all made out of ticky-tacky
And they all look just the same.

And they all play on the golf course
And drink their martinis dry
And they all have pretty children
And the children go to school.
And the children go to summer camp
And then to the university
And they all get put in boxes
And they come out all the same.

Stopping by Woods on a Snowy Evening

by Robert Frost

Whose woods these are I think I know.
His house is in the village though;
He will not see me stopping here
To watch his woods fill up with snow.

My little horse must think it queer
To stop without a farmhouse near
Between the woods and frozen lake
The darkest evening of the year.

He gives his harness bells a shake
To ask if there is some mistake.
The only other sound's the sweep
Of easy wind and downy flake.

The woods are lovely, dark and deep
But I have promises to keep,
And miles to go before I sleep,
And miles to go before I sleep.

THE SONG MY PADDLE SINGS

by E. Pauline Johnson

West wind blow from your prairie nest,
Blow from the mountains, blow from the west.
The sail is idle, the sailor too;
O! wind of the west, we wait for you.
Blow, blow!
I have wooed you so,
But never a favour you bestow.
You rock your cradle the hills between,
But scorn to notice my white lateen.

I stow the sail, unship the mast;
I wooed you long but my wooing's past;
My paddle will lull you into rest.
O! drowsy wind of the drowsy west,
Sleep, sleep,
By your mountain steep,
Or down where the prairie grasses sweep!
Now fold in slumber your laggard wings,
For soft is the song my paddle sings.

August is laughing across the sky,
Laughing while paddle, canoe and I,
Drift, drift,
Where the hills uplift
On either side of the current swift.

The river rolls in its rocky bed;
My paddle is plying its way ahead;
Dip, dip,
While the waters flip
In foam as over their breast we slip.

And oh, the river runs swifter now;
The eddies circle about my bow.
Swirl, swirl!
How the ripples curl
In many a dangerous pool awhirl!

And forward far the rapids roar,
Fretting their margin for evermore.
Dash, dash,
With a mighty crash,
They seethe, and boil, and bound, and splash!

Be strong, O paddle! be brave, canoe!
The reckless waves you must plunge into.
Reel, reel,
On your trembling keel,
But never a fear my craft will feel.

We've raced the rapid, we're far ahead!
The river slips through its silent bed.
Sway, sway,
As the bubbles spray
And fall in tinkling tunes away.

And up on the hills against the sky,
A fir tree rocking its lullaby,
Swings, swings,
Its emerald wings,
Swelling the song that my paddle sings.

"MY FATHER HURT"

by Fred Wah

my father hurt-
ing at the table
sitting hurting
at suppertime
deep inside very
far down inside
because I can't stand the ginger
in the beef and greens
he cooked for us tonight
and years later tonight
that look on his face
appears now on mine
my children
my food
their food
my father
their father
me mine
the father
very far
very very far
inside

THE WRECK OF THE EDMUND FITZGERALD

by Gordon Lightfoot

The legend lives on from the Chippewa on down of the big lake
they called Gitche Gumee.
The lake it is said never gives up her dead, when the skies of
November turn gloomy.
With a load of iron ore 26,000 tons more than the Edmund Fitzgerald
weighed empty
That good ship and true was a bone to be chewed when the gales of
November came early.

The ship was the pride of the American side, comin' back from some
mill in Wisconsin.
As the big freighters go it was bigger than most, with a crew
and good captain well seasoned,
Concluding some terms with a couple of steel firms, when they
left fully loaded for Cleveland,
And later that night when the ship's bell rang, could it be the
north wind they's bin feelin'.

The wind in the wires made a tattletale sound and a wave broke over
the railing,
And every man knew as the captain did too, 'twas the witch of
November come stealin'.
The dawn came late and the breakfast had to wait, when the gales
of November came slashin'.
When afternoon came it was freezin' rain, in the face of a hurricane
west wind.

When suppertime came the old cook came on deck saying, "Fellas
it's too rough to feed ya."

At seven p.m. a main hatchway caved in he said, "Fellas it's bin
good to know ya."
The captain wired in he had water comin' in and the good ship and
crew was in peril,
And later that night when its lights went out of sight came the
wreck of the Edmund Fitzgerald.

Does anyone know where the love of God goes when the waves turn
the minutes to hours?
The searchers all say they'd have made Whitefish Bay—if they'd
put fifteen more miles behind 'em.
They might have split up or they might have capsized, they may have
broke deep and took water,
And all that remains is the faces and the names of the wives and
the sons and the daughters.

Lake Huron rolls, Superior sings, in the rooms of her ice water
mansion,
Old Michigan steams like a young man's dreams, the islands and
bays are for sportsmen,
And farther below Lake Ontario takes in what Lake Erie can send
her,
And the Iron boats go as the mariners all know, with the gales of
November remembered.

In a musty old hall in Detroit they prayed in the maritime
sailors' cathedral,
The church bell chimed 'til it rang 29 times for each man on
the Edmund Fitzgerald.
The legend lives on from the Chippewa on down of the big lake
they called Gitche Gumee.
Superior they said never gives up her dead when the gales of
November come early.

[YOU ARE READING THIS TOO FAST.]

by Ken Norris

You are reading this too fast.
Slow down, for this is poetry
and poetry works slowly.
Unless you live with it a while
the spirit will never descend.
It's so easy to quickly cut across the surface
and then claim there was nothing to find.
Touch the poem gently with your eyes
just as you would touch a lover's flesh.
Poetry is an exercise in patience,
you must wait for it to come to you.
The spirit manifests in many guises;
some quiver with beauty,
some vibrate with song.
What is happening?
Slow down, slow down,
take a few deep breaths,
read the poem slowly,
read the lines one at a time,
read the words one by one,
read the spaces between the words,
get sleepy, this is poetry,
relax until your heart
is vulnerable, wide open.

TICHBORNE'S ELEGY

by Chidiock Tichborne

WRITTEN IN THE TOWER BEFORE HIS EXECUTION

My prime of youth is but a frost of cares,
My feast of joy is but a dish of pain,
My crop of corn is but a field of tares,
And all my good is but vain hope of gain;
The day is past, and yet I saw no sun,
And now I live, and now my life is done.

My tale was heard and yet it was not told,
My fruit is fallen and yet my leaves are green,
My youth is spent and yet I am not old,
I saw the world and yet I was not seen;
My thread is cut and yet it is not spun,
And now I live, and now my life is done.

I sought my death and found it in my womb,
I looked for life and saw it was a shade,
I trod the earth and knew it was my tomb,
And now I die, and now I was but made;
My glass is full, and now my glass is run,
And now I live, and now my life is done.

SONNET XVIII

by William Shakespeare

Shall I compare thee to a summer's day?
Thou art more lovely and more temperate:
Rough winds do shake the darling buds of May,
And summer's lease hath all too short a date:
Sometime too hot the eye of heaven shines,
And often is his gold complexion dimm'd;
And every fair from fair sometime declines,
By chance or nature's changing course untrimm'd;
But thy eternal summer shall not fade
Nor lose possession of that fair thou owest;
Nor shall Death brag thou wander'st in his shade,
When in eternal lines to time thou growest:
So long as men can breathe or eyes can see,
So long lives this and this gives life to thee.

A POISON TREE

by William Blake

I was angry with my friend:
I told my wrath, my wrath did end.
I was angry with my foe:
I told it not, my wrath did grow.

And I water'd it in fears,
Night and morning with my tears;
And I sunnèd it with smiles,
And with soft deceitful wiles.

And it grew both day and night,
Till it bore an apple bright;
And my foe beheld it shine,
And he knew that it was mine.

And into my garden stole
When the night had veil'd the pole:
In the morning glad I see
My foe outstretch'd beneath the tree.

THE SOLITARY REAPER

by William Wordsworth

Behold her, single in the field,
Yon solitary Highland lass!
Reaping and singing by herself;
Stop here, or gently pass!
Alone she cuts and binds the grain,
And sings a melancholy strain;
O listen! for the vale profound
Is overflowing with the sound.

No nightingale did ever chaunt
More welcome notes to weary bands
Of travellers in some shady haunt,
Among Arabian sands:
A voice so thrilling ne'er was heard
In spring-time from the cuckoo-bird,
Breaking the silence of the seas
Among the farthest Hebrides.

Will no one tell me what she sings?—
Perhaps the plaintive numbers flow
For old, unhappy, far-off things,
And battles long ago:
Or is it some more humble lay,
Familiar matter of to-day?
Some natural sorrow, loss, or pain,
That has been, and may be again?

Whate'er the theme, the maiden sang
As if her song could have no ending;
I saw her singing at her work,
And o'er the sickle bending;—
I listened, motionless and still;
And, as I mounted up the hill,
The music in my heart I bore,
Long after it was heard no more.

SONG

by Christina Rossetti

When I am dead, my dearest,
Sing no sad songs for me;
Plant thou no roses at my head,
Nor shady cypress tree:
Be the green grass above me
With showers and dewdrops wet;
And if thou wilt, remember,
And if thou wilt, forget.

I shall not see the shadows,
I shall not feel the rain;
I shall not hear the nightingale
Sing on, as if in pain;
And dreaming through the twilight
That doth nor rise nor set,
Haply I may remember,
And haply may forget.

ONE PERFECT ROSE

by Dorothy Parker

A single flow'r he sent me, since we met.
All tenderly his messenger he chose;
Deep-hearted, pure, with scented dew still wet—
One perfect rose.

I knew the language of the floweret;
"My fragile leaves," it said, "his heart enclose."
Love long has taken for his amulet
One perfect rose.

Why is it no one ever sent me yet
One perfect limousine, do you suppose?
Ah no, it's always just my luck to get
One perfect rose.

"ADIEU FOULARD..."

by Derek Walcott

I watched the island narrowing the fine
Writing of foam around the precipices then
The roads as small and casual as twine
Thrown on its mountains; I watched till the plane
Turned to the final north and turned above
The open channel with the grey sea between
The fishermen's islets until all that I love
Folded in cloud; I watched the shallow green
That broke in places where there would be reef,
The silver glinting on the fuselage, each mile
Dividing us and all fidelity strained
Till space would snap it. Then, after a while
I thought of nothing, nothing, I prayed would change;
When we set down at Seawell[1] it had rained.

1. Seawell: name of main airport in Barbados at time poem was written.

What Do I Remember of the Evacuation?

by Joy Kogawa

What do I remember of the evacuation?
I remember my father telling Tim and me
About the mountains and the train
And the excitement of going on a trip.
What do I remember of the evacuation?
I remember my mother wrapping
A blanket around me and my
Pretending to fall asleep so she would be happy
Although I was so excited I couldn't sleep
(I hear there were people herded
Into the Hastings Park like cattle.
Families were made to move in two hours
Abandoning everything, leaving pets
And possessions at gun point.
I hear families were broken up
Men were forced to work. I heard
It whispered late at night
That there was suffering) and
I missed my dolls.
What do I remember of the evacuation?
I remember Miss Foster and Miss Tucker
Who still live in Vancouver
And who did what they could
And loved the children and who gave me
A puzzle to play with on the train.
And I remember the mountains and I was
Six years old and I swear I saw a giant
Gulliver of Gulliver's Travels scanning the horizon
And when I told my mother she believed it too

And I remember how careful my parents were
Not to bruise us with bitterness
And I remember the puzzle of Lorraine Life
Who said "Don't insult me" when I
Proudly wrote my name in Japanese
And Tim flew the Union Jack
When the war was over but Lorraine
And her friends spat on us anyway
and I prayed to the God who loves
All the children in his sight
That I might be white.

BELLY GROWLS

by Cyril Dabydeen

There's an emptiness,
a wildness

deep yearning
for something
to swallow

fleshy—
mouth shape
wrapped around

eyes watching,
teeth sharp
with thoughts
(belly
growls)

the entire
forest listens
(understands
the belch
that follows)

promise of something
else
(more fleshy
carcass)
waiting—

life's end.

TRACTOR-FACTOR

by Gene Dawson

for Carl Ringe

When you're a

                            spreader.   If the

                      or

green hand on   field looks

                      harrow

a dirt farm   anything

                  8 bottom

and the boss   like this

                  shear plow

sends you   when you

                  weeders

out on a

                                    stop,

                drill

tractor alone,   you're in

                  disc

it doesn't

                              Big Trouble

                  pulling a

matter a damn

                            in any

                or Caterpillar—

whether it's   Case.

                Massey-Harris

a Ford

                Deere

           John

International

Drama

Drama is literature brought to life. All forms of drama, from monologues to large-scale theatre productions, are meant to be performed. When a well-written drama is performed by a talented cast, it can be a thrilling experience. Just watch audience members leaving a theatre after a good play—they'll be excited about what they've seen, eager to tell their friends that this is a show not to be missed.

The selections in this unit cover a variety of dramatic forms: monologues, one-act stage plays, teleplays, and radio plays. They are written by playwrights who have mastered key elements that have been a part of drama since ancient times.

You can read these selections silently or aloud with others. To bring alive the action, follow any stage directions provided and use props mentioned in the text. Where possible, use sound effects to make the action even more dramatic, especially if you are recording a reading of a play.

CHARACTERISTICS OF DRAMA

A drama
- contains elements such as setting, technique, characterization, conflict, and plot
- usually includes stage directions, notes on setting and props, and dialogue
- can be performed by one person or by a whole team of actors

Drama

CHAGALL

a one-act stage play by Rick McNair

CAST:

MARC CHAGALL, referred to as MARC

OLD CHAGALL, referred to as CHAGALL

YOUNG CHAGALL 1; YOUNG CHAGALL 2; YOUNG CHAGALL 3; YOUNG
  CHAGALL 4—who represent aspects of Old Chagall's subconscious

MOTHER of Marc Chagall

FATHER of Marc Chagall

TEACHERS: TEACHER 1; TEACHER 2

KIDS: GIRL; TOUGH KID 1; TOUGH KID 2

PHOTOGRAPHER

HUSBAND; WIFE; four children

PENNE, the art teacher

RINGMASTER 1; RINGMASTER 2; RINGMASTER 3; RINGMASTER 4;
  RINGMASTER 5

CIRCUS PERFORMERS: Petrov Georgi; the Georgi Family; elephants;
  female tightrope walker

BELLA, Chagall's wife, a smiling young woman

GUEST at the wedding

RELATIVE at the wedding

DISTANT COUSIN at the wedding

HUPAH HOLDER

RABBI

ACCUSER 1; ACCUSER 2; ACCUSER 3; ACCUSER 4

RUSSIAN OFFICIAL

SCENE: *The setting for the entire play is a circus. There should be about five round platforms of various sizes to stand or sit on. They will serve as tables and chairs. Coloured ladders and a monkey bar could be centre stage. Everything should be painted in the vibrant colours characteristic of Chagall's paintings.*

(OLD CHAGALL *enters and takes a blue handkerchief and turns it red.*)

CHAGALL: I would paint all of that *(pointing to something in the theatre)* the brightest red I could make. And over there I would have a small house with walls that bend a little, and on its roof would be an old man. He looks a little like me. He'd sit on a rocking chair and eat carrots. And there … no … more to the left, there would be a giant violin, or fiddle, or what-you-will. And right there would be a purple cow. Yes, mooing in its own colour. A rooster there, and a yellow fish there. And all the space in between will be blue, with stars living in it. I'll paint people everywhere. Some will walk, and some will fly … maybe we could even see through some of them. Some things look better upside down. And over there I will have an angel. The whole place will be my circus. Excuse me, I am being rude. I have forgotten to introduce myself. My name is Marc … Chagall. I paint pictures, make rugs, pots, coloured glass windows. Some people tell me I'm the most famous painter in the world. I bet you never heard of me or, if you did, you probably can't remember … But that's all right I can't even remember when I was born. Let me see … it was 1887 … or was it 1889? Well, it doesn't matter. But I do remember I always wanted to be a painter. *(YOUNG CHAGALL 1, YOUNG CHAGALL 2, and YOUNG CHAGALL 3 enter, dressed alike.)*

YOUNG CHAGALL 1: When I grow up, I'm going to be …

CHAGALL: I remember I said …

YOUNG CHAGALL 1: … a violinist.

YOUNG CHAGALL 2: What are you going to be?

YOUNG CHAGALL 1: A fiddler!

YOUNG CHAGALL 3: When you grow up?

CHAGALL AND YOUNG CHAGALL 1: A fiddler!

YOUNG CHAGALL 2: That's not a real job.

YOUNG CHAGALL 1: I'll study at the Academy of Music.

CHAGALL: My fiddle will make the stars dance. Yes, I wanted to be a violinist as well. A magic sound.

YOUNG CHAGALL 3: I am going to be a poet.

YOUNG CHAGALL 1: What?

YOUNG CHAGALL 3: To write words upon the wind … to spill magic from my heart … to make ink dance on a field of white.

CHAGALL: Yes—a poet! I'll study to be a …

(YOUNG CHAGALL 4 enters, singing.)

YOUNG CHAGALL 4: Singer. I want to sing out loud, let notes float to the sky.

CHAGALL *(singing a scale with the letters of his name):* C-H-A-G-A-L-L, Chagall! I want to be a …

YOUNG CHAGALL 2: A dancer. To dance across the roofs, to leap, to float, to fly! *(He dances but he falls.)*

YOUNG CHAGALL 3: To sink.

CHAGALL: I want to be a …

YOUNG CHAGALL 1, 2, 3, AND 4: Fiddler, poet, singer, dancer.

(The four young CHAGALLS exit, arguing.)

CHAGALL: A painter. Maybe I did want to be a lot of different things. Clowns and acrobats and bareback riders too. They all sound like fun.

(MARC, as a young boy, and his MOTHER enter.)

MOTHER: I have got you into school. It hasn't been easy.

CHAGALL: She had to bribe the school to take me. Not everyone was allowed to go to school then. Not such a bad idea you think?

MOTHER: Marc, sit down over there, learn as much as you can, and you will get a good job … a clerk perhaps. Now don't be frightened.

(MARC does as he is told and MOTHER exits.)

CHAGALL: She got me into school for better or worse. What can I say about my mother? We loved each other; we disappointed each other; we needed each other. Maybe all I can say is … tears.

(The KIDS enter. TEACHER 1 and TEACHER 2 enter, one on each side of MARC.)

TEACHER 1: Marc Chagall, sit there.

(MARC sits on one of the round platforms.)

TEACHER 2: Take this book.

TEACHER 1: Put your name in it.

TEACHER 2: Today we will study the names of the czars …

TEACHER 1: … and czarinas …

TEACHER 2: … of all of Russia.

TEACHERS: Ivan, Peter, Alexander, Ivan, Nicholas, Catherine, Ivan, Ivan, and more Ivans. Ivan, Alexander, and Anne.

MARC *(not paying attention to the teachers)*: Name—Marc Chagall. Address—Pokrowsskaja Street. The Town of Vitebsk. Russia. Europe. Northern Hemisphere. The World. The Solar System. The Milky Way. The Universe. Infinity.

TEACHER 1: Marc Chagall, name five Russian czars.

MARC: Um … Al, no, Al … Fred? … Um.

TEACHERS: Don't know them, eh?

TEACHER 1: Two black marks for bad behaviour.

TEACHER 2: Bad behaviour.

(TEACHERS 1 and 2 exit.)

CHAGALL: I really did know them. I wasn't going to say them out loud. To me, history smelled too dead. It was just lists of dead czars. But … geometry …

KIDS: Geometry!

CHAGALL: It was magic signs and shapes that flew through space. *(Throughout the following verses, various designs and shapes are made with a large loop of material. At least four students are involved in a kind of giant cat and cradle game. A large six-point star is the final result.)*

KIDS: Dots are moving to form two lines.

Parallel lines, they never touch.

All in the circle I say is mine.

Ninety degrees is much too much.

Circle, Line, Triangle, Square,

You can make them anywhere.

With your compass draw what you will,

Make a perfect star and hold it still.

Round and round the magic star goes,

Where it stops nobody knows.

CHAGALL: I liked geometry. I also liked girls.

GIRL: Hello.

MARC: Hello.

CHAGALL: I had rosy cheeks and I was cute. I couldn't help myself.

GIRL: I'm better now.

MARC: You look better.

CHAGALL: She had freckles. Do angels have freckles? Oh, I bet some of them do.

GIRL: I don't have the measles anymore.

MARC: Did they hurt?

GIRL: Not much.

MARC: Was it my fault you had the measles?

GIRL: How?

MARC: Because I kissed you?

GIRL: No, silly!

MARC: I can do it again … and I will. *(He does.)*

TOUGH KID 1: Hey! Who said you could do that?

CHAGALL: She did.

TOUGH KID 1: Where do you think you're going?

TOUGH KID 2: Yeah. Where do you think you're going?

MARC *(trying to sneak away)*: Oh … nowhere. *(He stops.)*

TOUGH KID 1: Are you trying to get tough with me?

TOUGH KID 2: Trying to get tough with me?

MARC: No.

TOUGH KID 1: You're the kid who paints.

MARC: Yup, that's me … well, I'd better get going now.

TOUGH KID 1: Trying to get away, eh?

TOUGH KID 2: Getting away, eh?

MARC: Oh … no.

TOUGH KID 1: We can paint your face … with a black eye.

TOUGH KID 2: A black eye.

MARC: Don't you mean purple?

TOUGH KIDS 1 AND 2: Huh?

MARC: An eye, if you hit it, turns purple. Not black, but purple.

(A chase scene ensues. It has a slapstick quality. MARC thinks he got away and from behind him TOUGH KID 1 taps MARC on the shoulder.)

TOUGH KID 1: Okay painter kid, we'll see if it turns black or purple. On the count of three. One … two … two and a half … two and five-eighths … *(TOUGH KIDS 1 and 2 start to exit but MARC does not see because he has his hands over his eyes.)* two and seven-eighths … two and ninety-nine one hundredths. *(They laugh.)*

(MARC slowly uncovers his eyes and sees he is alone.)

MARC: Don't come back or I'll give you a purple eye. *(He exits.)*

CHAGALL: Well, maybe I wasn't such a good fighter. Memories. Some of them you'd rather not remember. But in art class I could float away from others. In art class … in art class … I was king. In art class I was magic. In art class I was the only one who used a lot of purple. With my brush I made things come to life. I felt as if I was the brush. I touched the paint and I touched the paper and out of that came a cow that flew, a horse that rode on trails in the sky, and a giant that could take care of me and carry me on his shoulders over the town. All of these creatures I made into my very own circus. Yes, I made a whole circus, right in my painting.

MARC *(entering with circus drawing and MOTHER)*: Look Mother, look at what I made for you.

Mother: Oh thank you, Marc. What is it?

MARC: What do you think? Do you like it?

Mother: Yes I do. You have talent.

MARC: Take it, Mother, please.

Mother: Thank you, Marc. Where did you get such talent?

MARC: I want to be a painter.

Mother: It might be better if you get a job as a clerk. It is good, steady work and they will pay you for it.

MARC: But I don't want to be a clerk, Mother. I want to make pictures.

MOTHER: Pictures? Hmm. I could get you a job working with a photographer. Yes … in a year you will get paid. Pictures are pictures.

MARC: Thank you, Mother. Taking pictures could be all right.

CHAGALL: Taking pictures could be all right.

MOTHER: Pictures are pictures.

(MOTHER *exits and whispers to* PHOTOGRAPHER *as she goes.*
PHOTOGRAPHER *enters bringing a large portrait camera.*)

PHOTOGRAPHER: Yes? Could I help you?

MARC: I am Marc Chagall.

PHOTOGRAPHER: Oh yes. Your mother told me.

MARC: I want to make pictures.

PHOTOGRAPHER: Yes, yes. I will make you an artist. This will be a real
opportunity for you. In two years you may even be good enough
to be paid.

MARC: I will be …

CHAGALL: … an artist.

PHOTOGRAPHER: Yes, but quiet. Here comes a customer. Hello, hello.
Welcome to my studio.

(HUSBAND *and* WIFE *enter with four children.*)

HUSBAND: I want a picture of our family. A picture that will show all
our true qualities. Can you do that?

PHOTOGRAPHER: Surely you jest. My pictures are so true to life that
when your friends look at them, they will want to talk to them.

HUSBAND: It won't cost too much, will it?

PHOTOGRAPHER: No, no. Exactly the right amount.

HUSBAND: What do you think, dear?

WIFE: Well, I don't know, I … (*It seems as if she doesn't want to spend
the money.*)

PHOTOGRAPHER: And who is this lovely lady?

HUSBAND: Oh … this is my wife.

PHOTOGRAPHER: I didn't know you were married to a beautiful
model.

WIFE: I'm not really a …

PHOTOGRAPHER: Isn't she beautiful, Chagall?

MARC: Not really like a model, no.

PHOTOGRAPHER: Marc!

WIFE: We are so looking forward to seeing your pictures.

PHOTOGRAPHER: Yes, I'm looking forward to seeing them too.

CHAGALL: So you can get their money.

PHOTOGRAPHER: Stand there please, Marc.

(*MARC leads HUSBAND, WIFE, and children to position for the picture.*)

WIFE: Are you sure we look fine?

PHOTOGRAPHER: Wonderful, just wonderful. Now … big smiles. Look at the birdie. Ready, aim … (*They freeze with funny looks on their faces.*) How could they help but look wonderful? (*The family exits.*) Take this, Marc, and develop it. Oh, and Marc … you are a painter, aren't you?

MARC: Yes I am.

PHOTOGRAPHER: Well, they don't look as good as they think they do, so I'd like you to take your brush and touch them up a little.

MARC: But you said you took true to life pictures.

PHOTOGRAPHER: Never mind what I said! Just make them look pretty. (*He exits.*)

MARC: If that's what he wants, then that's what he'll get. Now let me see … a little bit here and a little bit there. I'll touch up her face, and I'll fill in his hair. I'll make a line over here, and another line there. I'll push in his nose, and fix up her hair.

(*MARC touches up the pictures and very funny faces result. PHOTOGRAPHER enters.*)

PHOTOGRAPHER: Are you finished, Chagall?

CHAGALL: I certainly was.

PHOTOGRAPHER (*taking pictures from behind MARC's back*): Wha … What have you done to my picture? You … you are … are…

CHAGALL: Fired?

PHOTOGRAPHER: Fired! (*He takes the camera and leaves.*)

MARC: Fired. Oh … fired.

CHAGALL: Well, one career down the drain.

MOTHER (*entering with a blanket and making him lie down on a bed which is another rostrum*): Forget about it. Sleep tonight, and we'll talk about it in the morning.

MARC: Yes, Mother.

(*MOTHER exits.*)

CHAGALL: I couldn't sleep that night … not after being fired from my very first job.

MARC: I can't paint just like everyone else.

CHAGALL: Good for you.

MARC: Maybe I should only paint what my eyes see?

CHAGALL: What about what the heart feels … what makes you laugh … what makes you cry … even what scares you.

MARC: Nothing scares me.

CHAGALL: Oh? Nothing in a dark room? When you are alone?

MARC: Alone? No, I'm not afraid.

CHAGALL: Of what's under your bed?

MARC: Under my bed?

CHAGALL: The creature that lives under your bed.

(MARC is worried now. He wants to look, but … He hears a strange sound.)

MARC: There is nothing under my bed.

CHAGALL: The creature that lives under your bed.

(There is a sound and MARC sees the creature.)

MARC: Ahh! *(He stands up on the bed, would like to leave but is afraid.)*

CHAGALL: Quick. Maybe you should run for the door.

MARC: No! He'll get my feet.

CHAGALL: On the count of three. One, two …

MARC: Two … oh what should I do?

MOTHER *(from off-stage)*: MARC? Are you having a dream?

MARC: Yes, Mother, I was only dreaming.

CHAGALL: Wouldn't you like to paint what is under your bed?

MARC: Don't be silly. There's nothing *(looking under)* under my bed.

CHAGALL: That's right. You just imagined it …

MARC: … in my head.

CHAGALL: Well? Wouldn't it be fun to paint what you imagined? Look around your room, Marc. What do you see?

MARC: It's only my room.

CHAGALL: Close your eyes. Remember? Your imagination?

MARC: It's my giant that carries me over the town. Or maybe an angel.

CHAGALL: Giants and angels. I remember once when I was alone, the roof blew apart, boards burst in all directions, lights …

MARC: … are pouring into my room, and an angel is flying down. It's beautiful.

(MOTHER enters in time to hear the last part. She puts breakfast things on the rostrum to make it a table. FATHER enters and sits down at the table.)

MOTHER: You certainly have an imagination, Marc.

CHAGALL: Imagination.

MARC: I can be a painter. Just let me take some classes with a painting teacher. I saw a sign that said a teacher gave painting lessons.

MOTHER: It won't be easy, Marc.

CHAGALL: Let me try.

MARC: I will work very hard.

MOTHER: We will see. What do you think, Father?

FATHER: It would be a waste of time and money. Who will pay a painter?

MOTHER: He could paint signs.

FATHER: Is that what you want to paint, Marc?

MARC: I want to be an artist.

MOTHER: Give him the money. Give him the lessons. He does have talent.

FATHER: If you want to paint … paint. Take my money.

(FATHER puts a small bag of money on the table and the parents exit.)

CHAGALL: My parents loved me. They wanted what was best for me. I think I knew that even way back then.

MARC: I will be an artist, and lots of people will want to see and buy my work.

(PENNE, the art teacher, enters with lumps of clay and a statue to copy. The statue and lumps of clay are actors in black body suits. They could be

pulled in a wagon. The lump that MARC uses could be more than one actor.)

PENNE: Ah, there you are. *(taking the money bag from MARC)* Welcome to Penne's School of Art. I will teach you everything there is to know about art. You can count on that.

MARC: I want to learn.

PENNE: Good. Well, just don't stand there. Take that lump of clay and do as I do.

MARC: Yes, sir.

PENNE: You must get the proportions correct.

(The statue is set up and they are trying to copy it. PENNE is getting his lump more like the statue than is MARC. MARC has a very interesting shape and is even able to pull coloured strands of material from his clay.)

MARC: I'm trying.

PENNE: No, no, no. Your work must look like the real thing.

MARC: Like the real thing looks like on the outside, or on the inside?

PENNE: Uh … copy this statue.

MARC: Yes, sir.

PENNE: Now, I want the features, details, and the proportions.

CHAGALL: I tried to see as he did. But …

(MARC pulls out a bunch of colours from the clay.)

PENNE: Now, let's see your finished work.

CHAGALL: But it was not like him.

MARC: Here it is.

PENNE: Are you trying to be smart?

MARC: Yes, sir. I mean no, sir.

PENNE: This does not look like that.

CHAGALL: It does in a way.

PENNE: Don't be silly. Remember, if you do as I do and copy that statue, someday you will be just like me.

MARC: But I don't want to be just like you.

PENNE: Pardon?

CHAGALL: I said I don't want to paint the way you do.

PENNE: Preposterous! You will never be an artist then.

MARC: Yes I will.

PENNE: I can make a face that looks like a face.

MARC: I can make a face that shows what it is dreaming.

PENNE: I can make a person come true to life.

MARC: I can draw a man who will float over the town.

PENNE: I can draw the world as it is.

MARC: I can make my own world. I turn everything upside down and inside out. I can make the world dance. I can make the world sing …

PENNE: I can …

MARC: I can make a circus where there is nothing; I can paint love in all its colours.

PENNE: You are a fool. Now give up. You'll never be an artist. (PENNE'S *lump of clay and the statue to be copied leave.*) Get out and stay out. Never come back again! You are a failure. Your mother has wasted her money. Your dreams are nothing.

CHAGALL: I can make a circus in my head.

(MARC's *sculpture exits with all its colours flying.* MARC *exits.*)

(*All the performers in the following circus scene are dressed in bright circus costumes. The one who is the ringmaster has a top hat and a megaphone. These are passed on to the next person when they become the ringmaster. There should be music with drums and trumpets, and the like.*)

RINGMASTER 1: Ladies and Gentlemen, I welcome you to the Circus Marc Chagall. All these brilliant acts are the finest, fanciest, funniest, most famous, most fantastic anywhere in the world. They are brought to you from us—thanks to that daring, dashing juggler of images, Marc Chagall.

(MARC *enters and juggles three brilliantly coloured scarves. If he drops one, it could be picked up by* CHAGALL *who is always watching and sometimes participating invisibly with* MARC.)

RINGMASTER 2: Ladies and Gentlemen, let's give a big welcome for the next attraction under the Big Top … the Georgi Family. They will perform one of the most difficult feats known in the circus, the full flip off the balance board.

(The GEORGI FAMILY runs on and constructs a balance board with a plank and something to act as a fulcrum.)

RINGMASTER 2: And now, let's give a really big hand for the star himself, the one, the only, the magnificent, Petrov Georgi … Here he is!

(PETROV GEORGI enters. He is a life-sized doll that can be made to do anything. He is manipulated as a kind of large puppet.)

RINGMASTER 2: Silence please, Ladies and Gentlemen. And now the dangerous full flip off the balance board … Maestro, a drum roll!

(When the drum roll ends, one of the family jumps with a yell on one end of the balance board and, with the help of the other family members, PETROV GEORGI does a flip and takes a bow.)

RINGMASTER 3: Ladies and Gentlemen, Mr. Marc Chagall, at great expense, has brought the largest trio of trained pachyderms, that means elephants to you, to be found in all Russia. All eyes on the centre ring.

(MARC enters as an animal trainer and gets the elephants [who are people] to do circus tricks. They perform a parade of holding one another's tails with their trunks. They even perform a dance. They could also show the courage of MARC by letting them stand on him. They exit, and MARC bows and exits.)

RINGMASTER 4: Ladies and Gentlemen, walk on the edge and float over your heads. You take a lady, add an umbrella, and you have an angel … on a tightrope.

(A girl performs the act on the ground. She shows the danger of walking on a tightrope by wobbling. The crowd and RINGMASTER respond with "oohs" and "ahhs.")

RINGMASTER 5: Ladies and Gentlemen, for our final act we have a man who will be shot from the mouth of a cannon. Yes, a man who will be shot from the mouth of this very cannon. He will be propelled through the air and land in the safety of our newly repaired net.

(A silk net is brought out which has an obvious patch. It is controlled by two people.)

The net! And here to perform this act is our very own star—Petrov Georgi!

(*The rag doll* PETROV GEORGI *enters and is bowing during the next speech.*)

Ladies and Gentlemen, you will see for the first time and maybe the last time this dangerous, dreaded, death-defying dive …

(PETROV GEORGI *looks like he has second thoughts.*)

The great Petrov will be shot from this cannon (a hollow tube) and land in this net … we hope.

(PETROV GEORGI *is being forced into the cannon.*)

Maestro, a drum roll please.

(*A drum roll sounds across the stage.*)

The fuse … the match.

(*The sound of the drum is followed by a big bang.* PETROV GEORGI *flies in a looping way, turned and twisted by the actors, toward the net. The net is moving all over the place and, of course, misses him.*)

The ambulance!

(*The ambulance siren sounds and there is a flashing light. The light could be as simple as the opening and closing of hands.* PETROV GEORGI *is loaded into the ambulance and …)*

To the hospital!

(*The circus exits to the hospital amidst much bowing and excitement.* MARC *enters as the circus exits.*)

MOTHER (*bringing back on the circus painting*): You did not do well in art school. You cannot be a painter, my son.

MARC: There are other schools. But I did learn something.

MOTHER: Don't worry, you can always get a real job … remember? A clerk.

CHAGALL: What are you doing?

(MOTHER *is taking the circus painting and putting it on the floor to be a rug.*)

MARC: My painting!

MOTHER: Yes, it's a good thick cloth. It makes a beautiful rug.

MARC: It was my painting.

CHAGALL: She just didn't understand.

MOTHER: I'm sorry, MARC.

(MOTHER *exits and* MARC *picks up the painting that has been walked on.*)

MARC: Maybe you are right. I can be a clerk.

CHAGALL: I still wanted to be a painter; but could I find my dream again?

(BELLA *enters. She is a smiling woman.*)

BELLA: Could I see what you're holding?

CHAGALL: Her name is Bella. An angel who walked.

BELLA: May I see it, please?

MARC: Why? Do you want to wipe your feet?

BELLA: What?

MARC: Oh … nothing.

BELLA: I'd just like to look at it.

CHAGALL: Will she laugh at my paintings?

(BELLA *laughs.*)

MARC: You think it's stupid, don't you?

BELLA: No. Your painting laughs, so I want to laugh too.

MARC: You mean you like it?

BELLA: Yes.

CHAGALL: She liked it!

BELLA: I wish I could have one just like it in my room.

MARC: I can fill your room with paintings. I can put you in my paintings … May I put you in my paintings?

CHAGALL: I thought I could paint her into my life. If she were in my pictures, I thought she would always be near. I'd help make her wings.

BELLA: You want to paint me?

MARC: Can you fly?

BELLA: If you show me.

CHAGALL: She didn't laugh. She knew what I meant. She was my angel. I could see her, touch her; I could soar with her. After we had taken some time together, I wanted to ask her to marry me.

(*While* CHAGALL *is talking,* MARC *and* BELLA *walk and talk with a lot of gestures. They sit together and … *)

MARC: Bella, would you …

BELLA: Would I what?

MARC: Would you … be interested …

CHAGALL: Go ahead. Ask her if she would marry you.

MARC: Will you …

BELLA: Will you marry me?

MARC: What? Yes! Sure! Mazel Tov!

(MARC and BELLA exit to get ready for the wedding.)

CHAGALL: Everyone has wedding pictures. I remember my wedding like a picture; well, more like a comic book. If Bella had asked me to paint a picture of our wedding, this is how I would have painted it. There would be relatives, and friends of relatives. You could see them talk.

(The following scene can be done with puppets or actors. If actors are used, they should use masks. Balloons with painted faces can also be used, including many different kinds of puppets.)

GUEST: When is Marc Chagall going to get here?

RELATIVE: The sooner the wedding is over, the sooner we can all eat.

DISTANT COUSIN: No, worse. Pictures. He says he's an artist.

GUEST: Yes, but what does he do for a living?

DISTANT COUSIN: That's just it! Nothing! He just paints.

RELATIVE: Poor Bella.

ALL: Tsk, tsk, tsk.

CHAGALL: Talk, talk, talk. Sometimes all that talk reminded me of so many geese. But now, there we are, coming down the centre of my wedding picture. And who comes along but my mother and father, holding me so I don't float away. There would be another picture of me … waiting under the Hupah.

(MARC enters as described. The Hupah is the tent-like covering used in Jewish weddings.)

HUPAH HOLDER: Here she comes.

CHAGALL: I remember she looked truly like an angel. *(The wedding music starts.)* I was frozen, as if my blood had stopped moving. If I smiled, my face would have cracked. The ceremony began. The Rabbi …

RABBI: Blessed be he that cometh in the name of the Lord, we have blessed you out of the house of the Lord.

CHAGALL: Ceremony, solemnity, and ritual mixed with a gaggle of relatives.

MARC: Behold, you are consecrated to me with this ring as my wife, according to the law of Moses and Israel.

CHAGALL: We looked inside of each other. We spoke without words.

RABBI: Soon may be heard in the cities of Judah …

RABBI, HUPAH HOLDER: … and the streets of Jerusalem …

RABBI, HUPAH HOLDER, CHAGALL: … the voice of joy and gladness …

RABBI, HUPAH HOLDER, CHAGALL, MARC: … the voice of the Bridegroom …

RABBI, HUPAH HOLDER, CHAGALL, MARC, BELLA: … and the voice of the Bride.

ALL: Mazel Tov!

CHAGALL: Ahh! And now the wedding dance begins, and all the guests join in, if not by dancing at least by clapping.
(*The entire cast joins in. The dancers gradually spin away leaving only MARC and BELLA.*)

CHAGALL: We went to the countryside for our honeymoon, to a place beside a field of cows. It was more like a milkmoon … cows, horses, Bella and I both flew over the moon.
(*BELLA dances as she exits off-stage.*)

CHAGALL: Too soon the war broke out, and Mother finally got her wish. I became a clerk in the army.
(*A sound collage of war sounds, a soldier with a gun runs by and gives MARC an army hat, coat, rifle, pen, and paper.*)

CHAGALL: Soldiers shooting, people fleeing, hurting, bleeding, dying. No food, fathers killed, children hungry. Anger festered all around. Tears washed the faces and fields of war.
(*ACCUSERS 1, 2, 3, and 4 run on from opposite sides of the stage and yell to one another in a relay of blame.*)

ACCUSER 1: The generals are to blame.

ACCUSER 2: No, It's the German's fault.

ACCUSER 3: It's the Czar's fault.

ACCUSER 4: It's their fault.

ACCUSERS (*to* MARC): It's the Jews' fault.

  (*They exit.*)

CHAGALL: My people are blamed, and fled as of old.

MARC (*starting to draw on the paper he has on a clipboard*): I want to paint my people into my pictures so they will be safe. I will make places in my pictures where they can hide.

  (RUSSIAN OFFICIAL, *dressed as pompously as possible, enters.*)

RUSSIAN OFFICIAL: Mr. Chagall? Mr. Marc Chagall? Oh, there you are. Mr. Chagall, we have a job from the government for you.

MARC: Oh? What kind of job?

RUSSIAN OFFICIAL: We would like you to be the art supervisor for your home town of Vitebsk.

MARC: Me? What could I do?

RUSSIAN OFFICIAL: You can make the town come alive with art of the people.

MARC: Well, that would be great!

CHAGALL: I thought I could make the whole town as magical as one of my paintings.

MARC: All you painters of Vitebsk! We are going to make this town fly.

CHAGALL: Most of them were the painters of the beautiful little signs that hung above the shops.

MARC: Get all your colours and we'll paint horses and cows and roosters and whatever we dream, all over the walls and roofs of our town. (*to the audience*) Now get all your colours.

CHAGALL: I brought my favourite colours, even good old purple.

RUSSIAN OFFICIAL: All we really want is some statues of the politicians.

MARC: Yes. (*not really listening to the Russian Official*) And we can have a school for all the artists in the community; a place where children can find a love of art. We can make giant kites and fly colours to the sky …

RUSSIAN OFFICIAL: Just a minute …

MARC: Every home shall be a gallery of art, and every person an artist.

RUSSIAN OFFICIAL: Stop!

MARC: What's the matter?

RUSSIAN OFFICIAL: You are going too far.

MARC: What do you mean? I'm doing what you asked. I am making the town come alive with the art of its people.

RUSSIAN OFFICIAL: That's all very well; but you see, all we really need is some statues of the political leaders to go in the park.

MARC: That's all you want?

RUSSIAN OFFICIAL: That, and no more!

(The RUSSIAN OFFICIAL exits.)

CHAGALL: He wanted so little. He turned my colours black. He was the kind who doesn't like stars because they don't line up in neat rows. Bella had warned me. But I still couldn't find my colours.

MARC: I don't want to paint anymore.

BELLA *(entering)*: Let your colours, your dreams, your heart, and your laugh—let them fly away in your paintings.

MARC: But …

BELLA: Let me feel your colours.

(She starts to exit.)

MARC: I've run out of colours.

BELLA: Feel all your colours.

(She is gone. MARC exits after her. There is a pause.)

CHAGALL: I can't stay sad forever. Circus clowns start bumping into my gloom, and stars follow me to work. I can paint anything. I see with more than my eyes. I see how I will paint you and even you! I need lots of purple for you. A dollop of red, a touch of green, maybe you have stripes and dots. Your feet don't touch the ground. Watch the roof! You're going to fly higher than my cows. You save a small space in your pictures for me to sneak into … and I will save a place for you in mine.

(For an example of Marc Chagall's paintings, please see page 337.)

THE HITCHHIKER

a radio play by Lucille Fletcher

CAST:

RONALD ADAMS

MRS. ADAMS

THE HITCHHIKER

FILLING STATION MAN

ROAD STAND PROPRIETOR

ROAD STAND PROPRIETOR'S WIFE

GIRL HITCHHIKER

LOCAL GALLUP OPERATOR

LONG DISTANCE OPERATOR

NEW YORK OPERATOR

ALBUQUERQUE OPERATOR

MRS. WHITNEY

TECHNICAL CREW:

DIRECTOR

MUSIC SOUND RECORDING

MANUAL RECORDINGS 1

MANUAL RECORDINGS 2

SCENE: *As curtains part, we see a stage set up for a 1940s' radio broadcast. RONALD ADAMS is standing at a central microphone. The rest of the cast is seated in a semicircle of chairs at the rear of the stage.*

Music: *Dark and ominous music fades in. It continues throughout the following, but fades down so that the words are audible.*

RONALD ADAMS: I am in an auto camp on Route Sixty-six just west of Gallup, New Mexico. If I tell it, perhaps it will help me. It will keep me from going mad. But I must tell this quickly. I am not mad now, I feel perfectly well, except that I am running a slight temperature. My name is Ronald Adams. I am thirty-six years of age, unmarried, tall, dark, with a black mustache. I drive a Buick, licence number 6Y-175-189. I was born in Brooklyn. All this I know. I know that I am at this moment perfectly sane. That it is not me who has gone mad—but something else—something utterly beyond my control. But I must speak quickly. At any moment the link may break. This may be the last thing I ever tell on earth ... the last night I ever see the stars ... (*Pause. Music fades out.*)

(Mrs. ADAMS *rises from chair, rear, and comes forward to microphone.*)
Six days ago I left Brooklyn, to drive to California.

MRS. ADAMS: Goodbye, son. Good luck to you, my boy.

ADAMS: Goodbye, Mother. Here—give me a kiss, and then I'll go.

MRS. ADAMS: I'll come out with you to the car.

ADAMS: No. It's raining. Stay here at the door. Hey—what's this? Tears? I thought you promised me you wouldn't cry.

MRS. ADAMS: I know, dear. I'm sorry. But I—do hate to see you go.

ADAMS: I'll be back. I'll only be on the Coast three months.

MRS. ADAMS: Oh—it isn't that. It's just—the trip. Ronald—I wish you weren't driving.

ADAMS: Oh, Mother. There you go again. People do it every day.

MRS. ADAMS: I know. But you'll be careful, won't you? Promise me you'll be extra careful. Don't fall asleep—or drive fast—or pick up any strangers on the road.

ADAMS: Gosh—no. You'd think I was still seventeen to hear you talk.

MRS. ADAMS: And wire me as soon as you get to Hollywood, won't you, son?

ADAMS: Of course I will. Now, don't you worry. There isn't anything going to happen. It's just eight days of perfectly simple driving on smooth civilized roads. (*Sound of car door slamming. Car starts and drives away. Sound of car driving continues under the following.*) With a hot dog or a hamburger stand every fifteen kilometres ... (*He chuckles slightly.*) (*calling*) G'bye, Mom—

(Mrs. ADAMS *leaves microphone, goes to row of chairs at rear of stage.*)

(*Sound of car driving continues.*) I was in excellent spirits. The drive ahead of me, even the loneliness, seemed like a lark. But I reckoned—without—*him.* (*Opening music fades to level of car noise.*) Crossing Brooklyn Bridge that morning in the rain, I saw a man leaning against the cables. He seemed to be waiting for a lift. There were spots of fresh rain on his shoulders. He was carrying a cheap overnight bag in one hand. He was thin, nondescript, with a cap pulled down over his eyes ... (*Music fades out. Sound of car continues.*) I would have forgotten him completely, except that just an hour later, while crossing the Pulaski Skyway over the Jersey flats, I saw him again. At least he looked like the same person. He was standing now, with one thumb pointing west. I couldn't figure how he'd got there, but I thought probably one of those fast trucks had picked him up, beaten me to the Skyway, and let him off. I didn't stop for him. Then—late that night—I saw him again. (*Opening theme music fades in.*) It was on the new Pennsylvania Turnpike between Harrisburg and Pittsburg, It's four hundred twenty-five kilometres long with a very high speed limit. I was just slowing down for one of the tunnels, when I saw him— standing under an arc light by the side of the road. I could see him quite distinctly. The bag, the cap, even the spots of fresh rain spattered over his shoulders. (*Music fades out.*) He hailed me this time.

HITCHHIKER (*off-stage*): Halloo ... (*slightly closer*) Hall ... llooo ...
(*Sound of car running faster.*)

ADAMS: I stepped on the gas like a shot. That's lonely country through the Alleghenies, and I had no intention of stopping. Besides, the coincidence, or whatever it was, gave me the willies. (*Sound of car fades.*) I stopped at the next gas station. (*Sound of nervous honking of horn.*)

(*The filling station attendant leaves chair and advances to microphone.*)

FILLING STATION MAN: Yes, sir.

ADAMS: Fill her up.

FILLING STATION MAN: Certainly, sir. Check your oil, sir?

ADAMS: No thanks. (*Gas station sounds—putting gas in car, etc. This continues behind the following.*)

FILLING STATION MAN: Nice night, isn't it?

ADAMS: Yes. It hasn't been raining here recently, has it?

FILLING STATION MAN: Not a drop of rain all week.

ADAMS: H'm. I suppose that hasn't done your business any harm?

FILLING STATION MAN: Oh—people drive through here in all kinds of weather. Mostly business, you know. There aren't many pleasure cars out on the Turnpike this season of the year.

ADAMS: I suppose not. (*casually*) What about hitchhikers?

FILLING STATION MAN: Hitchhikers—*here?*

ADAMS: What's the matter? Don't you ever see any?

FILLING STATION MAN: Not much. If we did, it'd be a sight for sore eyes.

ADAMS: Why?

FILLING STATION MAN: A guy'd be a fool who started out to hitch rides on this road. Look at it.

ADAMS: Then you've never seen anybody?

FILLING STATION MAN: Nope. Mebbe they get the lift before the Turnpike starts—I mean—you know—just before the toll-house— but then it'd be a mighty long ride. Most cars wouldn't want to pick up a guy for that long a ride. This is pretty lonesome country here—mountains and woods ... You ain't seen anybody like that, have you?

ADAMS: No. (*quickly*) Oh, no, not at all. It was—just a technical question.

FILLING STATION MAN: I see. Well—that'll be just fifteen forty-nine— with the tax ...

(*FILLING STATION MAN steps back from microphone and returns to seat at rear of stage.*) (*Sound of car fades in and continues.*)

ADAMS: The thing gradually passed from my mind, as sheer coincidence. I had a good night's sleep in Pittsburgh. I didn't think about the man all next day—until just outside of Zanesville, Ohio. I saw him again. (*eerie music*) It was a bright sunshiny afternoon.

The peaceful Ohio fields, brown with the autumn stubble, lay dreaming in the golden light. I was driving slowly, drinking it in, when the road suddenly ended in a detour. In front of the barrier—*he* was standing. (*Sound of car fades out. Music continues.*) Let me explain about his appearance before I go on. I repeat. There was nothing sinister about him. He was as drab as a mud fence. Nor was his attitude menacing. He merely stood there, waiting, almost drooping a little, the cheap overnight bag in his hand. He looked as though he had been waiting there for hours. Then he looked up—(*Music stops.*) He hailed me. He started to walk forward ...

HITCHHIKER (*off-stage*): Hallooo ... Halloo ... ooo ... (*Sound of car starting. Sound of gears jamming.*) Hall-ooo ... (*Sound of car stopping.*)

ADAMS (*panicky*): No. Not today. The other way. Going to New York. Sorry ... (*Automobile starts noisily.*) Sorry ... (*Automobile noise continues through the following.*) After I got the car back onto the road again, I felt like a fool. Yet the thought of picking him up, of having him sit beside me was somehow unbearable. Yet at the same time, I felt more than ever unspeakably alone ... (*Eerie music fades in above sound of automobile. It continues through the following.*) Hour after hour went by. The fields, the towns, ticked off one by one. The light changed. I knew now that I was going to see him again. And though I dreaded the sight, I caught myself searching the side of the road, waiting for him to appear ... (*Music and sound out. Horn honks two or three times; pause; nervous honk again.*) (ROAD STAND PROPRIETOR, *elderly rural type, comes forward to microphone.*) (*Creak of squeaky door.*)

PROPRIETOR (*querulous, mountain voice*): Yep? What is it? What do you want?

ADAMS (*breathless*): You sell sandwiches and pop here, don't you?

PROPRIETOR (*cranky*): Yep. We do. In the daytime. But we're closed up now for the night.

ADAMS: I know. But—I was wondering if you could possibly let me have a cup of coffee—black coffee.

PROPRIETOR: Not at this time of night, mister. My wife's the cook, and she's in bed. Mebbe further down the road, at the Honeysuckle Rest. (*Creak of door closing.*)

ADAMS: No—no—don't shut the door. Listen—just a minute ago, there was a man standing here—right beside this stand—a suspicious-looking man ...

PROPRIETOR's WIFE (*a quavery, whiny voice*): Hen-ry? Who is it, Hen-ry?

PROPRIETOR: It's nobuddy, Mother. Just a feller thinks he wants a cup of coffee. Go back into bed.

ADAMS: I don't mean to disturb you. But you see, I was driving along—when I just happened to look—and there he was ...

PROPRIETOR: What was he doing?

ADAMS: Nothing. He ran off—when I stopped the car.

PROPRIETOR: Then what of it? That's nothing to wake a man in the middle of his sleep about ...

WIFE: Mebbe he's been drinkin', Henry ... (*calling*)

PROPRIETOR (*sternly*): Young man, I've got a good mind to turn you over to the sheriff—

ADAMS: But—I—

PROPRIETOR: You've been taking a nip. That's what you've been doing. And you haven't got anything better to do than wake decent folk out of their hard-earned sleep. Get going. Go on.

WIFE (*calling*): Jes' shut the door on him, Henry—

ADAMS: But he looked as though he were going to rob you.

HENRY: I ain't got nothin' in this stand to lose. (*Sound of door creaking closed.*) Now—on your way before I call out Sheriff Oakes. (*Door slams shut; bolted.*) (PROPRIETOR *and his* WIFE *return to their seats at rear of stage.*)

(*Sound of auto starting and driving away.*)

ADAMS: I got into the car again, and drove on slowly. I was beginning to hate the car. If I could have found a place to stop ... to rest a little. But I was in the Ozark Mountains of Missouri now. The few resort places there were closed. Only an occasional log cabin, seemingly deserted, broke the monotony of the wild wooded landscape. I *had* seen him at that roadside stand. I knew I would see him again—perhaps at the next turn of the road. I knew that when I saw him next—I would run him down. (*Music fades in.*) But I did not see him again until late next afternoon. (*Sound of signal bell at railroad crossroads; continues through the following.*) I had stopped the car at a sleepy little junction just across the border into Oklahoma ... to let a train pass by—when he appeared across the tracks, leaning against a telephone pole ... It was a perfectly airless, dry day. The red clay of Oklahoma was baking under the southwestern sun. Yet there were spots of fresh rain on his shoulders ... (*Music fades out.*) I couldn't stand that. Without thinking, blindly, I started the car across the tracks. (*Distant cry of train whistle approaching. Signal bell continues.*) He didn't even look up at me. He was staring at the ground. I stepped on the gas hard, veering the wheel sharply toward him. (*Sound of train whistle closer; chugging of wheels fading in.*) I could hear the train in the distance now. But I didn't care. (*Sound of jamming of gears; clash of metal.*) Then—something went wrong with the car. (*Sound of gears jamming, then car dead. Train sound louder.*) The train was coming closer. I could hear the cry of its whistle. (*Sound of train chugging; cry of whistle closer; continues to grow louder.*) Still he stood there. And now—I knew that he was beckoning—beckoning me to my death ... (*Music fades in as train passes. ADAMS says breathlessly, quietly*) Well—frustrated him that time. The starter worked at last. I managed to back up. But when the train passed, he was gone. I was all alone, in the hot dry afternoon. (*Music continues; sound of car driving.*) After that, I knew I had to do something. I didn't know who this man was, or what he wanted of me. I only knew that from now on, I must not let myself be alone on the road for one moment. (*Music and sound of car fades.*)

(*GIRL HITCHHIKER comes forward to microphone.*) Hello, there. Like a ride?

GIRL: What do you think? How far are you going?

ADAMS: Where do you want to go?

GIRL: Amarillo, Texas. (*Sound of car door opening.*)

ADAMS: I'll drive you there.

GIRL: Gee! (*Car door slams and car drives away. It continues through the following.*) Mind if I take off my shoes? My dogs are killing me.

ADAMS: Go right ahead.

GIRL: Gee, what a break this is. A swell car, a decent guy, and driving all the way to Amarillo. All I been getting so far is trucks.

ADAMS: Hitchhike much?

GIRL: Sure. Only it's tough sometimes, in these great open spaces, to get the breaks.

ADAMS: I should think it would be. Though I'll bet if you get a good pickup in a fast car, you can get to places faster than, say, another person in another car.

GIRL: I don't get you.

ADAMS: Well, take me, for instance. Suppose I'm driving across the country, say at a nice steady clip of about seventy kilometres per hour. Couldn't a girl like you, just standing beside the road, waiting for lifts, beat me to town after town—provided she got picked up every time in a car doing from a hundred and five to one hundred ten kilometres per hour?

GIRL: I dunno. What difference does it make?

ADAMS: Oh—no difference. It's just—a crazy idea I had sitting here in the car.

GIRL (*laughing*): Imagine spending your time in a swell car and thinking of things like that.

ADAMS: What would you do instead?

GIRL (*admiringly*): What would I do? If I was a good-looking fellow like yourself? Why—I'd just *enjoy* myself—every minute of the time. I'd sit back and relax, and if I saw a good-looking girl along the side of the road ... (*sharply*) Hey—look out!

ADAMS (*breathlessly*): Did you see him, too?

GIRL: See who?

ADAMS: That man. Standing beside the barbed-wire fence.

GIRL: I didn't see—nobody. There wasn't nothing but a bunch of steer—and the wire fence. What did you think you was doing? Trying to run into the barbed-wire fence?

ADAMS: There was a man there, I tell you ... a thin grey man, with an overnight bag in his hand. And I was trying to run him down.

GIRL: Run him down? You mean—kill him?

ADAMS: But—(*desperately*) You say you didn't see him back there? You're sure?

GIRL (*strangely*): I didn't see a soul. And as far as I'm concerned, mister ...

ADAMS: Watch for him the next time then. Keep watching. Keep your eyes peeled on the road. He'll turn up again—maybe any minute now. (*excitedly*) There! Look there ... (*Sound of car skidding; screech; a crash of metals as of car going into barbed-wire fence. GIRL screams; door handle of car turning.*)

GIRL: How does this door work? I—I'm gettin' out of here.

ADAMS: Did you see him that time?

GIRL (*sharply, choked*): No. I didn't see him that time. And personally, mister, I don't expect never to see him. All I want to do is go on living—and I don't see how I will very long, driving with you.

ADAMS: I'm sorry. I—don't know what came over me. (*frightened*) Please ... don't go ...

GIRL: So if you'll excuse me, mister.

ADAMS: You can't go. Listen, how would you like to go to California? I'll drive you to California.

GIRL: Seeing pink elephants all the way? No, thanks. (*Sound of door handle turning.*)

ADAMS: Listen. Please. For just one moment—

GIRL: You know what I think you need, big boy? Not a girlfriend. Just a dose of good sleep. There. I got it now ... (*Sound of door opening; slams.*)

ADAMS: No. You can't go.

GIRL (*wildly*): Leave your hands offa me, do you hear? Leave your—
(*Sound of sharp slap; footsteps over gravel, running. They die away; pause.*)

ADAMS: She ran from me, as though I were a monster. A few minutes later, I saw a passing truck pick her up. I knew then that I was utterly alone. (*Sound of low mooing of steer.*) I was in the heart of the great Texas prairies. There wasn't a car on the road after the truck went by. I tried to figure out what to do, how to get hold of myself. If I could find a place to rest. Or even if I could sleep right there in the car for a few hours, along the side of the road. (*The eerie theme music fades in softly.*) I was getting my winter overcoat out of the back seat to use as a blanket, when I saw him coming toward me, emerging from the herd of moving steer ... (*Sound of mooing of steer, low. Out of it emerges a voice.*)

HITCHHIKER (*off-stage*): Hall ... ooo ... Hall ... oo ... (*Sound of auto starting and driving off. Music continues.*)

ADAMS: Perhaps I should have spoken to him then, fought it out then and there. For now he began to be everywhere. Wherever I stopped, even for a moment—for gas, for oil, for a drink of pop, a cup of coffee, a sandwich—he was there. I saw him standing out-side the auto camp in Amarillo, that night, when I dared to slow down. He was sitting near the drinking fountain in a little camping spot just inside the border of New Mexico ... He was waiting for me outside the Navajo Reservation where I stopped to check my tires. I saw him in Albuquerque, where I bought fifty litres of gas. I was afraid now, afraid to stop. I began to drive faster and faster. I was in a lunar landscape now—the great arid mesa country of New Mexico. I drove through it with the indifference of a fly crawling over the face of the moon ... (*Music becomes more and more eerie.*) But now he didn't even wait for me to stop. Unless I drove at one hundred thirty-five kilometres per hour over those endless roads, he waited for me at every other kilometre. I would see his figure, shadowless, flitting before me, still in its same atti-tude, over the cold lifeless ground, flitting over dried-up rivers, over broken stones cast up by old glacial upheavals, flitting in the pure and cloudless air … (*Music reaches eerie climax then stops. Sound of auto stops.*) I was beside myself when I finally reached Gallup, New Mexico, this morning. There is an auto camp here— cold, almost deserted at this time of year. I went inside and asked if there was a telephone … (*sound of footsteps on wood, heavy, echoing*) I had the feeling that if only I could speak to someone familiar, someone I loved, I could pull myself together. (*LOCAL GALLUP OPERATOR rises, comes forward to microphone.*) (*Sound of money put into payphone.*)

LOCAL GALLUP OPERATOR: Number, please?

ADAMS: Long distance.

LOCAL GALLUP OPERATOR: Thank you. (*LONG DISTANCE OPERATOR comes forward to microphone.*) (*Sound of return of money from phone; buzz.*)

LONG DISTANCE OPERATOR: This is Long Distance.

ADAMS: I'd like to put in a call to my home in Brooklyn, New York. I'm Ronald Adams. The number is 232–0828.

LONG DISTANCE OPERATOR: Thank you. What is your number? (*A mechanical tone.*)

ADAMS: My number … 312. (*ALBUQUERQUE OPERATOR rises from chair, remaining at rear of stage.*)

ALBUQUERQUE OPERATOR (*from distance*): Albuquerque.

LONG DISTANCE OPERATOR: New York For Gallup. (*NEW YORK OPERATOR rises, stands beside chair at rear of stage.*)

NEW YORK OPERATOR: New York.

LONG DISTANCE OPERATOR: Gallup, New Mexico, calling 232–0828.

ADAMS: I had read somewhere that love could banish demons. It was the middle of the morning. I knew Mother would be home. I pictured her tall, white-haired, in her crisp housedress, going about her tasks. It would be enough, I thought, merely to hear the even calmness of her voice.

LONG DISTANCE OPERATOR: Will you please deposit three dollars and eighty-five cents for the first three minutes? When you have deposited a dollar and a half will you wait until I have collected the money? (*Other three* OPERATORS *sit down.*) (*Sound of clunk of six quarters going through telephone.*) All right, deposit another dollar and a half. (*Sound of clunk of six quarters.*) Will you please deposit the remaining eighty-five cents (*Sound of clunk of three quarters and one dime*). Ready with Brooklyn—go ahead, please. (*MRS.* WHITNEY *comes forward to centre microphone.*)

ADAMS: Hello.

Mrs. WHITNEY: Mrs. Adams' residence.

ADAMS: Hello. Hello—Mother?

Mrs. WHITNEY (*very flat and proper*): This is Mrs. Adams' residence. Who is it you wished to speak to, please?

ADAMS: Why—who's this?

Mrs. WHITNEY: This is Mrs. Whitney.

ADAMS: Mrs. Whitney? I don't know any Mrs. Whitney. Is this 232–0828?

Mrs. WHITNEY: Yes.

ADAMS: Where's my mother? Where's Mrs. Adams?

Mrs. WHITNEY: Mrs. Adams is not at home. She is still in the hospital.

ADAMS: The hospital?

Mrs. WHITNEY: Yes. Who is this calling, please? Is it a member of the family?

ADAMS: What's she in the hospital for?

Mrs. WHITNEY: She's been prostrated for five days. Nervous break-down. But who is this calling?

ADAMS: Nervous breakdown? But—my mother was never nervous.

Mrs. WHITNEY: It's all taken place since the death of her oldest son, Ronald.

ADAMS: Death of her oldest son, Ronald ...? Hey—what is this? What number is this?

Mrs. WHITNEY: This is 232–0828. It's all been very sudden. He was killed just six days ago in an automobile accident on the Brooklyn Bridge.

LONG DISTANCE OPERATOR: Your three minutes are up, sir. (*pause*) Your three minutes are up, sir ... (LONG DISTANCE OPERATOR *and* MRS. WHITNEY *sit down.*)

(*Softly. A pause; fade in eerie theme music softly.*)

ADAMS (*a strange voice*): And so, I am sitting here in this deserted auto camp in Gallup, New Mexico. I am trying to think. I am trying to get hold of myself. Otherwise I shall go mad ... Outside it is night—the vast, soulless night of New Mexico. A million stars are in the sky. Ahead of me stretch fifteen hundred kilometres of empty mesa, mountains, prairies, desert. Somewhere, among them, he is waiting for me ... (*He turns slowly from microphone, looking off-stage, in direction of* HITCHHIKER'S *voice.*) Somewhere I shall know who he is—and who ... I am ... (*Music continues to an eerie climax.*) (ADAMS *walks slowly away from microphone, and off-stage.*)

MONOLOGUES FOR TEENAGERS

by Roger Karshner

LARRY speaks of his father's passing, expressing his sense of abandonment and loss.

It was two years ago today that my dad died. Yep, already two years. And, you know, it's still hard to believe. I mean, like I still look for him to come walking in the back door every night with this big grin on his face.

He died unexpectedly. I mean, like he was always so healthy and strong. Indestructible, you know? I don't remember him ever being sick a day. Then one night he comes home complaining of this pain, this burning sensation in his chest. Like, right here ... (*He presses a spot near the base of his sternum.*)

He thought it was the stomach flu or heartburn, or something. So he got a whole bunch of stuff from the drugstore and started watching his diet. But the pain didn't go away. In fact, it kept getting worse. To the point where one morning he couldn't go in to work.

He finally broke down and went to the doctor, and he sent him to this specialist who said he had to have an operation because of this dark spot that showed up in the X-rays.

The night before he went to the hospital was the first time I ever remember seeing him afraid. It was in his eyes, the fear, you could see it. We all sat up real late that night because he didn't want to go to bed. Poor guy. He must have suspected something.

When they operated they found that cancer was eating him alive and they told us he had maybe six months. It was a terrible thing. I remember how sick I got inside.

Mom decided to close up the house and rent us a place in Florida so Dad could be someplace warm and sunny till ... Then, unexpectedly, he died three days later—just like that.

It was an awful shock. It was the first time I'd ever been around death. I mean, at close hand. It was the first time I'd felt the sudden jolt of it. It was kind of like this hot knife going right through me. It took me a long time to get over it. The shock of it nailed me down for awhile, you know? But I got over it, I mean the grieving part, that is. You have to. But I still think of him and I still miss him. It just isn't like the same without him around. Like there's this place inside me that's empty, you know, a place he filled. I really miss him. And I always will, I guess. I mean, after all—he was my dad.

MARCIE

MARCIE speaks of the importance of her room. It is her sanctuary, her haven, her special place.

It's the very best place in the world. I go there whenever things get crazy. Like they seem to get a lot of the time. I go there and close the door and lock myself in with all my stuff and I feel safe and like nobody or anything can hurt me. It's my special place. A place where I can dream and hang out and think personal thoughts and be free.

If it wasn't for my room I don't know what I'd do. Sometimes when I'm real sad I go there and cry where nobody can see me and I can let it all out. It's a place where I'm happy, too. It's very important to have a place that's all yours; a place where it's like your own world, kind of; a place where you can be alone with the things that are important to you: your clothes, your magazines, your sounds, your phone, your pictures. And your special secret stuff that nobody knows anything about but you. Sometimes I get into this fantasy thing in my room and create stories and situations in my mind. It's neat. It makes me feel good to make up things and dream and go far out mentally.

I think everybody needs a place where they can go and be alone and away from other people for awhile and be private and do and think what they like. I think older people—my parents, for example, our world leaders for sure—should have a room, a special room of their own where they can get off by themselves. Maybe if they did, they wouldn't be so uptight all the time, so crazed.

Every person in the world should have their private place where they can go and let down and be just plain them for a few minutes every day. I think it would help them get perspective. Everybody's so rushed and intense. It seems like nobody wants to be private anymore.

Words on a Page

an episode from "Spirit Bay," a teleplay by Keith Ross Leckie

CAST:

LENORE GREEN, an Ojibway[1] teenager

PETE GREEN, Lenore's father, a fisherman and trapper

CONNIE GREEN, Lenore's mother

SADIE GREEN, Lenore's younger sister

MISS WALKER, Lenore's grade 10 teacher

PRINCIPAL, Mr. Crankhurst, the principal of Lenore's high school

VARIOUS STUDENTS

DRIVER

MAN

CREWMAN

PANEL OF SIX JUDGES

ACT ONE

SCENE 1: Interior. Classroom. Day.

It is a sunny fall afternoon in LENORE'S *grade 10 English class. The sun's rays filter through dust particles in the air. There are a dozen classmates, a mixture of white and Native, listening as* LENORE *reads a story she has written.*

LENORE: "So on that morning before she left, they went by canoe one last time to those favourite places. It was at first light, when the water is a mirror and the trees are still, as if nature is holding her breath. (*A variety of young faces listen, all enthralled with her story. Camera moves slowly, panning across the classroom, holding on different faces.*)

"And there was the beaver and the loon and the hawk circling above the treetops. And below, the trout and the sturgeon slipped silently through the black water. (*Camera stops on one girl, listening intently, then moves again. Camera holds on two boys slouching close together, almost touching, but their eyes and attention are on* LENORE *at the front of the class.)*

"Creatures as powerful as the great moose, as small as a minnow. She and her father took their place among them. (*Camera cuts to* MISS WALKER, *the Native teacher. She sits to one side of* LENORE *listening as intently as the rest. She is very impressed. Camera pans and pulls focus to hold finally on* LENORE *as she finishes the story. She has memorized most of it and hardly has to look at the page. She speaks very well with skilled emphasis and a personal passion for her words.*)

"And in this world there was a peace and harmony that she knew no matter how far she travelled, she would never find again. She understood now why her father had brought her here. She felt the morning sun on her face and the gentle rocking of the canoe and smiled because she knew that here would always be her home."

LENORE *stops speaking, holds the few pages against her chest with both arms, and looks at* MISS WALKER *a little anxiously. There is a hushed silence for a moment.*

MISS WALKER (*quietly*): Lenore, that was beautiful! (*Lenore gives a shy, tentative smile.*) What did you think, class?

(*The class gives a collective chatter of positive response, then ...)*

GIRL #1: It was real sad.

BOY: It reminded me of ... like around Shadow River.

GIRL #2: It was just like a book.

(*There is a silent moment after this pronouncement.* LENORE *looks at the other students, trying to suppress her excitement. The bell rings, signalling the end of class, and the students quickly exit the classroom. When the wave of students has passed,* LENORE *is left still standing there.* MISS WALKER *puts a hand on her shoulder.)*

MISS WALKER: I'm really impressed, Lenore. Leave your story on my desk. There are some people I'd like to show it to.

(MISS WALKER *then exits, leaving* LENORE *alone. She takes a deep breath then allows herself a beaming smile as she hugs her story against herself.*)

SCENE 2A: Exterior. Stream. Afternoon.

The prow of a cedar canoe cuts through the calm water. LENORE and her father PETE, in the stern, are canoeing their way up a quiet stream. It is late in the afternoon. The shadows are lengthening, and the sunlight retains the shimmering intensity of this time of day as it filters through the autumn foliage.

PETE: Good here for beaver. Heavy willow growth. Lots of food.
   (*LENORE notices a beaver swimming. She points.*)
LENORE: Look, Baba[2]. (*The camera shows a beaver swimming. The beaver suddenly slaps his tail loudly and dives underwater. [stock shot]*). He's warning his friends about us.
PETE (*seriously*): You know that a long time ago the beaver only had a little skinny tail.
LENORE: Oh yeah? (*LENORE looks back, smiling expectantly. She knows this is the opening to one of her father's crazy stories.*)
PETE (*in a storytelling tone*): You see, one day Nanabozho[3] was out paddling his big canoe. He's pretty lazy, so he decided if he gave the beaver a big paddle tail, he could tie them on the back and they would push his canoe. But once he had given the beaver a paddle tail, the beaver was too quick to catch. So he didn't get a chance to try it.
LENORE (*only half-serious*): D'you think it would work?
PETE: Cheemo and I tried it once.
LENORE: Really?
PETE: Sure! Roped a couple seventy-pound beavers on the back of his canoe.
LENORE: What happened?
PETE: Well, they chewed a hole in the canoe and we all sank and they got away!
   (*LENORE laughs at this image and turns to look back at her father.*)
LENORE: Serves you right.
   (*PETE laughs, too. They continue paddling slowly, quietly.*)

Scene 2B: Exterior. Beaver Pond. Afternoon.

PETE and LENORE canoe near a bubbling beaver dam with beaver houses visible.

PETE: You said you had a dream to tell.

LENORE: Yes. (*She turns around in the canoe, facing him.*) It's pretty simple, I guess. I'm standing in the woods. There's a raven flying just above my head. It hovers there. It has something to tell me. (*pause, while she thinks*) It wants to land ... but it can't. It only hovers there. It never lands.

(*PETE thinks about the dream very seriously for a moment.*)

PETE: Sounds like a good dream. Can't tell you what it means. Maybe it isn't finished with you yet. (*LENORE smiles. Pause.*) You know Cheemo had the same dream for five nights in a row. He dreamed he was swimming underwater.

LENORE: Yeah?

PETE: Every night, same thing. Swimming underwater!

LENORE: Yeah?

PETE: On the sixth day, he couldn't stand it anymore. He jumped in the lake! And no more dream. (*They both laugh again.*) We'll go upstream to the next pond and ...

LENORE (*hesitant*): Baba, I ...

PETE: What?

LENORE (*feeling badly*): I've got all kinds of homework to do. We've got a lot of tests coming up ...

PETE: Isn't it enough they have you all day at that school?

LENORE: I'm sorry, Baba.

PETE (*gruffly*): Never mind.

PETE quickly backpaddles to turn the canoe around and they head back the way they came. LENORE looks unhappy.

SCENE 3: Exterior. Schoolyard. Day.

It is the lunch break at school. A number of students are sitting around on the grass and walls eating lunch. Some play volleyball nearby. LENORE is sitting on a bench reading some poetry to a classmate. SADIE (LENORE's sister) is listening in. LENORE reads with feeling from the book.

LENORE:
"Up on the hill against the sky,
A fir tree rocking its lullaby,
Swings, swings,
Its emerald wings,
Swelling the song that my paddle sings."

CLASSMATE: That's neat!

LENORE: Yeah. Pauline Johnson. She's a Native poet who travelled all around these lakes almost one hundred years ago. Musta been hard to get gas for her outboard then, eh?
(They laugh. MISS WALKER comes up behind them with a letter in her hand. She crouches behind them.)

MISS WALKER *(excited, smiling)*: LENORE? I've got some news for you. I sent your story into the District Writing Competitions. You've been accepted as a finalist! *(She shows LENORE the letter. LENORE and SADIE read it together. LENORE is both excited and disbelieving.)* Next week you go down to Thunder Bay to read your story to the judges! *(LENORE and SADIE look at each other in amazement.)* This is wonderful! If you do well there, they could send you to a special high school in the south. Then maybe to study English at university!

LENORE *(with mixed emotions)*: University!

MISS WALKER: Well, let's see how Thunder Bay goes. We just need a letter of permission from your parents and we're all set! *(LENORE looks at the letter again, confused and excited. MISS WALKER smiles at her, then leans forward and gives her a little hug.)* I'm proud of you. *MISS WALKER gets up and leaves them. Again SADIE and LENORE look at each other.*

SADIE: Nice going!

LENORE *(grinning)*: Yeah! I can't believe it! *(frowning)* I just wonder what Baba's going to say.

SCENE 4: Interior. Kitchen (LENORE's home). Evening.

LENORE, SADIE, their mother CONNIE, and PETE are having a fish dinner. PETE eats his food hungrily. LENORE looks up at him once, then again. Then she notices SADIE staring at her impatiently. LENORE glares at SADIE and they both resume eating.

PETE (*to all*): Good trout, eh? We caught them way north of Mulligan Bay. Cold and deep. (*He takes a huge mouthful.*)

CONNIE: We should have enough in the freezer to last until Christmas.

PETE: The King of France never ate better than this.

    (*There is a moment of silence. SADIE can wait no longer.*)

SADIE: Baba, Lenore has something to ask you.

    PETE and CONNIE look up. LENORE glares at SADIE.

PETE: Uh huh?

LENORE (*bolstering her courage*): Well ... I've been doing some work at school ...

PETE: Yeah. So?

LENORE: You know ... like writing. (*PETE takes another large bite of fish, only vaguely interested.*) Anyway ... the new teacher, Miss Walker, said I've been doing real well ... and there was a story I wrote ...

PETE: A what?

LENORE (*hesitating*): Well, a story ... and they, ah ...

SADIE (*interrupting*): The story won a contest and now she has to go to Thunder Bay to read it and then they'll send her away to university!

    (*LENORE "looks daggers" at SADIE. Both PETE and CONNIE look at LENORE in surprise.*)

LENORE: Can't you shut up?

PETE: University!

    (*LENORE passes PETE the letter.*)

LENORE: Well, no! It's only if I win, but ...

    (*PETE glances at the letter, then pushes it away.*)

PETE: That's crazy! You're only a young girl! You can forget about going to Thunder Bay.

LENORE: But I have to! I'm representing the school!

PETE: They can find someone else.

LENORE: But they want my story!

PETE: Then send the story to Thunder Bay.

LENORE (*approaching tears*): But I want to go!

PETE: "Want" and "can" are not always the same thing. (*He goes back to his dinner.*)

LENORE: You never ...!

(*LENORE is about to continue her argument but her mother is signalling her not to continue along these lines. LENORE stands up and quickly exits the kitchen.*)

ACT TWO

SCENE 5: Interior. Classroom. Day.

The classroom is empty except for LENORE standing at the front and MISS WALKER sitting at a desk several rows back. LENORE is practising reading her story with a compelling intensity.

LENORE: "She found her father out behind the shed laying the steaming cedar strips across the frame of a new canoe, his strong hands moulding the soft wood. 'Baba,' she said, 'Why can't I visit Aunt Doreen for the summer? I'm not a child anymore. I want to ride a subway, Baba! I want to climb to the top of a skyscraper, and see a museum and go to a play. I want to see the world!' But her father turned away and would not look at her."

(*LENORE stops and thinks about her father for a moment.*)

MISS WALKER (*quietly*): Yes. Go on.

(*Suddenly all of LENORE's momentum is gone. She appears weary.*)

LENORE: Can we stop now?

MISS WALKER: Sure. Sure, that's fine. It's coming along really well, Lenore. Parents' Night will be a good rehearsal for the finals. (*She pauses, looking at LENORE, who appears distracted.*) Is everything all right?

LENORE: Yes. I'm just tired.

MISS WALKER: Good. You get a good sleep. I'll see you tomorrow.

(LENORE gives her a half-hearted smile and leaves the classroom. MISS WALKER looks after her, wondering if there is anything wrong.)

SCENE 6: Interior. Kitchen, (LENORE's home). Day.
LENORE comes into the kitchen, tosses down her books and flops down at the table. Her mother is making bannock⁴. They are alone. Her mother notices her unhappiness.

CONNIE: How was school?
LENORE: Okay. *(pause)* Actually it was lousy. *(suddenly angry)* I just don't understand! Why won't he let me go?!
   (CONNIE stops working and sits down across from her.)
CONNIE *(after a moment)*: He is afraid of what will happen to you.
LENORE: He wants to trap me!
CONNIE: It might seem like that, but he believes he's protecting you.
LENORE *(deflated)*: What am I going to do, Mom?
CONNIE: He's stubborn. The harder you push, the more he digs in his heels. *(pause)* D'you remember the story of the Sun and the Wind, how they had a contest to see who could get the coat off a passing man? The Wind blew as hard as he could, but the man held the coat on tightly. When the Sun had his turn, he shone warm and bright and the man just took off his coat.
LENORE: I should be the sun?
CONNIE *(nods)*: Maybe you can read your story to him.
LENORE: I have to read it on Parents' Night. But he'll never come.
CONNIE: Maybe this time, if you ask, he will.
LENORE *(looking suddenly hopeful)*: You think so?
CONNIE *(smiling)*: Maybe.
   (LENORE smiles happily.)

SCENE 7: Exterior. Woods. Day.
A small cedar tree crashes to the ground near the banks of a stream. PETE stands beside the stump, axe in hand. He wipes a sleeve across his sweating forehead, then quickly begins to trim the branches.

With a smaller axe, LENORE competently trims the branches of another downed cedar in the foreground. In the background we see a sturdy lean-to, three-quarters completed, large enough to sleep two or three people with provisions—side walls, open front, firepit. LENORE lifts her three-metre cedar pole, takes it to the structure and fits it in place, resting on the centre beam nailed between two trees.

PETE is suddenly beside her and places his pole beside hers, which almost completes the superstructure of the roof. He smiles at her.

PETE: Now the tarp and a good layer of cedar boughs. One snowfall will make it warm and dry. Ron and I'll live here a week for trapping. (*looking at LENORE*) What d'you think? You want to come?

LENORE: Where?

PETE: Out on the new trapline in November with Ron and me?

LENORE (*excited*): Yeah! (*then subdued*) But I've got school. (*hopefully*) But maybe I can get off for a couple of days.

(*PETE turns away to adjust the poles on the crosspiece*).

PETE (*not looking at her*): You think about it.

SCENE 8: Exterior. Rocky stream bed. Day.

LENORE kneels down on a flat rock. Holding her hair back she drinks from the surface of the black, bubbling stream. The camera is at stream level. She looks up, satisfied, her face wet. She watches her father who puts his face right down in the water and shakes his head, splashing and blowing bubbles. He looks up at her and they both laugh, water dripping off their faces. PETE cups some water in his hand and brings it to his lips to drink. LENORE watches him a moment.

LENORE: Sometimes I wish I could be a son for you, Baba.

(*PETE looks up at her curiously at this statement out of the blue.*)

PETE: A son?

LENORE: Yes. I know every father wants a son.

(*PETE considers this as he fills a canteen with water.*)

PETE: I would like a son. Maybe someday … (*pause*) but the first time I saw you and you smiled at me, I wouldn't have traded you for ten sons!

(*LENORE smiles at this, watching him fill the canteen.*)

LENORE: Baba?

PETE: Hmmm?

LENORE: Parents' Night is on Wednesday.

PETE (*distastefully*): Parents' Night?!

LENORE: Yeah. I'm going to read something. Be real nice if you were there.

PETE: I don't have anything to say to those teachers.

LENORE: You don't have to say anything.

PETE (*resisting*): And we're fishing the next day. We'll be outfitting the boat.

LENORE: Just for a little while? Maybe? (*pause*) Please?

PETE: Okay, I'm not promising, but I'll try.

(*LENORE smiles, her eyes sparkling.*)

SCENE 9: (Dream) Exterior. Open Sky. Day.

In slow motion against a blue sky background, a single bird comes into frame. It hovers above the camera. After a moment it is joined by other birds … two, three, four, all hovering in frame above the camera. It is not a threatening image. The motion is beautiful to watch. The sound of the wings becomes steadily louder.

SCENE 10A: Interior. LENORE's bedroom. Night.

LENORE, with a little gasp, suddenly sits up in bed, staring out in front of her. Her tense body relaxes. She thinks for a moment about the images of the dream. She lies down again and rolls over, her face toward the camera. She smiles with excitement and anticipation.

SCENE 10B: Exterior. Spirit Bay docks. Late day.

A pickup truck stops beside the docks. PETE is waiting. The DRIVER gets out and opens the tailgate.

DRIVER: Got your new nets, Pete.

(PETE inspects the three bundles of nets as the DRIVER drops them on the ground.)

PETE: Hey, they don't have floats!

DRIVER *(handing him the bill)*: See? Nothing about floats.

(PETE looks at the bill. The DRIVER looks at him, then turns the bill right side up for him to read. PETE glances at it and stuffs it into his pocket.)

PETE: Gonna take me all night to sew floats on these nets.

DRIVER: You want 'em or not?

(PETE nods. The DRIVER drops the last net on the ground, gets back in the truck, and drives off. PETE checks his watch, looks unhappy, then carries the first bundle toward the boat.)

SCENE 11: Interior. School auditorium. Evening.

It's Parents' Night in the small auditorium. There are about two dozen parents present, Native and white. Tables display artwork of various kinds and highly graded tests and essays. There is a coffee and pastry table where parents stand in small groups, talking with four or five teachers.

There is a podium at the front of the auditorium. LENORE stands near it anxiously watching the doorway, holding the pages of her story.

SADIE: 'Becha he doesn't come.

LENORE: He'll come.

(MISS WALKER approaches them.)

MISS WALKER: Hi, Lenore. Are you ready?

LENORE *(anxious)*: I think so.

MISS WALKER: You'll do great! Are your parents here yet? I was looking forward to meeting them.

LENORE *(eyeing the doorway)*: They'll be here any minute.

(The PRINCIPAL moves behind the podium to address those present. Conversation dwindles.)

PRINCIPAL: Good evening, and welcome to the first Parents' Night of the year at Nipigon District Junior High School. Glad you could come out. In a moment I'll ask one of our students to come up and read a prize-winning story she's written ... (*The PRINCIPAL's talk continues over dialogue between LENORE and MISS WALKER, below.*) But first I would like to say a few words about the challenges facing us in the coming year. Never before has there been such an abundance of information and communication in our world ...

LENORE (*whispering anxiously to MISS WALKER*): Wait! I can't do it yet!

MISS WALKER: Don't worry. I'll stall him if necessary. (*smiling*) Mr. Crankhurst goes on forever, anyway.

(*LENORE tries to smile. She looks at the PRINCIPAL.*)

PRINCIPAL: It is almost overwhelming when you consider it. In the face of this, a sound education has never been more important. And so, our goal will remain a high standard of academic achievement and individual excellence in all our endeavours. We are deeply aware of our responsibility here at Beardmore to mould the bright minds of young men and women who will in a few short years forge the destiny of our world! (*CONNIE comes through the door into the auditorium. She is alone. LENORE watches her. CONNIE stops, looks around the room, and sees LENORE. She looks at her and shakes her head sadly. PETE is not coming. LENORE appears as if she's about to cry. SADIE takes this all in.*) So now let me introduce one of those bright young minds, to read her story that has been selected for the finals of the District Writing Competition ... Lenore Green.

(*There is polite applause. LENORE turns to MISS WALKER in anger and frustration.*)

LENORE: I'm not going to do it.

MISS WALKER (*suddenly alarmed*): What?

LENORE: Why bother!

(*The applause dies out. The principal and all others are looking expectantly at LENORE. With story in hand, LENORE turns and exits the auditorium. There are whispered comments in the audience of parents. MISS WALKER quickly follows LENORE.*)

SCENE 12: Interior. School hallway. Evening.

The hallway is deserted. LENORE walks determinedly away from the auditorium. MISS WALKER comes out the door and calls after her.

MISS WALKER: Lenore! Lenore! (*LENORE stops and turns back. MISS WALKER comes up to her.*) What's wrong? I don't understand.

LENORE: I don't want to read my story. And I don't want to go to Thunder Bay!

MISS WALKER: But Lenore! This is a great opportunity! This is the first big step in your career.

LENORE: What career?

MISS WALKER: You could do anything—go to university, become a journalist or an English professor or a playwright. You've been given a talent. You can't turn your back on it!

LENORE: It's only a stupid story. I'm sorry I even wrote it.

(*LENORE throws the story down on the floor, turns, and walks away. After a beat, MISS WALKER reaches down and picks up the spilled pages. She looks at them, then watches LENORE walking away from her.*)

ACT THREE

SCENE 13: Interior. Classroom. Afternoon.

MISS WALKER is sitting at her desk, marking tests in the empty classroom. She works quickly for a moment, but then her momentum slows, her eyes leave her work, and, brows knitted, she begins to think again about LENORE. She can't figure it out.

SADIE and CONNIE enter the room behind her. CONNIE is intimidated by a woman of her own generation with a university education. She looks uncomfortably around the room.

SADIE: Miss Walker?

MISS WALKER (*turning around and standing*): Hi, Sadie ... and Mrs. Green. How are you?

(*CONNIE nods shyly. It takes a moment to find the words, but she speaks them with determination.*)

CONNIE: There is something you should know. Lenore loves to write more than anything. And she wants to go to Thunder Bay. But my husband ... (*a little ashamed*) ... he won't let her.

SADIE: Baba doesn't believe in schools and books and stuff.

MISS WALKER (*reflectively*): I see. Please sit. (*She gestures to a chair for* CONNIE *and another for* SADIE.)

SCENE 14: Exterior. Spirit Bay docks. Afternoon.

PETE *is unloading his catch after a good day's fishing. He is on the dock. A* CREWMAN *hands him a tub full of ice and fish from the deck on the boat. There are several tubs on the dock.*

PETE (*feigning pain*): Uhhh! The only trouble with a good catch is it's bad for my back!

(*The* CREWMAN *laughs.* PETE *lifts the tub of fish and walks a few steps to the other tubs when he notices* LENORE. LENORE *stands, with school books, at the far end of the dock, watching* PETE *from a distance. Other students pass by behind her on their way home.* LENORE *and* PETE *look at each other a moment.* PETE *puts the tub down with the others and, wiping his hands with a rag, takes a step toward her.* LENORE *turns and quickly walks away.* PETE *stops and watches her, feeling badly.*)

SCENE 15: Interior. Classroom. Afternoon.

CONNIE *and* SADIE *are talking to* MISS WALKER. CONNIE *is more relaxed now. She is reflective.*

CONNIE: When I was Lenore's age, I was real good at school, too. Top of my class. I might have gone on to university, even! But I couldn't decide ... and then I met Pete ... (*pauses, then says with conviction*) I want this for Lenore!

MISS WALKER: So do I.

CONNIE: We're having a roast, Sunday. Why don't you come by?

(CONNIE *and* MISS WALKER *and* SADIE *share a conspiratorial smile.*)

MISS WALKER: Good! I will.

SCENE 16: Exterior. LENORE's home. Day.

A car and a pickup truck are parked outside LENORE's *house. (This scene establishes the passing of time.)*

SCENE 17: Interior. LENORE's house. Day.

The table is nicely laid out with a bright plastic tablecloth, flowers, and a variety of food—fish, slices of moose, potatoes and other vegetables, and bannock. MISS WALKER sits at one end of the table, PETE at the other. SADIE and CONNIE sit on one side, LENORE on the other.

LENORE is very quiet. She is angry at her father and embarrassed by MISS WALKER being there. She is uncomfortable to be at the table with both of them. MISS WALKER takes a platter of meat from LENORE.

MISS WALKER: Thanks, Lenore. (*PETE is eating his food hungrily, eyes on his plate. MISS WALKER is talking mostly to CONNIE, though she watches PETE for any response.*) ... and we're getting in a new portable classroom and adding to the library ... (*PETE, without looking up, grunts his disfavour over this.*) And what I'm hoping for by the end of the year is a computer terminal for the students to use ...

PETE (*grunts again*): Pass the moose.

(*MISS WALKER finds the platter of moose beside her and passes it. PETE piles moose meat on his plate. MISS WALKER looks at him, is about to say something to him, then thinks better of it.*)

MISS WALKER: One thing I'm excited about ... (*looking at PETE*) and Mr. Crankhurst seems open to it ... is an Ojibway Studies course.

(*PETE looks up at this.*)

PETE (*with disdain*): Ojibway Studies?

MISS WALKER: Yes. The language and customs and history ...

PETE: Like one of them dead civilizations in a museum.

MISS WALKER: No! Not at all. In fact, you trap and fish. Maybe you'd come in and give demonstrations of your expertise?

PETE: Expertise! If you get paid by the word, that's a ten-dollar one for sure!

(*SADIE giggles at this. MISS WALKER is angry. The gloves are off.*)

MISS WALKER: I can see you don't think much of education, but it can give all kinds of things to a girl like Lenore.

PETE: You mean like a one-way ticket out of here.

(Miss Walker takes out the folded pages of Lenore's story and unfolds them.)

Miss Walker: Have you read this?

Pete: No.

(Connie looks worried.)

Miss Walker: Well, I think you should read it!

Pete *(suddenly awkward)*: I will … later.

Miss Walker: Read it now! Just the first page. *(She stands up, reaches over and puts the manuscript down in front of him. Pete moves it away. Miss Walker stays standing.)*

Pete: No.

Miss Walker: Well, if you don't care enough to even read …

Pete *(standing up angrily)*: You saying I don't care about my daughter?!

Miss Walker: She has talent and imagination and desire! You can't imprison her here!

Pete: Prison!

Miss Walker: There's a whole world waiting for her out there!

(Lenore sits there becoming angry and frustrated listening to this exchange.)

Pete: In that world she'll be an outsider! She'll be alone and unhappy and forget who she is!

Lenore *(stands up and looks at Pete)*: You don't care who I am! *(then looks at Miss Walker)* Neither of you! No one even cares what *I* want! *(She turns away and exits the house.)*

(Pete and Miss Walker look at each other, now sorry that they have been so insensitive.)

Scene 18: Exterior. End of dock. Day.

Lenore *crouches on the end of the dock. She looks down at her reflection in the black water. She holds out a pebble and lets it drop into the reflection. When it clears a moment later, her father's reflection can be seen behind her. He stands there a moment.*

LENORE (*with residual anger*): Why won't you read my story?
  (*PETE crouches down beside her and looks out at the water movement.*
  He doesn't look at her as he speaks.)
PETE: Because ... I can't. (*LENORE looks at him in surprise.*) I never
  learned to read so good. You never knew, eh? (*LENORE shakes her*
  head. PETE pauses, then continues, bitterly.) When I went to school
  there was a teacher ... If I didn't learn my lessons or talked Indian,
  he'd beat me with a switch and call me names. One day I took the
  switch away from him and never went back. Never been in a
  school since.
LENORE (*As she watches her father, her expression softens.*): Come for a
  walk?
  (*PETE looks up at her for the first time, smiles, and nods.*)

SCENE 19A: Exterior. Spirit Bay field. Day.
A telephoto lens shows PETE and LENORE walking side by side toward the
camera. The background shows the picturesque village of Spirit Bay on the
edge of the lake. They walk in silence for a moment.

PETE: I'm afraid. (*pause*) Afraid that you'll go away and become a
  stranger to us.
LENORE: How could I do that?
PETE: If you go south to school. It's very different there.

SCENE 19B: Exterior. Spirit Bay road. Day.
PETE and LENORE walk towards the camera, shooting with a telephoto lens.
LENORE: I'll always be Nisnabe[5], Baba. And Spirit Bay is my home.
PETE: Others have said that and not come back.
LENORE: I'll come back! I want to learn to write better so I can live
  here and tell about our people! That's why I want to write!
  (*PETE thinks about this hard as they walk along. They fall silent again.*)

SCENE 20: Exterior. Dreamer's Rock. Afternoon.

PETE and LENORE sit atop Dreamer's Rock, facing the lake that stretches out before them to the horizon. The village can be seen below, and distant islands in the lake.

LENORE: I've been waiting to tell you the last of the dreams. The dreams of the bird that wants to land.

PETE (*very interested*): Yes! Is it finished?

LENORE: It's finished.

PETE: How did it end?

LENORE: Remember I told you the bird was hovering and trying to land? (*PETE nods.*) Well then, each night there were more birds—a few and then dozens ... then hundreds of birds! (*She pauses, remembering.*) And there was a wide open field of snow! And there they began to land, black against the white snow.
  (*PETE is listening intently.*)

PETE: They all landed?

LENORE: Yes! And as each bird landed it became a letter. And the snow was like a page. And the bird-letters formed words. And the words, sentences. (*looking at him*) They were my words, Baba! They were the words I wrote!
  (*LENORE stops, thinking about the images. PETE smiles at her, excited by the dream but saddened by its meaning.*)

PETE: Sounds like you are meant to be a writer. I won't stop you.
  (*LENORE is not satisfied.*)

LENORE: But I need more, Baba. I don't know if I can do it alone. I need your help.

PETE: *My* help? I can't even read!

LENORE: Not that kind. I need your ... (*she pauses, finding the right word*) ... courage. Will you come to Thunder Bay and hear me read my story?

PETE (*unhappily*): At the university? (*LENORE nods. PETE hesitates, then answers.*) I'll come.
  (*LENORE takes his hand and smiles at him happily.*)

SCENE 21A: Exterior. Lakehead University. Day.
A shot of the university, with an identifying sign, is shown to establish locale.

SCENE 21B: Interior. University hallway. Day.
PETE, LENORE, SADIE, CONNIE, and MISS WALKER approach a man in a suit outside the lecture room doors. PETE looks around uncomfortably.

MISS WALKER (*to man*): Is this the District Writing Finals?
MAN (*officious*): Yes. They're about to begin.
  (*LENORE is excited and scared. She hesitates at the door.*)
LENORE: I ... I don't think ...
  (*PETE puts a hand on her shoulder. She looks up at him.*)
PETE (*smiling*): Read it to me. Just to me.
  (*LENORE takes heart in these instructions. She smiles and goes quickly inside, followed by the others.*)

SCENE 22: Interior. Lecture hall. Day.
The lecture hall is quite full of people. A panel of six judges sits at a table at the front listening as LENORE reads her story.

LENORE: "So on that morning before she left, they went by canoe one last time to those favourite places. It was at first light, when the water is a mirror and the trees are still, as if nature is holding her breath. (*Near the front rows sit MISS WALKER, PETE, CONNIE, and SADIE listening. LENORE reads directly to her father, inspired by his presence. PETE listens intently.*)
  "And there was the beaver and the loon and the hawk circling above the treetops. And below, the trout and the sturgeon slipped silently through the black water. Creatures as powerful as the great moose, as small as the minnow. She and her father took their place among them. (*PETE, in his solemn features, reveals amazement at his daughter's ability and the touching sentiments of the story.*)

"And in this world there was peace and harmony that she knew no matter how far she travelled, she would never find again. She understood now why her father had brought her here. She felt the morning sun on her face and the gentle rocking of the canoe and smiled because she knew that here would always be her home."

(When LENORE finishes, the hall is silent. PETE, very moved by his daughter's story, rises immediately to his feet. He begins to applaud loudly—the only one in the hall. The judges look at him with disfavour. But then SADIE applauds and stands and CONNIE and MISS WALKER stand applauding and then others and finally the whole hall is on its feet, applauding. Even two of the judges give polite applause. CONNIE, MISS WALKER, and SADIE smile at PETE. PETE looks only at LENORE.

PETE and LENORE, who has tears in her eyes, look at each other and smile meaningfully.)

1. Ojibway (also Ojibwa): members of the Amerindian people living in the region around Lake Superior and westward. They formerly occupied an area stretching from the Ottawa Valley to the prairies.
2. Baba: an Ojibway term for "dad."
3. Nanabozho (also Nanabush, Manabozo, and other names): in the myths of the Ojibway, a powerful creator and saviour of the people.
4. bannock: a flat round bread made of unleavened flour, salt, water, and sometimes baking powder
5. Nishnabe: another word for Ojibway: It means "our people."

WEIRD KID

a one-act stage play by Rex Deverell

CAST:

VOICE

TIM

TRISH

BEN

JENNIFER

ACTOR

SCENE: *The suggestion of a school classroom in shambles.*

VOICE *(amplified over a P.A. system):* Your attention please. The following students will report to the principal's office immediately: Tim Kowalchuck, Ben MacFarlane, Trish Klein, and Jennifer Small. Tim Kowalchuck, Ben MacFarlane, Trish Klein, and Jennifer Small please report to the principal's office immediately.

(The students are lined up as if in the towering presence of a school principal.)

TIM: No, Sir, I didn't.

TRISH: No!

BEN: No, Sir.

JENNIFER: I wouldn't do anything like that, honest!

TIM: The first we knew about it was when we walked in this morning.

TRISH: We were just as surprised as everybody else.

BEN: Why would we want to wreck our own classroom?

TIM: I know but—

JENNIFER: We didn't even see each other over the weekend—except that Trish and me went to a movie Saturday afternoon. *(pause)* Trish and I.

TRISH: Why would we do that? I mean if we did it why would we leave our names on the board?

BEN: Yeah.

TIM: Right.

(The invisible Mr. Phillips walks across his office and produces certain objects. The eyes of the students widen in surprise.)

JENNIFER: Yes, Mr. Phillips. That's my notebook.

TRISH: Yes, Mr. Phillips, that's my pencil case. I lost it a long time ago.

TIM: Yes, Mr. Phillips, that's my math text.

BEN: Yes, Sir. That's my library card.

TRISH: Where did you get all that?

TIM AND JENNIFER: Hall floor?

BEN: Mr. Phillips, if we had done it—and we didn't, honest—it would have been really stupid to drop our stuff all down the hall.

TRISH: Running? You think we were running? But we weren't even there.

TIM: We weren't. I don't know what else to say.

BEN: We didn't trash the room.

TRISH: Somebody else must've left those things there. Maybe they just wanted to make it look like we did it.

JENNIFER: Yeah.

BEN: Right.

TRISH: I don't know why.

TIM: But it wasn't us.

TRISH: That's all we know. It wasn't us.

(After a moment of listening they all groan.)

TIM: But there's nothing more we can—*(pause)* yes, Sir.

(They stand aside as he leaves the office and then they follow along in a depressed procession back to the classroom.)

TRISH: But this isn't fair! It isn't! It isn't! Why the—

(The others try to shut her up.)

Why should we have to clean it up when we didn't wreck it in the first place? *(pause)* Yes, Sir.

(The sound of a door slamming. They are jolted. It is like a sentence of death.)

Dork brain.

TIM: Don't make it worse.

TRISH: Well he is. *(imitating the principal)* "Maybe you should just stay in here for a while, clean up the damage, and think about things." Thanks a lot.

BEN: "Come and see me when you have reconsidered your position."

JENNIFER: He isn't ever going to believe us.

TIM: Probably not.

TRISH: I'm not gonna apologize for something I didn't do. He can leave me here until I'm a toothless old lady before I'll do that.

JENNIFER: Speak for yourself. I want to get out of here.

BEN *(mock hysterics)*: I've gotta get outa here! I've gotta get out, I tell you!

JENNIFER: Ben.

BEN: I can't take it. I've got claustrophobia—I'm going to break. I'll tell them anything they want. I'm going berserk in here! The walls are closing in. To be locked up in a classroom forever. A fate worse than death. Arrrgggh!

TIM: Unless they expel us.

(This sobers everyone up.)

BEN: I didn't think of that.

(pause)

JENNIFER *(clearly distressed)*: What'll we do?

TIM: It's okay, Jen. We'll come up with something, eh?

BEN: Sure we will.

TRISH: We'd better.

JENNIFER: Like what?

TIM: Well—like—

BEN: Like—

TRISH: Like—

(There is a long pause.)

JENNIFER: Well?

BEN: If we could only think of who did it.

TIM *(after a moment)*: It really wasn't any of you guys, was it?

   (Everybody protests at the same time.)

TRISH: Oh, come on!

BEN: Are you kidding?

JENNIFER: You know us better than that.

TIM: I didn't really think so. *(pause)* Can you prove it?

TRISH: Can you?

TIM: I was away over the weekend with my parents.

BEN: When did you get back?

TIM: Last night.

BEN: Maybe that's when it happened. It could have happened anytime over the last forty-eight hours. You could have done it.

TIM *(conceding)*: Yeah.

BEN: I could have. Any of us could have.

OTHERS. But we didn't.

BEN: Of course not but—*(surveying the wreckage)* somebody sure did
   and, Ladies and Gentlemen of the Jury …

OTHERS: Ben.

BEN: I can't help it. This calls for a great criminal lawyer and I'm it.
   So—I ask you, Ladies and Gentlemen of the Jury, since none of us
   committed this heinous crime, who in fact did?

TIM: That's the question alright.

BEN: Think.

TIM: I'm thinking—I'm thinking.

TRISH: I'm too mad to think.

BEN: Think!

JENNIFER: I don't know. There's no way we can know. It could have
   been anybody.

TRISH: No, not just anybody. *(after a moment)* Somebody who wanted
   to get us real bad.

BEN: Now you're thinking.

JENNIFER: Oh, come off it.

TRISH: Why else would they leave our names on the board and our stuff around the place?

TIM: A frame-up?

TRISH: Of course.

JENNIFER: Who'd want to do that? We're nice.

BEN: Right. We're the most popular kids in the school. Least I am.

TIM: You're the most popular jerk in the school.

BEN: Speak for yourself.

JENNIFER: You'd have to be weird to hate anybody that much.

TIM: I think we're dealing with somebody pretty weird here.

TRISH: That's it. Think—who might be psycho enough to do stuff like this.

JENNIFER: Out of the whole school?

TRISH: No.

TIM: Probably just out of our class, right?

BEN: Probably.

TRISH: Exactly. Somebody in our class who knows us. The one person who is just weird enough to do something this strange. There's only one person who would do something like this.

(Pause. Realization dawns on the others almost simultaneously.)

JENNIFER: Babs?

BEN: Babs.

TIM: Babs.

TRISH: Babs Story.

BEN: That's it—it couldn't have been anyone else.

JENNIFER: She'd have to be the one.

TIM: Makes sense.

Ben *(heading for the door)*: Let's go tell Mr. Phillips.

JENNIFER: Yeah.

(JENNIFER and TRISH follow him.)

TIM: Hold it, hold it!

Ben AND JENNIFER: What?

TIM: Let's think about this. We don't have any proof. All we've got is our suspicions.

TRISH: Well, we can—(pause). He's right.

JENNIFER: But it's all we've got. Better than nothing.

BEN: Least it'll take the heat off us.

TIM: Okay—I'm old Phillips—(setting up a scene) and you come in—Yes, MacFarlane? You're ready to confess?

BEN (falling into line): Yes, Sir—I mean no, Sir. We've just figured out who—er—

TIM (ominous): Vandalized?

BEN: Our classroom. It was Babs Story.

TIM: Yes?

BEN: That's all. It wasn't us. It was Babs Story.

TIM: Are you sure?

BEN: Yes. (pause) Sort of.

TIM: Be careful, young man.

BEN: Pardon?

TIM: This is a serious accusation. You are already in very deep trouble. Don't add to your list of crimes. Now why do you believe Babs Story is the vandal?

BEN: She's the only one wacko enough to do it.

TIM: I beg your pardon?

BEN (hesitating): There's nobody else in our class who's that—that—wacko.

TIM: In your opinion.

BEN: Ask anybody.

TIM: That is not good enough.

TRISH: And he thinks we left our things at the scene of the crime.

TIM: And you left your things at the scene of the crime. All of the evidence points to you.

JENNIFER (bursting in): She was out to get us.

TIM: Why?

(pause)

BEN: I don't know.

JENNIFER: Well—like she acts like she's mad all the time—and—

TIM: Yes?

JENNIFER: —and she's not like normal.

TIM: Yes.

JENNIFER: For instance she's kind of dozy a lot—

TIM: Yes.

JENNIFER: And sometimes she's—*(lamely)* kinda smelly.

TIM *(exploding)*: This is despicable! You children have been picking on this girl ever since she came to this school last fall.

JENNIFER: We have not.

TIM: I think you have. I'm ashamed of you. Ashamed! Have you anything else to say for yourselves or shall I call your parents down here? *(pause)* Well?

BEN *(slumping)*: I see what you mean. We're sunk. We don't have anything.

JENNIFER: We haven't been picking on her ever since she came to school.

TRISH: Yes we have. Think about it.

JENNIFER: Not me.

BEN: Not me—well, maybe a little.

TIM: Maybe a lot.

BEN: Come on—she brought it on herself. Remember that first day—when she first came into the class? *(doing a somewhat unpleasant caricature)* So what's it to ya—I couldn't care less if it's your book. Gimme that—how'm I supposed to do my homework if I don't have a book—you're a bunch of jerk faces—you guys—I'm gonna be a movie star when I grow up. I was already in two movies where I useta live …

TRISH *(aside to JENNIFER)*: Yeah, *The Bride of Frankenstein* and *Return of the Blob*.

(They both laugh.)

BEN *(as Babs)*: I heard that.

TRISH: See?

JENNIFER: What?

TRISH: You did pick on her.

JENNIFER: All I did was …

TIM: Laugh, right?

JENNIFER *(weakly)*: Laugh. At Trish's stupid joke.

BEN: We all laughed. *(to TIM)* You too.

TIM: I guess I did.

TRISH: I thought I was kinda witty.

JENNIFER: We tried to make friends—I did, anyway.

BEN: Yeah, we weren't really cruel or anything.

JENNIFER: I remember the first day she was there I walked right up to her and I said, "Wanna eat lunch with me?"

TRISH: Yeah and she said—"Forget it—I don't want to eat lunch with you."

TIM: No—she said—she said—I can't remember—wasn't it like—I can't today. I gotta go home.

JENNIFER: And I said "Don't you have your lunch?"

TIM: I forgot it. Why don't you just leave me alone?

JENNIFER: I was just trying to be nice.

TIM: Well forget it—You don't have to be nice to me. And *(with TRISH)* what makes you think I'd want to eat lunch with you anyway?

TRISH: … *(with TIM)* what makes you think I'd want to eat lunch with you anyway?

JENNIFER: There, see?

BEN: So what's your point?

TIM: That this is complicated—more complicated than you—

TRISH: It's not complicated at all—Babs Story is just a spoilt brat—

TIM: Sure she's gross and everything. But if we really want to show that she's the one who did all this we have to sort it all out—get all the facts straight. Then we can go to Mr. Phillips with the whole story.

BEN: Like what she's done to us up to now.

TIM: Yeah—or even what we've done to her. Then he might believe us.

JENNIFER: Brilliant.

TRISH: I coulda thought of that.

BEN: Oh yeah?

TIM: All we have to do is remember every time any of us had anything to do with her.

TRISH *(dismayed)*: Oh boy.

JENNIFER: Where do we start?

TIM: Anywhere, I guess. Whatever we remember.

BEN: Okay, let's start with this. *(resuming his role as a criminal lawyer)* Mr. Phillips, Your Honour—Your Dishonour, Your Fatheadedness—

OTHERS: Ben!

BEN: Whatever—Ladies and Gentlemen of the Jury—I intend beyond a shadow of a doubt to expose the defendant, Babs Story, for the criminal she is. I call as my first witness, Patricia Klein. *(to TRISH)* Do you swear to tell the truth, the whole truth and nothing but the truth, so help you God?

TRISH: This is serious, Ben.

BEN: I'm serious. What were you doing on or about … the lunch room about a month ago?

TRISH: Eating lunch?

TIM: Give the lady a cigar.

BEN: This day in particular, there was only one place left and you had to sit beside someone you didn't particularly want to sit beside—

TRISH *(remembering)*: Oh yeah.

JENNIFER *(remembering)*: Right.

BEN: Who was that person?

TRISH: Babs.

BEN: Exactly. *(arranging the stage)* Now, Your Honour, with the court's permission I'd like to arrange a little demonstration here. *(He has pulled chairs up to a table or desk.)* Jennifer—you play the part of the defendant, Babs Story.

JENNIFER: But I wasn't there—I just heard about it after.

BEN: You are eating your lunch—

TIM: This time you have a lunch.

(She pretends to be eating.)

BEN: Yes, this time she has a lunch. And Trish comes in. She sits down beside her. Observe, Your Honour …

(TRISH squeezes in beside Babs and they look to BEN for more direction.

BEN: Did she say anything?

TRISH: Yeah, I think so—

JENNIFER: Hi.

TRISH: I couldn't find any place else—

JENNIFER: What do I do now?

TRISH *(pause)*: And then you just get up and throw my lunch on the floor and say I hate you, I hate you.

JENNIFER *(giggling as she does it)*: I hate you, I hate you.

BEN: M'Lord, the Crown rests its case.

TIM: Wait a minute. Are you sure that's what happened?

BEN: Precisely, I saw it myself.

TIM *(to the girls)*: Would you do it again?

TRISH: Come on, Tim. That's what happened.

TIM: It's like something's been left out.

TRISH: Well, I can't remember every itty bitty detail—but that's more or less what—

TIM: She wouldn't get that upset over nothing—

BEN: That's what she's like—

TIM: You guys, do it right, okay? I mean nothing is going to come out of this unless we remember all the details. It's the only way Phillips is going to believe us. It's the only way he'll know we aren't just giving our version of it—if we've worked it all out. Now there's gotta be more to it than that, isn't there, Trish?

TRISH: Maybe a little.

TIM: Okay, you were here. Babs was sitting there. You sat down. What did she do right when you sat down?

TRISH: She just kept eating, I guess—

JENNIFER: Like what?

TRISH: Like something kinda smelly—

TIM: You said something, didn't you?

BEN: Your Worship, my friend is badgering the witness.

TIM (*to* BEN): Buzz off.

BEN (*protesting*): Your Worship!

TIM (*showing him a fist*): Ben.

   (BEN *is quiet.*)

TIM: Okay.

TRISH (*a certain amount of disdain*): What's that?

JENNIFER: A sandwich.

TRISH: I know that, stu- (*catching herself*). What's in it?

JENNIFER: Onions and garlic sausage.

BEN: And, Mr. Judge, Sir—sitting at close quarters with this—this
   person who is eating onions and garlic sausage, Patricia didn't
   even wrinkle her nose—

TRISH: Well, maybe I did a little … I don't know what she was
   eating—but it stunk. I mean what would you do if you were
   sitting beside this slob and she was eating yuck.

BEN (*annoyed*): You're not helping our case.

TIM: The absolute truth, Ben. It's the only thing that'll save us.

TRISH: Okay, okay. We'll do it right. This is my lunch. (*miming*)

JENNIFER: This is my lunch.

   (*Once more* TRISH *sits down. This time they try to play it as it happened.*)

JENNIFER: Hi.

TRISH: Hello.

   (*They eat away at their lunches for a time.* JENNIFER *becomes aware that*
   TRISH *is watching her.*)

TRISH (*nasty*): What's that?

JENNIFER: A sandwich.

TRISH: I know that, stupid. What's in it?

JENNIFER: Onions and garlic sausage.

   (TRISH *makes a face.*)

JENNIFER: You didn't have to sit here, you know.

TRISH: I didn't have any choice.

   (*They eat in silence. The tension is growing between them.*)

JENNIFER: Keep your garbage on your own side of the table, okay?

TRISH: I didn't do anything. You're the one eating garbage.

(JENNIFER explodes and throws over the desk they were using as a table.)

JENNIFER: I hate you! I hate you!

TIM: Hey, take it easy.

BEN: Are you alright?

JENNIFER: Yeah, I'm okay.

TRISH: You sure?

JENNIFER: Yeah. It got kinda real there.

TRISH *(with the others)*: Yeah, it did. *(to the others)* Anyway there, you see? That's exactly what happened.

JENNIFER: Well, you see why, doncha?

TRISH: She is just basically a nasty person.

JENNIFER: What was the girl supposed to do?

TRISH: She doesn't like me and I don't like her.

BEN: Your Honour—in this situation there wasn't any need for this kind of violent behaviour. You can see now what sort of person we are dealing with here—

TRISH: The sort of person who'd wreck a classroom just to get back at us …

TIM: The person who might have some reason to get back at us.

BEN: I guess we might have been mean to her sometimes …

TIM: So that was one situation. Okay. Who remembers another one?

BEN: The video project.

JENNIFER: What did Babs have to do with that?

TIM: She was in our group.

TRISH: No she wasn't. We didn't choose her …

BEN: She came in late. *(to TRISH)* You be Babs.

TRISH: No way.

BEN: Why not.

TRISH: I don't want to be her.

TIM: Somebody's gotta be.

TRISH: We don't have to act it out—we can just try to remember what happened.

JENNIFER: No—this is good. You find out a lot this way.

TRISH: Like what?

JENNIFER: Believe me.

TIM: Let's just try it, okay?

TRISH: You do it then.

(*Everybody laughs.*)

TIM: Alright. I'll be Babs.

TRISH: No. That'd be just silly.

TIM: Silly? Just watch. Remember what we were doing? We were just getting our idea together for rock videos—and how that'd be what we'd do for the class, right? And—

BEN (*to* TRISH): You were up on the desk and we were all making like … (*he names a popular rock group*).

JENNIFER: Right. We were doing … (*a current hit*).

(*They all get into recreating the song.*)

TRISH (*at the peak of the fun*): And then Babs came in.

TIM: Right. Babs came in.

(*His version of Babs is not an impersonation so much as how he would act if he were in Babs's situation. When the others play Babs later they fall into this style of role playing. TIM as Babs is standing at the entranceway watching the others carry on.*)

TIM: What are you doing?

(*They don't hear.*)

Tim (*louder*): I said, what are you doing?

BEN: A rock video. What's it look like?

TIM: Stupid.

TRISH: What are you doing here?

TIM: Mrs. Graham.

JENNIFER: You're supposed to be in group 5.

TIM: There were too many in group 5. Mrs. Graham told me to come here.

BEN: But we've already started.

TIM: Why are you doing a rock video? I thought we were supposed to do something about—like—what makes our lives different from—like other peoples' lives—

JENNIFER: Like that's what we're doing, aren't we?

BEN: What is the big symbol of our generation?

TIM: A moving van.

TRISH: Rock videos.

JENNIFER: Come on. You can be the drummer.

TIM: I don't want to be no drummer.

BEN: Any drummer.

TIM: Shut up. All I know is we're supposed to be making up something about our lives today.

BEN: I just said that's what we are doing. Rock videos. Come on. We don't have a lot of time. Are you going to join in or not?

TIM: What if I got a different idea?

TRISH: We don't have enou—

JENNIFER: Well, we should listen—

TIM: You won't want to do it—

BEN: Sure, if it's better than our idea—.*(to the others)* Right?

JENNIFER: Sure.

TRISH: We're wasting time. What's your idea?

TIM: I said a moving van.

TRISH: I don't get it.

TIM: I think a lot of people—like families—like—move around the country a lot more than they useta.

BEN *(to the others):* Do you want to do "moving around the country" instead of rock videos?

(The reply is silence.)

BEN: That's what I thought. *(to TIM/Babs)* See? Okay, let's get on with it.

(They start back into the song.)

TIM *(interrupting)*: Could you do the rock video about moving?

BEN: No.

TIM: Why not?

TRISH: There's no song like that—

TIM: There could be. We could—

JENNIFER: Either help or keep quiet, alright? *(pause)* Well, we didn't have any time, did we?

TRISH: She just wanted her own way.

TIM: She wrote the song, you know.

   (*The others do not know how to respond.*)

TRISH: Babs?

TIM (*fishing in his school bag and mumbling*): I don't have any place to go … But I'm just movin' on … Something, something …

BEN: It's a song?

TIM: Yeah … (*consulting a piece of paper*). They told me it'd be good here …

TRISH: How does it go?

TIM (*trying to remember the tune*): Just a minute … (*With growing confidence he begins to sing.*)

I don't have any place to go
but I'm just movin' on

They told me it'd be good here maybe
Dad and Mom might get along here
Dad might even get a job here maybe

Now we're movin' on from here
Don't have any better place to go

No place worse though,
Movin' on.

Don't know where to go
but I'm goin'.

BEN: Babs wrote that?

JENNIFER: How did you learn it?

TIM: A cassette. She gave me a cassette a couple weeks after the video project. I guess she wanted to show us.

BEN: We might've gotten a better mark with that.

TRISH: When we get an F minus, any direction is up. Geeze, Babs Story. Who woulda thought.

BEN: Did she move a lot?

JENNIFER: Kinda obvious, eh?

TIM: I asked around. They say her family isn't too together—her dad doesn't show up much.

TRISH: We all have problems. That's no excuse.

BEN: Well, Your Honour—we admit that we looked down on the defendant. We admit we misjudged her. In fact it's getting to look more and more like she's the only one who had enough reasons to want to get us into deep—er—difficulty, Sir.

TRISH: That's right.

TIM: Okay. What else have we got? Jen—what about the time—

JENNIFER: Isn't this enough? *(starting for the door)*. Hey, Ben, that sounds good, eh? Let's go.

TIM: What's your hurry?

JENNIFER: Let's get it over with.

TIM: What about the time you were best friends with her.

JENNIFER: It didn't last very long.

BEN: Yeah—what was that about, anyway?

JENNIFER: Nothing.

TIM: Well, tell us then.

JENNIFER: It's my business.

TRISH: What is?

JENNIFER: It's not something I'm proud of, okay?

(pause)

JENNIFER: Alright, you know how last year I was new at this school—and it took a long time to make friends with anybody and finally you guys got to be my friends. Well for a while this year Trish started to act kinda strange—

TRISH: I did not!

JENNIFER: I mean you were going to movies and stuff with Ben and Tim—and you wouldn't call me up or anything and see if I might want to go, you know what I mean?

TRISH *(surprised)*: Really?

JENNIFER: Yes, really. So I kinda made up with Babs.

TRISH: What a choice.

JENNIFER: To get back at you.

TRISH: Oh. But I didn't do that on purpose—

JENNIFER: I know that now—

TRISH: Oh, Jen …

JENNIFER: Oh, Trish …

(The boys are about to vomit.)

TIM: I hate to break in on this intimate scene—but we're talking about Babs.

JENNIFER: Yeah, Babs. Well, she just got caught in the middle. I guess the worst part of it was when I made arrangements to go shopping with her.

TRISH: The day I ran into you at Market Square Mall?

JENNIFER: I kinda planned that too. I knew you'd probably show up. *(to BEN)* You be Babs this time.

BEN: Yucky girls' stuff. Let Trish do it. She hasn't done it yet—

JENNIFER: No, Trish is in this.

BEN *(resigned)*: What do I do?

JENNIFER: Well, it took me a while to persuade her to come. She said she didn't want to buy anything and she didn't have the money to take the bus downtown—and I said come on anyway because I'd gotten a lot of money for my birthday from my grandmother and I still need to buy a pair of jeans or something and *(to BEN)* you have such great taste …

TRISH: Oh-boy.

JENNIFER: Right. Anyway that's what I told her and *(to BEN)* you fall for it and my mom gives us a ride and drops us off … but you still don't have any money … What are you going to get, Babs?

BEN *(playing the part realistically)*: I told you I couldn't buy anything.

JENNIFER *(keeping an eye out for TRISH)*: I know—but I thought you probably could buy some little thing.

BEN: Well, I can't. Let's go and get your—boy, look at that.

JENNIFER: What?

BEN: That dirt bike—no, she wouldn't be interested in a dirt bike—

JENNIFER: It was one of those keyboard things—electronic piano or something. How did you know she stopped like that?

BEN: If she's like me—whenever I don't have any money I always see something really expensive I'd really like. That really bugs me.

JENNIFER: She looked at it like she'd never be able to buy it—not in a thousand years.

BEN (as Babs): Those keyboards—you can make any sound you could ever want. You don't even have to write it down or anything. You just play it and it plays back whatever you think up.

JENNIFER: It's probably not that easy, Babs. Let's start with Chez Lean Jeans—and if they don't have anything maybe Jiffy Sports and then I'll try Eaton's and maybe Zellers, okay? Hey, look at those …

BEN: They're nice …

JENNIFER: No—they're too ordinary …

BEN: Are you sure you want me to help?

JENNIFER: I wouldn't have asked you, would I?

BEN: I guess not …

JENNIFER (suddenly): There's Trish Klein. (waving) Hi, Trish.

TRISH (coming over): Hi, Jenny. Fancy meeting you.

JENNIFER: Say hello to my very good friend Babs.

TRISH: Hello, Babs.

BEN: Hullo.

TRISH: So what are you doing?

JENNIFER: Buying some jeans. Babs is helping me, aren't you, Babs?

BEN: I guess so.

TRISH: How come I haven't heard from you?

JENNIFER: How come I haven't heard from you?

TRISH: I thought you'd call.

JENNIFER: I thought *you'd* call.

(pause)

TRISH: Are you going to the party tonight?

JENNIFER: What party?

TRISH: Ben and Tim are cooking something up. They said they were inviting you.

JENNIFER: I don't know …

TRISH: You can come. Hey, I'll stop on the way and we can walk over together, okay?

JENNIFER: I'll think about it. I'll probably come. Yeah, I'll come. What time?

TRISH: Eight.

JENNIFER: Great!

TRISH: What sort of jeans are you going to buy?

JENNIFER: I don't know. Got any ideas?

TRISH: To tell you the truth there's this new brand over at the Slack Shack? I've been thinking about—you know—at least trying on a pair. Wanna go over there?

JENNIFER: Sure! *(to Babs as an afterthought)* Coming?

BEN: No, it's alright. Go ahead.

JENNIFER *(breaking out of the scene):* That's exactly the way it sounded. You could have been there. How did you know?

BEN: I sorta guessed.

TIM: There's a picture coming clear.

BEN: And so, Your Honour, Sir, perhaps you can see a history of meanness, a building up of hurt and little insults, a powder keg, as they say, just waiting to explode.

JENNIFER: Yeah.

TRISH: Still, didn't give her any right to—

BEN: And then there was the great tease episode. I started that myself.

JENNIFER: Oh, no. I hate this, Ben: It makes us sound so awful.

BEN: Truth, Jen. It's the only thing that'll save us. Right, Tim?

TIM: Go ahead.

Ben *(going up to TRISH)*: Hey, Babs!

TRISH: Go 'way.

BEN: Babs!

TRISH: I don't want to.

BEN: Babs.

TRISH: No, Ben.

BEN: Know what I heard, Babs?

TRISH: Ben, go away.

BEN: Somebody likes you.

TRISH: Not interested. *(but she falls into the role in spite of herself)*

BEN: Okay, I'll tell him you're not interested.

TRISH: Who?

BEN: Guess.

TRISH: I can't guess.

BEN: He told me not to tell you. But I'll tell you his initials.

TRISH *(softly)*: Okay.

BEN: Pardon?

TRISH: Okay.

BEN: Okay what?

TRISH: Tell me his initials.

BEN: Whose initials?

TRISH: Whoever—likes me.

BEN: T. K.

TIM: Oh no.

BEN *(aside)*: Sorry, Tim.

TRISH: Tim likes me?

JENNIFER: He told me, too. He's told everybody in the school. Tim
    Kowalchuck likes Babs Story.

TRISH: Everybody knows?

JENNIFER: Everybody knows.

BEN: Everybody in the school.

TRISH: And everybody is laughing.

BEN: I wouldn't say everybody.

JENNIFER: Not everybody. Look, there he is.

BEN: Tell him to come over here.

TRISH: No.

BEN: Go on. It won't hurt you.

JENNIFER: Go on.

TRISH: Tim?

TIM: What?

BEN (too loudly): Come over here, Tim. Babs wants to ask you something.

TIM (coming closer): What?

JENNIFER: Ask him for a date, Babs.

(BEN and JENNIFER burst into laughter.)

TIM: What is this?

TRISH: Did you tell Ben that you liked me?

TIM: No way. Why?

TRISH (seeing that it is all fictitious): Oh, nothing.

(More laughter.)

TIM (walking away in disgust): Give up, you guys.

TRISH: This isn't funny.

BEN: Babs didn't say that.

TRISH: She said it to herself.

TIM: Yeah, she must've …

TRISH: Why did you do that, Ben?

BEN: I was just having fun. You're the one to talk.

TRISH: This is different.

BEN: Why?

JENNIFER: Because you were being Babs this time?

TRISH: Yeah. (pause) And what if she liked Tim a little? Lots of people do.

TIM: Of course.

BEN: Especially if they are weird.

TRISH: Don't let it go to your head but people think you're nice.

JENNIFER: I don't think that any of us are so nice.

TIM: Agreed. Not now.

BEN: I'll dispute that. (The others glare at him.) Lighten up, everybody. I just wanted to have a little fun. (pause) Okay, you're right. It wasn't the most terrific—but okay, so look … (to TRISH) You're a girl—

TIM: Observant.

BEN: Shut up. (to TRISH) Trish, if we'd done that to you instead of Babs, what would you have done?

TRISH: Me? I would have gotten mad, for sure. I would have told you all off and then I might have laughed but inside I'd still be really hurt.

BEN: Right. But you wouldn't have gone and tried to tear the school down.

TIM: But if you were Babs?

TRISH: If I were Babs? Well, I guess I'd've gone home and cried a lot and then I might have remembered all the other times stuff was done to me—and I'd probably not be thinking too clearly, and I might decide to take it out on the school—just anything to hurt back for a change—instead of taking it all the time and then I might have thought about the four of us and written our names on the board and taken a few things of ours and thrown them around just to make it look like we had done it—because I might have been trying to say that we were responsible—and I guess maybe we were.

BEN: So, there you are, Your Honour. I rest my case.

JENNIFER: Pretty convincing.

TIM: Right. She was an unhappy person and we made her—

TRISH: Unhappier.

(pause)

BEN: Can we go to Phillips with all this?

TIM: If we tell it like we told ourselves.

(The intercom beeps.)

VOICE: Room 4?

TIM: Yes, Sir?

VOICE: Have you cleaned up in there?

JENNIFER: Yes, Sir.

BEN: More or less.

VOICE: I beg your pardon?

TRISH: Yes, Sir.

TIM: We've thought things over—and I think we know what happened.

VOICE: Very well, come to the office.

(Intercom clicks off.)

JENNIFER: Let's go.

BEN: Yeah, let's go.

(But none of them want to move.)

TRISH *(after a time)*: Maybe we should tell him we did it?

JENNIFER: Are you crazy?

TRISH: It's just an idea.

TIM: What would it accomplish?

TRISH: Nothing, I guess. *(pause)* No. For one thing it might give us a chance to make it up to Babs—maybe we could help her somehow.

BEN *(getting up)*: She did it. She should take the consequences. Let's go.

TIM: Help her?

BEN: Nothing's going to help Babs.

JENNIFER: Nothing we could do.

TRISH: Nothing easy. *(pause)* I can't believe it's me saying this.

BEN: Me neither.

TIM: I like it.

BEN *(in pain)*: Tim.

TIM: We'd all have to stick together on it.

JENNIFER: But it would be lying.

BEN: Right. No way, man. I'm telling it like it happened.

TRISH: But we don't know that's what happened. Not for sure.

BEN: Oh yes we do. Yes we do. We know that is exactly what happened. We tell it any different and we get punished for what she did …

TRISH: That's the idea.

JENNIFER: Trish!

BEN: It doesn't make any sense.

TIM: You don't think it makes sense for us to take her punishment.

BEN: Of course not.

TIM: You sure?

(This brings BEN up short. There is a long pause.)

JENNIFER: Suppose we do. She won't thank us.

TRISH: Probably not.

BEN: It'd probably be the first time anybody ever did anything for her. *(pause)* Trish ...

TRISH: What?

BEN: This is the most ridiculous thing I ever heard.

TRISH. I know. I must be going weird. Let's do it, okay?

JENNIFER: I'm scared.

TIM: Me too.

BEN: Are we going to do it or not?

(Intercom beeps.)

VOICE: Room 4?

EVERYONE: Coming.

(They leave the room and their voices are heard echoing down the hallway.)

The End

In the first production, an actor would step forward after the curtain call.

ACTOR: Thanks a lot. We have some time left and we would like to hear what you think is going to happen in the principal's office once the students get there. Please turn to your neighbours and talk about it for a few minutes.

After a certain amount of discussion the actor may ask for reports from the groups or the cast may circulate among the audience and hear what they have to say. At the end of the time, it would be good to have a brief summary of the range of possibilities that have been talked about.

ACTOR: Thank you for your comments. Most of us have probably felt like Babs Story from time to time—and we've probably been like the other kids, too. Maybe the next time we can make it different.

Media. We all know the term, but what does it mean? Essentially, media includes all forms of mass communication — what we hear on radio, what we view on television and at the movies, and what we read in magazines, newspapers, books, and on the Internet. These channels of communication can be read, heard, or viewed by large numbers — often millions — of people at the same time.

Media entertains, informs, amuses, and persuades us. Chances are you sometimes use a form of media to create messages. You send an e-mail to a friend, for example, or you make a video for a class project.

This unit is organized into five sections: *Print Media, Audio Media, Visual Media, Advertising and Design,* and *Technology.* In each section, you'll find selections that explore how each form of media presents a particular view of people, products, and situations. Keep this in mind the next time you hear a news story about another part of the world or watch an advertisement for a new product—even when a celebrity you admire gives a testimonial to that product or uses it in a movie you're enjoying. (You may already know the term for this: product placement.)

Consider also *different reactions* to media. Have you ever thought a comedian was funny but a friend did not agree with you? Your reaction may be due to your cultural background, family background, gender, age, or lifestyle. Creators of media works are very conscious of these factors when they target a product to a particular group of consumers.

And, as you'll read in the coming sections, each media form has its own key *elements and production practices,* such as the creative use of camera shots and storyboards in videos and films; how newspaper and magazine articles are designed for maximum effect; and how advertisers target the high school market. Keep these elements and practices in mind as you analyze the media messages you encounter and as you create your own media works.

PRINT MEDIA

A newspaper provides us with a wealth of information, including news on local, national, and international events, entertainment, and sports, as well as opinions on current issues, information about the latest technologies, and classified advertisements. Papers offer both factual articles and opinion pieces, and it is important to recognize the differences between these two types of writing.

Factual articles (sometimes called hard news stories) usually provide objective information and answer the questions who, what, when, where, why, and how. Many factual articles come from news agency wire services, such as Canadian Press, that sell their stories and photographs to newspapers. The article on page 152, reproduced in part on the next page, is an example of a factual article.

Opinion pieces reflect the writer's point of view and, in some cases, that of the newspaper's owner. The opinion of the newspaper on an issue is expressed in an editorial. Other opinion pieces include columns that offer the beliefs of individual writers. Movie and concert reviews are examples of opinion pieces. "Dogs and Books," on page 168 of this anthology, is an opinion piece.

Magazines, like newspapers, are popular with Canadians. Some magazines are of general interest and cover a range of topics. Most magazines published today, however, are special interest magazines that focus on a specific topic such as cars, fashion, or sports. Each special interest magazine targets a certain group in society, and the type of writing used and the advertisements included will depend on the intended readership. "Tom Longboat" on page 121, "Hesquiaht" on page 134, "Invaders from Mars" on page 286, "Lights, Camera, Frostbite!" on page 295, and "Cyberspace Studios" on page 325 are examples of magazine articles.

As you read newspaper and magazine articles in this book and from other sources, pay attention to the use of layout and design, and look for examples of key terms highlighted on the following pages.

ANATOMY OF AN ARTICLE

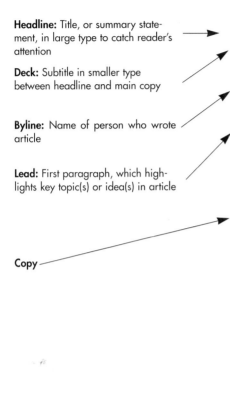

Headline: Title, or summary statement, in large type to catch reader's attention

Deck: Subtitle in smaller type between headline and main copy

Byline: Name of person who wrote article

Lead: First paragraph, which highlights key topic(s) or idea(s) in article

Copy

Mr. Preston (and Mr. Rawat) go to New Delhi
CONTRASTS/The congress brimmed with products that few Indians could afford

by John Stackhouse, New Delhi

LEWIS T. PRESTON AND D. S. RAWAT came to New Delhi this month for the same reason: development.

Mr. Preston is president of the World Bank, the Washington-based juggernaut that has about $90 billion (U.S.) in loans outstanding to developing countries. He earns $285 000 a year, tax-free. And at 65, the career banker is getting his first taste of development.

Mr. Rawat scrapes by on a metal worker's income in a southern Indian city. He is infected with the AIDS-causing human immunodeficiency virus. And at 28, he too is getting his first taste of development.

This was Mr. Preston's first visit to southern Asia since assuming the president's job in 1991, and he was accorded all the privileges of a head of state. There were the armed escorts, the prime minister's lunch, the five-star hotels and a visit to the Taj Mahal under a full moon. There was a private plane, too, arranged by the Indian government to avoid the pain that Indian Airlines inflicts on most other air travellers. And there were the carefully planned project visits: family planning in Rajasthan, irrigation in Haryana, slum upgrading in Bombay...

Also to note when reading a newspaper or magazine article:

Fact: Statement or data presented as objective information (e.g., in the second paragraph above, "He earns $285 000 a year, tax-free").

Five W's: Key questions being answered in article: who? what? when? where? why? how?

Inverted Pyramid: Information presented in descending order of importance or interest.

Opinion: A point of view or judgment expressed in an article about the information presented. This can be explicit (e.g., if the writer above had stated, "I think that Mr. Preston earns too much"), or it can be inferred from the connotations of words and phrases used by the writer (e.g., in the fourth paragraph above, " ... to avoid the pain that Indian Airlines inflicts on most other air travellers").

Caption or Cutline: Short description or explanation accompanying a photograph or illustration.

AUDIO MEDIA

Sound plays a major role in the media. Imagine going to see a movie without sound, or pressing the mute button during your favourite television show. Think about how often you listen to the radio for news, weather reports, and the latest music releases. Can you imagine a world without recorded music?

Sound can be used to inform, entertain, and persuade you. You can use sound for these same purposes when you create media works: for example, when you tape-record yourself reading a poem, when you interview someone for a class project, or when you include background music for a video you're making. When you use sound creatively in these ways, your audience is more likely to pay close attention to the material you are presenting.

INVADERS FROM MARS

by Carla Magor

IT WAS HALLOWE'EN NIGHT, 1938. Just as people today relax for the evening in front of their TV sets and VCRs, millions of people all over the United States were relaxing in front of their radios.

Most listeners were enjoying *Edgar Bergen's Comedy Hour*. Edgar Bergen (father of actress Candice Bergen) was a ventriloquist, who always made people laugh. Then Bergen introduced an unpopular singer, and people got up to turn the dial. In 1938, there were no remote controls, but changing stations was just as popular as it is today.

Suddenly, people heard the sobbing, terror-stricken voice of a radio announcer. The news was from New Jersey, and it was chilling. Reporting live from the scene, the announcer said that a cylinder of unknown origin had just slammed into the earth "with earthquake force" near Grover's Mill, New Jersey.

Listeners in millions of living rooms froze in their seats as the announcer's voice shook.

Ladies and gentlemen, this is the most terrifying thing I have ever witnessed—wait a minute! Someone's crawling out of the hollow top—someone or ... something. I can see peering out of that black hole two luminous discs. Maybe eyes, might be a face ... Good heavens, something wriggling out of the shadow like a grey snake. Now it's another one ... They look like tentacles ... I can see the thing's body now—it's as large as a bear. It glistens like wet leather. But that face, it's ... it's ... ladies and gentlemen, it's indescribable; I can hardly force myself to keep looking at it, it's so awful. The eyes are black and gleam like a serpent; the mouth is ... kind of V-shaped, with saliva dripping from its rimless lips that seem to quiver and pulsate. The monster or whatever it is can hardly move; it seems weighted down possibly by gravity or something ...

There was more. Much more. The monster turned its deadly heat ray on advancing soldiers and turned them into screaming pillars of fire. The fire was spreading—then, abruptly, the announcer's voice was cut off. There was a brief musical break, and then bulletins started to pour in:

"Red Cross emergency workers dispatched to the scene ..."
"Bridges hopelessly clogged with human traffic ..."
"The strange beings who landed in the Jersey farmland tonight are the vanguard of an invading army from the planet Mars ..."
"The monster is now in control of the middle section of New Jersey ..."

Air-force bombers, the report continued, were melting out of the sky. New York City itself was now under attack. Smoke and poisonous gas filled the night air, drifting across the city.

By this time, people listening to the radio had leapt to their feet and were calling the police and running through the streets. Like wildfire, the word spread to those who weren't listening to the radio—the United States was being invaded by Martians!

Inside Studio One at CBS in New York, Orson Welles and his fellow actors kept on broadcasting. They had no idea what was happening outside their door, in the city's streets, and across the country. They continued with their radio adaptation of *The War of the Worlds*, H. G. Wells's science-fiction novel. Little did they realize that most of their listeners had missed the opening of *Mercury Theater on the Air*, when Orson Welles explained that the program was a dramatization.

Toward the end of the radio play, Welles, playing a professor named Pierson, described the scene. He was in Times Square, he said, staggering through the destruction caused by the Martian heat rays. The city was deserted. He pressed on to Central Park. There he found the remains of the Martians themselves. They were dead—victims of Earth germs! The Martians, said Professor Pierson, had no immunity to Earth diseases and had all been destroyed. Earth was now safe.

Even before the end of the broadcast, Welles and the other actors had begun to realize that something was wrong. At one point, CBS had interrupted the broadcast to announce that it was just a play. Welles closed the show by calling it "Mercury Theater's own radio version of dressing up in a sheet and jumping out of a bush and saying boo" for Hallowe'en.

But it was too late. Police, wielding clubs, stormed through the halls of CBS. Outside the studio a huge swarm of reporters and police were waiting for Welles. Reports were coming in from other media that panic-stricken listeners, convinced that the broadcast was real, not fiction, had died or committed suicide.

Welles went to face the crowd, certain that his acting career was finished. But, although millions were badly frightened that Hallowe'en night, miraculously, no one died or was even badly injured. And, as a result of the publicity, Orson Welles was an overnight sensation. He went on to become one of Hollywood's most celebrated directors and actors, and *The War of the Worlds* became the most famous radio show ever broadcast.

RAP

RAP IS A TERM adopted from the jazz tradition, where it indicates "speaking" or "talking." Musically, too, the development of rap into a billion-dollar industry in the '80s and '90s can be traced to "jazz poets" such as Gil Scott-Heron and the Last Poets.

In its modern form, rap began with the 1979 single "Rapper's Delight," released by the Sugarhill Gang on Sylvia Robinson's Sugarhill Records. The first line of this song: "A hip-hop, the hi-be, To the hi-be, The hip-hip-hop, You don't stop rockin'," also coined the term which denotes rap's parent movement—hip hop (which embraces graffiti art, music, break dancing, and inner-city culture).

Rap music generally relies on two components—the MC or rapper, and the DJ, responsible for constructing musical accompaniment, often with the aid of "samples" from other records. Originally rap was an entirely street-linked phenomenon, as rival troupes competed at street parties and warehouses in a manner similar to that of the reggae sound systems.

There are other similarities between the two musics—one of the first to pioneer hip hop was Jamaican Kool Here, and the rap MC has similarities to reggae's DJ or toaster. Other "old school" artists including Afrika Bambaataa and Grandmaster Flash subsequently took rap into the political arena, Flash's *The Message* being a particularly evocative record in the early '80s.

By the mid-1990s, the dominant force in rap became "B-Boy" culture, epitomized by Run DMC of Def Jam Records and LL Cool J. Other originators such as KRS-1 of Boogie Down Productions continued to produce quality recordings. By the late '80s, NWA and Public Enemy had taken the music to, in hip-hop parlance, "the next level." As the deeply politicized voice of dispossessed black youth culture, both groups were viewed with suspicion by the white music industry and traded on the fact (Public Enemy memorably titling one of their albums *Fear of a Black Planet*, NWA sponsoring the development of gangsta rap). Though NWA's vitriol soon became artistically sterile, Public Enemy have persevered to become rap's single most important commentators.

A former member of NWA, Ice Cube, became a potent commercial force in the '90s, alongside his near namesake Ice T. Both were dogged by accusations of misogyny and the glorification of violence. However, at their best, each had something valuable to say about the society in which they lived and its representation in the media— unlike a slew of egomaniacal exhibitionists such as the Geto Boys.

Gang Starr successfully reiterated the link between jazz and rap with a series of lauded experiments throughout the '90s. Mere commercial acts, including Vanilla Ice and MC Hammer, brought rap to MTV cameras and a wider public, but they were consistently denigrated by purists. Of the white rappers, the only act to appeal across the racial board remained the consistently innovative Beastie Boys.

By the mid-1990s, Dr. Dre and his protégé Snoop Doggy Dogg had relocated rap's epicentre to Los Angeles, framing the G-Funk sound, which became the dominant urban mantra of the period. The west coast's ascendancy has subsequently been challenged by the dynamic creative forces within the Wu-Tang Clan, as well as Nas and Fat Joe Da Gangsta.

Rap has developed at an astonishing pace since its inception, retaining its position as the preferred outlet for those in America's depressed inner cities and articulating views which would otherwise remain unheard. That it thrives on a diet of adverse publicity and notoriety should come as no surprise to those familiar with the conditions that have bred it.

Chasing Down the News

by Barbara Frum

No matter how you get it, the news is always a selection, a gerry-mandered slice of reality. Your favourite newscaster signing off with "… and that's the news" is having you; "that's the news we've chosen to give you" would be more like it. Most of the world and its events are almost permanently ignored.

Far from being a replica of the day's events, the news is a highly organized creation; you could even call it a distortion. In truth many sketches of the unfolding universe are possible, each containing only the information that a particular news team has wanted or has managed to get.

What we set out to get is decided by the democratic vote of our production staff. Out of the clash of different outlooks, backgrounds, and personal styles, we shape our show. And, let me tell you, it's a clash. We are in constant internal disagreement. In fact, the first clue that we are onto something good is the amount of argument a story suggestion will spark among ourselves.

What we don't argue about are certain general principles. We're always hard on phoney Canadian angles to international news, when the heart of a given story lies elsewhere. We don't cover political disputes as though the only interest in the world is Uncle Sam's. We're as interested in why a story is being leaked as in the story itself. And we always try to get to the people directly involved.

It's a wired world, as somebody has already noted, and we take advantage. If there are deep-sea divers under the ice at Frobisher Bay, you can be sure that they're not without a telephone. I've even talked to a bank robber in the midst of his own hold-up. A young man calling himself Cat was holding 11 hostages at a bank in Greenwich Village,

New York City. We got the branch's number from the bank's head office and cut right by the army of battle-dressed policemen sealing off the area—right into the bank. The phone rang once, twice, a third time. Then a cheerful male voice came on the line.

"Hull-low."

"Hello." I chirped, guessing that this had to be the holdup man: a hostage wouldn't sound so relaxed. "I'm calling for the Canadian Broadcasting Corporation—"

"Canada," he exulted. "Far out. How're ya doin' up there in Canada? It's cold, huh?"

"We'd like to know what's going on there," I said, briskly moving past the small talk. Obligingly, he got down to business.

Fortunately for a program dependent on it, bank robbers aren't the only people unable to leave a ringing phone alone. During the Cod War (Part One), the Icelanders, furious at Britain for fishing in what the Icelanders considered their territorial waters, spent their frustration in stoning the British embassy. We thought we'd try to get through to the embattled diplomats. Not only did we get through, the ambassador himself picked up the phone.

"I'd like to speak to the British ambassador," I announced.

"I am the ambassador," came the reply over the sound of shattering glass.

"We understand there's a riot going on," I said obtusely. "What is that terrible noise in the background?"

"My windows, Madame."

"Ambassador," I went on, "we'd like your view of the current dispute between your country and Iceland." The ambassador was now a little upset.

"My dear Madame," he ordered frostily, "will you please get off my line. I have to telephone my Foreign Office."

"Please, just one moment," I persisted. "I need only one comment—"

"Madame," he pleaded, now barely able to conceal the edge of hysteria creeping into his cultured tones, "Madame, you don't seem to understand. I haven't yet reported to my own government. There's only one line out of here, which you are rudely monopolizing."

I proposed a solution. "Well, if you'll just answer my one question, I'll be glad to leave you to your duties."

Having no choice, the poor man did. And that's how listeners that night got to hear the views of a besieged British diplomat, with the sound of his own embassy being stoned in the background.

Sometimes you chase down eyewitnesses, only to discover that they have completely forgotten what they saw. We can miss the story of the night because the coup or guerilla hijacking happens twenty minutes after the program is put to bed. We're limited, as well, by the competence of people on the scene to describe a given day's events, and by their capacity to make the story meaningful. After the 1976 Italian earthquake, for example, with hundreds dead, thousands homeless, whole communities destroyed, and plague in the offing, I asked a British major who was there doing relief work to describe the tragedy and horror he saw around him.

"How does it look to you?" I asked, wanting to be subtle.

"Well, it's a broad plain that winds upwards into snowcapped mountains. One could say it's both plains and mountains."

Thanks, Major.

As hard as we try to report only what is true, there's no reporter who doesn't occasionally get caught by invented news. Once, a memo from our London office suggested that we might want to do a piece sometime on how Heathrow Airport protects itself against terrorists. By the time that idea had been relayed through three different staffers to a new and very keen story producer, it had become a hot tip: the IRA was about to attack Heathrow. Naively, the producer checked out the details by calling a colleague at the London *Daily Mirror.*

"We just learned that the IRA is about to launch a missile attack against Heathrow," he probed.

"Really," said the *Daily Mirror,* and promptly alerted Scotland Yard. Two days later, after we'd all forgotten the incident, our copy of the London *Times* arrived with this front-page story: tipped off by "sources" in Canada, the British Army took defensive action today at Heathrow. That was one credit we have never wanted to claim.

VISUAL MEDIA

Television was first introduced in North America in 1939 at the World's Fair in New York City, but it wasn't until 1952 that the CBC launched the first Canadian television network. Since then, hundreds of new channels have been introduced (see the sample television listings chart on page 339). Satellites have further enhanced television viewing — now we can view events around the world as they happen.

Films, or motion pictures, were the first form of visual entertainment. In the late 1800s short, silent films began to be shown as part of live stage shows. In 1927, the first talkie, a movie with sound, was released. Movie attendance during the 1930s and 1940s was extremely high, but it lessened with the introduction of the television in the 1950s. Today, television is the favourite form of entertainment, but movie makers continue to entice people to theatres with the promise of dazzling special effects and digital sound.

The word *video* is Latin for "I see" and is now a word we use every day. We rent videos to watch movies, we videotape television shows to see at a later time, and we watch music videos. The selections in this section cover two of the most important visual media today—film and television.

THE NEWS

by Ben Wicks

"That wraps up the good news. Now for
the rest of the news."

LIGHTS, CAMERA, FROSTBITE!

by Liz Crompton

A FROZEN LAKE SOMEWHERE IN THE YUKON.
A half-dozen people huddle together on a snow-covered tarn in the brutal chill of late November. At –45°C, any desire to move is killed by the cold; instead, they remain as motionless as possible inside their clothing cocoons. And although they tell themselves they should be indoors, they continue with the task at hand: shooting film.

Elaborate measures have been taken to keep the camera equipment operational. A generator powers a microwave, which in turn heats hot gel packs. The heated packs are then placed inside a beer cooler to warm the camera batteries it houses. A few cables run through a hole in the cooler, connecting the cozy batteries to the camera, which is entombed in an insulated cover. Several individual hand warmers are strapped onto the camera body at critical points to keep it running.

"I have a few tricks for dealing with the cold," says Robert Toohey, the Whitehorse-based production manager who concocted this elaborate assembly line for a commercial for winter boots. When making moving pictures in the often hostile climate of Canada's Northern reaches, tricks such as Toohey's often spell the difference between cinematic success and failure.

The list of obstacles is long. In the winter, filmmakers must deal with extreme cold, short daylight hours, and bone-chilling winds. Summertime comes with its own challenges, unrelenting swarms of bugs that have been known to drive people insane. "The logistics of working in the remoteness of the North need particular attention to detail," he notes. In other words, it ain't Hollywood.

In addition to devising imaginative ways to keep equipment running, individuals like Toohey face an equally daunting task: ensuring the safety and well-being of people unfamiliar with the North. He pays particular attention to the needs of camera crews, actors, and production staff who sometimes don't have a clue what shooting in the North entails. "I've had people arrive in city shoes ... and we had 25 centimetres of snow," Toohey says, adding that non-Northerners are often surprised at the enormous amount of survival gear he packs along for even the shortest shoots.

For all his care, though, Toohey must also be flexible enough to fulfill the oddest requests from his world-wide battery of clients. One of the more bizarre pictures he worked on was a Chinese science fiction B-movie, where only one or two members of the company spoke English. One evening Toohey learned that he had to locate and outfit a couple hundred extras for the next day's shooting, no small feat under the best of circumstances. The ingenious freelancer sought out marching bands, hockey teams, and even can-can dancers. The members of the Chinese company must have been satisfied: they came for five days and stayed for 24.

A RIVERBANK NEAR THE TOWN OF WRIGLEY ON A PERFECT SUMMER EVENING.

A pair of Yellowknife filmmakers set their gear on the banks of the Mackenzie River. Mountains rise across the river, glowing from the touch of the lingering sun. The filmmakers are looking for a powerful image for a video they are making: a scene that illustrates Aboriginal spirituality in this Northern land.

A local man known for his drumming skill stands silhouetted against the setting sun. He beats the skin drum with a wooden stick, the sound echoing through the evening air. He begins to sing. The filmmakers race around, filming their subject from every possible angle. They know it's more than they hoped for.

"He exuded an aura of mystical understanding about his experience in life, and I think that came across in the film. We used it as the showcase ending for the film," says Alan Booth, who founded Yellowknife Films when he couldn't find another job. That was 15 years ago. Since then, Booth has become well-versed in Northern filmmaking, working in places like Northern Canada, the former USSR, Norway, and Alaska. Over the years, the company has won a variety of national and international awards. One of its productions, *The Northern Lights*, became a bestseller in the United States for the National Film Board of Canada. The NFB co-produced the film, which examines the aurora borealis from the viewpoints of both Aboriginal legend and traditional science.

These days Booth opts for a safer and steadier line of business producing videos that are underwritten by a sponsor. Having a paying sponsor alleviates the substantial risk faced by independent Northern filmmakers. High-priced equipment, travel to remote communities, and the exorbitant cost of accommodation makes the North as expensive as it is romantic.

Booth knows not to look to the government for much assistance. In the world of over-inflated deficits, grants for the arts community are hard to come by when budgets for education and health are being cut drastically. Nonetheless, maintaining a cultural identity helps keep society strong.

"Cultural industries are the glue that bonds us together as a society. There's a certain sense of comfort when you can have a violin player at your wedding, there's a certain sense of wonderment when you can watch a great play. The same thing goes for a good movie that interprets what we are. It gives us a sense of belonging, a sense of understanding about who we are," Booth says. "Art is a very important part of our lives and it's highly underrated. Life would be very boring without art."

A FOGGY ISLAND NEAR THE EASTERN ARCTIC COMMUNITY OF IGLOOLIK.

Members of a film crew prepare for a walrus-hunting scene for a television series they're shooting. Children playing nearby suddenly raise the alarm: a polar bear is lumbering dangerously close to the set. Dogs bark furiously at the bear. Men throw rocks at it, but the bear refuses to leave. The anxiety is palpable, since a polar bear—probably the same one—has visited the set before. The cast and crew have been sleeping in their canvas tents with rifles as their bedfellows.

The bear's demeanour takes a turn for the worse, and it attacks the dogs. Sensing the impending danger, an Inuit elder shoots and kills the bear. One of the filmmakers captures the scene on camera. The bear has presented an unexpected opportunity for the filmmakers, since it is illegal to kill a polar bear at this time of year, unless the bear poses a danger. The crew immediately creates a scene that incorporates the footage of the polar bear's death to show how Inuit living on the land would deal with a similar situation.

"That was not in the script," says Zacharias Kunuk as he recalls the incident, which took place last year during the filming of the 13-part TV series, *Nunavut*.

Nunavut follows the lives of five Inuit families in Igloolik in the 1940s. It was made by Igloolik Isuma Productions Ltd., an independent Inuit-owned production company operated by Kunuk and his partners, Paul Quitalki and Norman Cohn.

Igloolik Isuma had its beginnings before the settlement had any television service, in 1981. That's when Kunuk went to Montreal and bought a video recorder, a VCR, and a colour television. "I didn't know what I was doing," he exclaims. For two years, until the town received television service, children would gather outside his windows to watch his TV.

And while Igloolik may be small and isolated, it's just fine for video makers specializing in dramatic re-creations of traditional Inuit lifestyles, even those trying to penetrate international markets. Indeed, *Nunavut* has stirred interest on a global scale. Cohn said that apart from being shown on television networks north and south of the 60th parallel, the company has sold the series to Turkish TV and was negotiating earlier this fall to bring it to European countries.

Igloolik Isuma has also developed somewhat of a cult following in the slick environs of New York City, reports Faye Ginsburg, the director of Culture, Media, and History in New York University's anthropology department. Ginsburg shows Isuma's work in one of her courses; not bad for a company that incorporated itself in 1991.

Isuma, which means "to have an idea" in Inuktitut, has altruistic goals as well. The company wants to reverse the trend of outsiders coming in to make films of local culture. To that end, it trains local residents and employs them for its productions. The company is even planning to hold professional development workshops in town. The idea is to keep as much creative control in the hands of the Inuit," Cohn says. "We're offering something very unusual."

AN OFFICE WHOSE WINDOWS LOOK OUT ONTO A TYPICAL NORTHERN SCENE ... SNOW AND ICE.

Northern filmmakers diligently ply their trade in spite of the harsh environmental and financial obstacles thrown in their path.

Would they have it any other way? In the words of Robert Toohey "I think it's a decent way to earn a living."

MY AMERICAN COUSIN

by Sandy Wilson

IT ALL BEGAN with "The Battle of New Orleans" in August 1959 when Johnny Horton's hit song topped the charts and my American cousin George "Butch" Warren Jr. drove up in a big fancy convertible. Whenever "The Battle of New Orleans" came on the radio, Butch would turn the radio up and my father would shout, "Turn that damn noise off!" I couldn't believe I was related to anyone so bold, so glamorous, so American!

Then his parents came to take him home because he was a runaway and I never saw him again. I forgot all about him more or less, until Mom wrote me that he'd been killed in a car accident a couple of days after his wedding. He hit a tree or something. But it was 1965 and I was all caught up in the '60s so his memory faded.

Until I heard "The Battle of New Orleans" on my ghetto blaster, first week of August 1982 with Phil Schmidt and our four-year-old son Willie. I started telling Phil about my American cousin and we both got very excited: "Let's make a movie!" we said. I wrote *My American Cousin* first in Hollywood Pink lipstick on the cabin window looking south down Okanagan Lake. It looked perfect. And then I began typing *My American Cousin* on a secondhand Empire Aristocrat typewriter. Starting with what I remembered—my family and Butch's arrival and departure.

FADE IN:

1. EXT. LONG SHOT RANCH HOUSE—LATE EVENING.
It is a hot summer night in 1959. The light has almost left the sky. We are looking down a long, flat-roofed wooden house, situated over the Okanagan lake and surrounded by green lawns, pine trees, and a few fruit trees.

In the distance we can hear a radio playing Slim Whitman's "Suddenly There's a Valley." A screen door slams, the sprinklers and crickets round out the summer sound.

The lights inside the house look bright and welcoming.

2. INT. RANCH HOUSE OFFICE—LATE EVENING.
Queen's speech continues on the radio. Major John Wilcox, a handsome man in his late forties, sits behind a bare officious-looking desk adding numbers on an old adding machine. The Major pauses to pick up a letter and look at it in a worried way.

Kitty enters from the living room, book in hand; she is distracted by a light on down the hall and with an impatient sigh she says:

KITTY: You children are all supposed to be sleeping. Now stop playing and Sandra, turn off your light.

The Major quickly hides the letter.

CUT TO:

3. INT. SANDY'S BEDROOM—LATE EVENING.
Sandy, a plain 12-year-old, in rollers and pink baby doll pajamas, is sitting up in bed, writing in her diary. She has written "Nothing Ever Happens." Her room is littered with clothes, toys, photos of Elvis going off to the Army, Marilyn Monroe, James Dean, and Tab Hunter.

SANDY: Aw, Mom I'm still writing.

Kitty appears in the doorway.

KITTY: Lights off. Now.

Sandy looks very annoyed, sighs, and puts her diary away and turns off the light.

4. EXT. RANCH HOUSE—NIGHT. (SAME AS 1).
The ranch house is in the distance. We see the lights go off. Distant coyote cries fill the silent summer night.

5. INT. SANDY'S BEDROOM—NIGHT.

Sounds of Sandy fumbling around in the dark. Sandy finally fishes out a flashlight from underneath her mattress and shines it on a small Phillips radio next to her bed. She turns the dial until she gets an American station.

DJ's VOICE: And now KRKO, in Spokane, Washington, the heart of the great American Northwest, is pleased to spin that old, country classic, "Young Love, First Love." So pucker up, all you back-seat Romeos, here we go.

Sandy sets up the flashlight under the sheet, fishes in her bed until she gets a "True Confessions" magazine out and sits up to do some reading. She pauses to look out the window.

SANDY's VOICE: I'd always known we had American cousins. They sent us the biggest and the best Christmas cards of all our Canadian or English cousins.

6. EXT. RANCH ROAD—NIGHT.

A Cadillac is driving past lush green orchards. Sound of car radio in the distance, playing "Young Love, First Love." There is a metallic sound. The Cadillac loses its muffler. The Cadillac stops.

7. INT. SANDY'S BEDROOM—NIGHT. (SAME AS 2).

Now Sandy is reading her magazine. The song on the radio ends.

DJ's VOICE: Wasn't that romantic, kids? You bet it was. And now, to change the pace a little, the Number One hit from Coast to Coast again this week, Johnny Horton and you guessed it, "The Battle of New Orleans."

Song begins.

8. EXT. RANCH ROAD—NIGHT.

In the distance we see the Cadillac start up again. A car door slams and the Cadillac drives on down the road. The car makes a lot of noise now.

9. INT. SANDY'S BEDROOM—NIGHT.

"Battle of New Orleans" is still on and Sandy is reading. Suddenly there is the loud noise of the Cadillac driving up outside and squealing to a stop. Car radio is playing "The Battle of New Orleans" loudly. Sandy jumps in her bed and freezes for a moment.

SANDY'S VOICE: I first saw my American cousin in the summer of 1959.

Sandy quickly throws her magazine into the bed, switches off the radio, and tucks the flashlight under the mattress.

There is a loud knock on the screen door. Sandy goes to her bedroom door and opens it slightly. A light goes on down the hall.

MAJOR'S VOICE: I'm coming. I'M COMING.

10. EXT. RANCH HOUSE FRONT PORCH—NIGHT.

A front porch light goes on, car headlights shine on the front porch steps, a light at the corner of the house goes on. The Major, tying up a tartan gown, stands in the porch light.

MAJOR: What is it man, speak up.

BUTCH: Ah Sir, Uncle John, I'm Butch Walker.

The Major relaxes a little and studies Butch.

MAJOR: Of course, Al's boy. Must be about 17. What a surprise.

The Major and Butch shake hands.

MAJOR: Are Al and Dolly with you?

BUTCH: No Sir. I'm here alone. On a vacation.

MAJOR: I see. Alone. Well, you're family so you're welcome here son. Now please turn that damn radio and those lights off. You'll wake up the whole house.

Butch runs off to his car. Kitty steps into the light, tying up her dressing gown. She yawns.

MAJOR: It's Al and Dolly's boy Butch. Alone, on vacation. Were you expecting him?

KITTY: No one has written to me about it. But then there's a lot of things no one bothers to tell me. Now if we had a telephone ...

The radio and lights go off.

MAJOR: Kitty we simply can't afford it.

Butch reappears.

BUTCH: Hello Aunt Kitty, sorry to get you up like this.

KITTY: Hello Butch. Does your mother know you're here?

BUTCH: Oh yes, I'm surprised she didn't write you a letter. But then she's been busy.

KITTY: Must be in the mail. I'll make you a bed in the spare room.

Kitty goes into the house.

KITTY'S VOICE: Maybe you can help pick cherries.

BUTCH: Glad to help out.

MAJOR: You're not in trouble with the police?

BUTCH: Oh no, Sir.

MAJOR: You could tell me if you were.

BUTCH: No, Sir, I'm not.

MAJOR: Good.

The Major guides Butch inside the house.

MAJOR: Haven't got a girl in trouble have you?

The Major and Butch disappear. Sound of door closing and the lights go off. The Major stops Kitty in the hallway.

MAJOR: Kitty, please, you go back to bed. I'll handle this.

Sleepily, Kitty shrugs, turns to go back to her room, pauses, turns to the Major.

KITTY: Perhaps Al could help us. They've got lots of money.

MAJOR: Absolutely not.

Sound of car radio stops. Screen door slams. Kitty shrugs and goes off to bed. The Major disappears into the doorway opposite the bedroom. Sandy, Eddie, and Danny reappear.

KITTY'S VOICE: Maybe he can help pick cherries.

MAJOR'S VOICE: Quietly, man. You'll wake up the whole house.

11. INT. SANDY'S BEDROOM—NIGHT.
Sandy runs from the window to her bedroom door and peeks out.

12. INT. RANCH HALLWAY—NIGHT.
There are three doors on one side of the hallway, two on the right. Sandy's middle bedroom opens and she peeks out.

Another door opens and out peeks Danny—14 and wearing pj bottoms. A third door opens and Eddie—12 and wearing pj bottoms—stumbles out.

MAJOR'S VOICE: Come this way son.

The three kids scoot back into their rooms. The Major walks by. Butch follows the Major. Butch looks terrific. As soon as the Major has walked by, the kids come out again. The Major turns, the kids disappear, the Major goes into the spare room, the kids come out again, Butch turns and grins at them. Sandy, Eddie, and Danny stop dead in their tracks.

MAJOR'S VOICE: If the girls wake you up too early, you might be better in your car but you can sleep here for tonight.

The kids scramble out of the way, the Major crosses the hallway, lights go out.

JOHNNY'S VOICE: Sandy?

SANDY'S VOICE: Ya?

JOHNNY'S VOICE: Who is it?

SANDY'S VOICE: Our American cousin Butch.

JOHNNY'S VOICE: Wonder how long he'll stay.

SANDY'S VOICE: Forever I hope.

13. EXT. RANCH DRIVEWAY—DAY.

Butch is standing next to an enormous gleaming red '57 Cadillac El Dorado Biarritz with Pixie—a six-year-old girl with an enormous doll—and Ruth, an eight-year-old girl with blonde hair. Sandy is posing the girls and Butch in front of the car and taking photos.

PIXIE: Are you really from California?

BUTCH: That's right. Drove up yesterday.

Danny comes out pushing Johnny in a wheelchair. Johnny is about 16 and handicapped.

EDDIE: Wow. What kind of a car is that?

DANNY: Cadillac, El Dorado Biarritz. I saw a picture in a magazine.

JOHNNY: Can you take a picture of us too?

SANDY: Sure.

The boys pose with Butch for photos. The Major comes along, dressed in khakis and carrying a clipboard.

MAJOR: Well, Butch. This is a pretty big car, son.

BUTCH: My mom gave it to me.

SANDY: Dad, can you take a photo of me and Butch?

The Major smiles and puts down his clipboard. Sandy gives him the camera and runs next to Butch.

SANDY: Alright you guys, get lost.

EDDIE: Why?

SANDY: Because if you don't I'll kiss you dipstick. Now go jump in the lake.

Danny wheels Johnny away. Eddie reluctantly stands back while Sandy and Butch pose in front of the Caddy. Kitty comes outside wearing an apron and carrying a wooden spoon.

KITTY: Ah, here you all are. Such an extravagant car for one so young. It's so American.

MAJOR: Now Kitty, I know they're Americans, but still, he's from a decent family.

The Major snaps the photo.

BUTCH: Can I take a picture of you all together to send back home?

The Major and Kitty share a smile. Kitty takes off her apron, Danny pushes Johnny next to the car. Eddie, Pixie, Ruth, and Sandy all pose for Butch. The Major talks quietly to Kitty.

MAJOR: Kitty, Jim Van Weston is coming out today to examine the frost damage done last January.

KITTY: Is he here for lunch?

MAJOR: Yes and tea.

Butch snaps the photo and the family relaxes.

MAJOR: Come along Danny and Eddie. Butch, it's time to get up to the orchards.

KITTY: Alright Sandra, we have cherries to can this morning.

SANDY: Can't I stay outside a little longer?

KITTY: No dear. I need you in the kitchen, let's go.

Everyone leaves and the Cadillac is left alone, gleaming in the morning sunshine.

14. INT. RANCH KITCHEN—DAY.

The large kitchen table is covered with Mason jars, Mason lids, bags of sugar, and boxes of cherries. Huge vats of boiling water are steaming on the stove. Kitty is using metal forceps to lift the jars into the boiling water. Pixie and Ruth are putting fistfuls of cherries into the jars on the table. Sandy, wearing an apron, is measuring sugar and adding the sugar to the jars. Sandy catches something out of the corner of her eye. She goes to the window and looks out.

15. INT. RANCH HOUSE KITCHEN—DAY.

Still gazing out the window, Sandy asks her mother:

SANDY: Mom, how old were you when you started going out on dates?

Kitty pauses mid-movement to let her mind wander. She smiles to herself.

KITTY: Not until I went away to McGill. I went out with a boy from Trinidad. He was in my Contemporary Literature class. I wonder if ...

Sandy turns around to look at her mother and grimace.

SANDY: You never went out till they shipped you off to university?

KITTY: I was not shipped off. Back to work.

Both Kitty and Sandy resume their duties. Sandy pauses.

SANDY: If you weren't allowed to go out on DATES, what did you DO?

KITTY: Well, your Aunt Lid and I were always putting on plays and ...

SANDY: (*Disgusted*) Ew yuk. That is so dumb.

Kitty turns from the boiling vat of water to face Sandy, forceps in hand.

KITTY: (*Slowly*) Sandra. You really are the most unpleasant child I could ever imagine.

SANDY: (*Staring at her mother*) I am not a child.

As if on cue, Pixie and Ruth stand back together, holding hands. Kitty walks closer to Sandy, forceps raised. Sandy puts down the measuring cup filled with sugar and stands facing her mother with her hands on her hips. They glare at each other.

KITTY: Believe me, you most certainly are. You are the most selfish, self-centred ...

Kitty points the forceps accusingly at Sandy, coming closer and closer. Sandy quickly throws up her arms, spins around, and moves quickly to the other side of the table. She rests her hands on the table and leans toward her mother.

SANDY: I know. I know. Let me see, "selfish, self-centred, sloppy, silly," oh yes, and "cheap" and let's not forget the old favourite, "inconsiderate" ... Let me see, did I forget any?

Sandy pretends to consider, picks up a handful of cherries, and pops one in her mouth. Kitty glares at her. Now her hands are on her hips and she is shaking her head.

KITTY: (*Slowly*) That is IT. That is really IT. If you can't say anything nice ...

Sandy puts her hands on her hips. They are facing each other over the table.

The timer rings and continues to ring.

SANDY/KITTY: (*In unison*) ... DON'T SAY ANYTHING AT ALL.

Immediately Kitty spins around to grab the timer and turn it off. Sandy shakes her fistful of cherries at her mother's back and turns to go outside.

KITTY: (*Keeping her back to Sandy*) Get out. Get out. Before I ...

SANDY: I'M GONE!

Sandy slams the screen door. Kitty slams the kitchen timer down on the counter and its alarm goes off again.

CUT TO:

16. EXT. KITCHEN PORCH—DAY.
Sound of alarm ringing. Sandy throws her fistful of cherries at the kitchen door and screams out.

SANDY: I wish I lived anywhere else but here! This place is a PRISON. Some day I'll just run away. Then you'll be sorry.

KITTY'S VOICE: (*offstage*) Go right ahead.

CUT TO:

17. INT. CAB OF THE TRUCK—DAY.
Sandy is hanging around her father who is filling up cherry boxes and making notes on his clipboard.

MAJOR: Your mother grew up in a quiet house. She always thought she would be a librarian. So you must understand that she's not, well, she's ... it's just that you children are a bit much for her sometimes.

The Major walks away. Sandy throws her arms in the air.

SANDY: I'm not a child.

The Major returns to look at Sandy.

MAJOR: Oh yes you are.

Sandy looks disbelieving and shakes her head.

MAJOR: Exactly how old are you anyway? I lose track of you all.

SANDY: Oh Dad, really. I'll be 13 in three months. I'm practically a teenager.

MAJOR: (*Surprised*) Really? A teenager. Oh dear.

The Major looks at his clipboard. He looks up at Sandy.

MAJOR: Perhaps you should come with me today, I think we'd better have a talk.

The Major walks to the driver's side of the truck. Happily Sandy heads for the truck.

SANDY: Okay Dad, I wasn't doing anything anyway.

SOME HOW-TO'S OF MAKING VIDEOS,

OR HOW DO I GET FROM FILMING *HOW TO FIX A FLAT TIRE* TO *HOME ALONE?*

by Todd Mercer

Do your home movies turn out looking like comedy horror flicks? Have you ever wondered how to improve your video storytelling skills?

I did, and decided to talk with an expert. My research took me to the Media Arts Department of Sheridan College in Oakville, Ont. There I met Didier Kennel, a teacher of ENG—electronic news gathering. In Didier's course students learn the basics of camera movement, among other video-making techniques.

What advice did Didier give to a budding Spielberg like myself? Start small. Real small! In fact, one of his students' first assignments is to create a 5- to 10-minute how-to video. Some of the class's recent blockbusters include, *How to Make Jello, How to Give a Massage, How to Blow Glass*, and the unforgettable epic— *How to Fix a Flat Tire.*

What can you learn about video storytelling by making low-budget productions? Stay tuned. Lights ... camera ... action ... read on ...!

WHAT THE CRITICS ARE SAYING ABOUT
HOW TO CHANGE A FLAT TIRE ...
"... full of ups and downs ..."
Tex Reed, *Road and Tack Magazine*

"... A Triumph! ... er, maybe it was a Toyota ..."
  Janet Michelin, *Vanity Tire*

"... Riveting! ..."
  Ms. Goodyear, *Better Homes and Hubcaps*

"... Uplifting ..."
  M. R. Goodyear, *Rolling Rubber Magazine*

"At last ... a film that won't leave you flat! ..."
  Fredia Firestone *Snap, Crackle, Popular Mechanics*

TODD MERCER: **Tell me about the "how-to" video assignment.**
DIDIER KENNEL: Basically students take a normal event, such as changing a tire, and make a video about it. They have to assume they are presenting information to somebody who knows absolutely nothing about how to change a tire, make macaroni, clean a fish tank, or any number of little things.

TM: **Why do you have the students start on such a small-scale production?**
DK: With the "how-to's," they learn the basics of video-making: where the camera will be, where the actors will be, and how they'll put everything together. It's really storytelling at its most basic.

  I stress simplicity. I don't want them doing something they can't handle by trying marvellous tricks. We're not looking for *Star Wars*. If students do that, it takes away from the meaning of the video. Still, with the "how-to's," the students follow the same basic process as professionals do.

TM: **What is that process?**
DK: There are three major stages. The first stage is *pre-production*, where students plan their videos on paper. Pre-production involves all the planning until the day they take out the camera. Once they handle the equipment, they're in the *production* stage. *Post-production*, the final

stage, involves pulling all the shots together and making sense of the video footage.

TM: **What planning takes place?**

DK: It's important for the students to visualize and write down what they want to capture on tape. When they enter the program, some of them think they'll just take out the camera and shoot. But that's very wasteful. Pre-production should be the most time-consuming stage of the process.

One of the first things to do is make a *storyboard*, which breaks the story down into *scenes* (like a comic strip), and includes a script or written description for each scene. The storyboard is usually drawn, either by hand or by using a computer graphics program if one is available. You don't have to be an accomplished artist. Stick figures can often be sufficient. You can also use clips of pictures from magazines or photographs. For my own "how-to" video, for example, I did the storyboard by pasting photographs on index cards (one per card), with descriptions of the scenes on the backs of the cards.

The important point is to show and write down your ideas and what you visualize for the video. Professionals working on larger projects will go through much more detailed planning. The makers of music videos, for example, provide what are called *treatments* (see music video section) when they are pitching their projects to a band or a record company. They do this *before* storyboarding. Before production of a music video begins, the director must also do a song breakdown and work out a detailed *shot list* (see page 315 for a definition of the term).

Music Videos: Treatments and Song Breakdowns

A *treatment* is usually a three- to five-page written proposal in which a music-video director describes the setting, action, and "look and feel" of the song that he or she wants to film.

Once the director's proposal is accepted, a *song breakdown* is required. This is a detailed outline of a song in terms of *what exactly* is happening (vocals, instrumental solos, musical effects) and *when exactly* (to the second) they are happening. CD and audiotape machines have time codes, which track every second in a song.

PRODUCTION

TM: What advice do you give students in the production stage of the process?

DK: They should be trying to get across the message, so everything must be clear and precise. For example, with the *How to Fix a Flat Tire* video, when the actor removes the nuts off the wheel, the camera *angle* has to show the viewer what's happening.

I always recommend a *tripod* when shooting "how-to's." Never hand-hold your camera because you get too much movement. With a tripod you can *zoom* in to a point of interest, such as fitting the wrench on the first nut. You can *pan* to a point of interest, such as the actor walking with the jack from the trunk to the wheel. Or the student might want to add *tilt*, to show where the actor is positioned in relation to the wheel.

POST-PRODUCTION

TM: What happens in post-production?

DK: Unless students have equipment that allows them to shift the video and audio around, post-production is extremely difficult. It's probably the most difficult part of production at an amateur level.

I always stress there's an invisible link between pre-production and post-production. Unless they've gone through those planning stages carefully, they'll face unnecessary problems in post-production.

Post-production starts with viewing of the footage. First, you screen the footage to choose the good shots, and decide which shots have the best audio quality.

TM: How do you keep track of all the footage?

DK: With a *log sheet*, where you record the *time code*. The time code is the number assigned to each *frame* of video. Video runs in 30 frames

A Glossary of Terms

Angle: The angle from which the camera is directed at the subject, usually at eye level. If the camera looks down on the subject, this is called a *high-angle shot*. If the camera looks up, it is called a *low-angle shot*.

Close up (CU): A camera shot in which a part of a subject (e.g., a face) is the focus. An *extreme close up* (ECU) focuses even more closely on the subject (e.g., eyes in a face). On television, close ups are frequently used because of the focus on individuals. Extreme close ups are often used in horror movies.

Cut: Quick change from one shot or scene to another.

Editing Log Sheet: A record of important information about footage such as the time code and comments about the quality of the shots.

Frame: A single film image as it appears on a screen or through a viewfinder.

Long, or wide, shot (LS): A camera shot in which the whole subject and much or most of the surroundings are shown. In movies and on television, long shots are often used at the beginning of scenes and are called "establishing shots."

Medium shot (MS): A camera shot in which only part of the subject and some of the surroundings are shown. This provides a balance between the subject and the surroundings. This is the most common shot.

Pan: A camera shot in which the camera is rotated horizontally on a tripod from left to right or vice versa.

Point of view (POV): A camera shot that shows a scene as a character in the action would see it.

Scene: A unified action that may consist of a single shot, but usually is a group of shots.

Shot: A single piece of film from the time the camera starts running to the time it stops running.

Shot list: A list of camera shots that is especially critical in planning the many shots used to film the fast-paced action of most music videos.

Storyboard: A script that contains illustrations of the main visual elements.

Tilt: A camera shot in which the camera is moved up and down.

Time Code: Identifies each frame in terms of hour, minute, second, frame.

Tracking shot: A shot in which the camera moves in the same direction and at the same speed as the subject.

Tripod: A stand with three legs used to support a camera.

Zoom: A camera shot in which the camera's field of focus quickly changes. In a *zoom in*, the subject quickly fills more of the frame. In a *zoom out*, the subject quickly fills less of the frame. In a zoom shot, unlike a tracking shot, the camera itself does not move.

per second. Each frame has numbers, which indicate hour, minute, second, and frame.

If you have these time code numbers, you know exactly where your *shot* is, and you don't have to spend hours looking for it. On a large, professional production, you might have 30 or more tapes, so it's important to know where each shot is.

Even if you don't have time codes, you can still record the order of the shots. For example, in the changing-a-tire video, your first shot might be a *long shot* removing a nut. You could enter "#1 l.s. removing the nut" on the log sheet. Even if you don't have the time code, at least you have a list showing the order of the shots. The log is like a database of all your shots.

TM: **What editing can be done on home equipment?**
DK: In high school, I was asked to do a video for my school. All I had was a camera and a VCR. I shot all my film with the camera. Then I hooked up the camera to the VCR. As the shot I wanted appeared, I would put it into the VCR by pushing PAUSE. Of course this is not how editing is done in a real studio, but it allowed me to make some editing decisions.

With most video cameras, you can make a direct hook-up with the VCR. That's probably the best way for an amateur to learn some very simple post-production editing techniques. But the best way to edit is using an *editing board.*

THE MAKING OF A CAR COMMERCIAL

THE SAMPLE BELOW IS from the storyboard for a car advertisement. It mentions a few of the camera shots that are listed and explained on page 315. What other kinds of shots do you recognize? What other kinds of shots would you add?

Trans Am Promotional

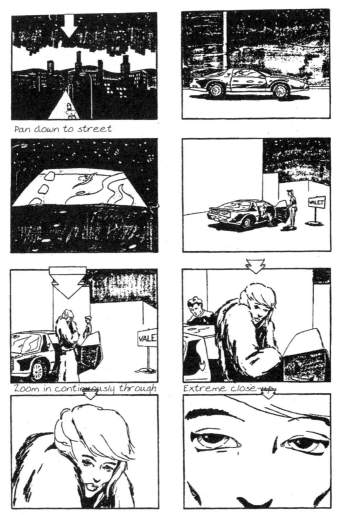

Pan down to street

Zoom in continuously through

Extreme close-up

ADVERTISING AND DESIGN

Each day, most of us purchase at least one item, whether it is something small (like a pack of gum) or something large (like a new jacket). Often, our purchases are influenced by advertisements and package and product design.

The term *advertising* used to refer to advertisements in magazines and newspapers or on television or radio. Today, you'll find advertisements on T-shirts, on billboards, on the sides of buildings, on (and in) forms of public transportation, on posters, on the Internet, at the theatre — even on fresh fruit that you buy at the supermarket. Look at page 333 to see an example of an innovative food advertisement and page 336 for an example of a movie poster.

Another popular form of advertising is the brochure. These sales tools usually include some detailed information about the product or service they are promoting, as well as pictures that support the text. Look at pages 334–335. What do the producers of the brochure want you to do after you have read their material?

How a package or product is designed will also influence our buying decisions. When a design captures our eye, we are more likely to pause and consider the suggested product. The result—a higher chance that we will buy it. Look at the book covers on page 340. Each cover is designed to appeal to a different audience. Can you list the features that would make younger children buy one version of the book and older children the second version?

The next time you are about to buy a product think about your purchase. Do you need the product or do you want it because you are being influenced by advertising and the product's appearance?

HIGH SCHOOL RULES
by Doug Stewart

THE FIRST STEP in gaining a solid understanding of teenagers is to grasp the significant role that high schools play within youth culture.

High schools and their environment are "mini-cities" where teenagers are citizens, complete with their own language and value system. Including their home, there is no location where teens spend more time than in school. Teenagers are at school for 10 months of the year, five days a week, for a minimum of seven hours a day. Almost 50 per cent of a teen's waking hours are spent inside their school.

Due to the sheer size and overwhelming concentration of the teen population within the high school environment, high schools are natural youth culture centres. They are the gathering places where teens communicate, evaluate, and determine the traits and values of their culture.

Beginning in April 1997, *Watch Magazine*'s circulation department surveyed each of Canada's 546 boards of education in order to gain a clearer picture of Canada's high school composition. In Canada, there are 1662 English-language high schools that have grades between 9 and 12. The population of these schools is a combined 1.4 million teenagers. Most importantly, the vast majority of these students (almost 90 per cent) fall on or between the ages of 14 and 18. (Traditionally, the "teen demographic" has been grouped within the 12 to 17 range. But this grouping skews too young to be accurate. Given the powerful role that the high school experience plays in shaping youth culture, it follows that the 14- to 18-year-old high school demographic is the engine of youth culture and correspondingly, the most valuable target group.)

More important, however, than understanding the demographic breakdown of high schools is understanding the teenage mindset or psychographic. Manifest in the expression of today's youth culture are common psychographic traits such as language, value system, and shared experiences that determine this group classification. Our research indicates that within the 14 to 18 age group exist five key shared experiences:

- The common schedule of the high school curriculum;
- The physical transformation from adolescence to adulthood;
- The impulse to create a strong identity separate from the family;
- The desire to bond with those sharing similar attitudes and preferences;
- The need to learn and the willingness to try new things.

Note that the underlying theme of these common experiences is change and exploration. That teens "explore" is found in the myriad of tribes that youth culture has spawned (ravers, trip-hoppers, Hip-Hop-headz, goths, jock rockers, etc.). This tribal diversity is united by a core set of values: The Teen Value System.

Central to the teen experience, to the culture of the 14- to-18-year-olds, are three characteristics that comprise the Teen Value System: Integrity, Passion, and Attitude. Understanding this system is fundamental to successfully communicating with teenagers. Why? Because it is how teens measure and perceive value.

Integrity: With so much change and so many options to explore while creating an individual identity, teenagers value an adherence to core principles. Integrity embodies "staying true" and "keeping it real" in the face of change. (Clothing companies such as Helly Hansen and Ecko Unltd. maintain integrity by incorporating specific elements of youth culture, namely the core Hip-Hop style and those that embody it, into their creative messages.)

Passion: Passion is the energy and dedication, the enthusiasm, behind loving what you do and who you are—in spite of the risks. Teens embody passion, they're fervent about their likes and dislikes and they let it show. The snowboard industry, for instance, was built on passion. (Industry leader Burton Snowboards's message is simple: "We love what we're doing.")

Attitude: To maintain energy and dedication requires attitude. Teens value attitude as a defence mechanism against the rigours of the teen world, as well as the outside world. They understand that attitude, right or wrong, "gets you through." (Rap/hip-hop artists are notorious for deriving success from their "I can't lose," challenge-the-establishment attitude.)

Communicating with teenagers requires an understanding of the role of high schools as immensely valuable cultural centres, as well as an understanding of the 14 to 18 high school/teenage demographic reality.

To be effective, marketers must also understand the psychographic of 14- to 18-year-olds, their common experiences and common values. Understanding youth culture is central to creating successful youth marketing programs.

EINBINDER FLYPAPER

by Bob Elliott and Ray Goulding

RAY: Now ... an important message from the makers of Einbinder Flypaper. Friends—despite our rigid quality control system at the Einbinder factory, several thousand rolls of flypaper have been released to the public with stickum that could become defective under certain conditions.

BOB: If you've bought flypaper recently that bears the manufacturer's code number 3-8-2-9-3 ... or 3-8-2-9-4 ... return it to the plant for new stickum at once. And while you're waiting for it to be returned to you— better protect your family by going out and buying some new flypaper.

RAY: When you do, be sure you insist on genuine Einbinder ... the brand you've gradually grown to trust over the course of three generations.

BOB: By the way, there's still time to order Einbinder's beautiful lapel pin. It's a lifelike replica of a giant horsefly ... a pin that makes an ideal accessory for either ladies or gentlemen ... with all eight of its legs painted in gleaming black enamel.

RAY: The wings are a lovely transparent mother-of-pearl and there's a simulated emerald set right in the insect's hind quarters that's sure to gain compliments from all your friends.

BOB: You'll want to have one of these gorgeous pins for yourself and several more to give as gifts for almost any occasion. So stock up on Einbinder Flypaper now ... and send in your proof-of-purchase tickets.

RAY: But be sure you insist on genuine Einbinder ... the flypaper you've gradually grown to trust over the course of three generations!

A PRODUCT ADVERTISEMENT

An advertisement can be effective in both black and white and full colour. Can you think of an ad in black and white that appeals to you? What about a full-colour ad that has recently caught your attention? The advertisement below is meant to be in full colour, and you can see it on page 333 as it was intended to be viewed. Compare the two versions. Which do you think is more effective? Why?

EVALUATING A WEB SITE

THE INTERNET OFFERS a vast array of Web sites and services. You can find sites set up to entertain, increasing numbers of them pitching products, and lots filled with information and ideas you can quickly access for your classroom work. Many Web sites are of high quality, but be particularly careful when you log on to a site looking for information for a school project. You'll be requiring material—people's names, dates, statistics, titles of resources, and so on—that is reliable and accurate. Don't just accept at face value what you see and read on the site, no matter how impressive it looks. Take the time to access what the site offers. Here are some key questions to help you do so.

Authority

- Is it clear who is sponsoring the page?
- Is the author and his/her qualifications for writing on the topic clearly stated?
- Is there a way of verifying the legitimacy of the page's sponsor (e.g., address, phone number), in addition to an e-mail address?

Accuracy

- Are sources for any factual information clearly listed so they can be verified?
- Are there many grammatical, spelling, or other errors?
- Is it clear who has the responsibility for the accuracy of the content of the material?

Objectivity

- Is the information provided as a public service?
- Is the information free of advertising?
- If there are ads, are they clearly differentiated from the informational content?

Currency

- Are there dates on the page to indicate:
  When the page was written?
  When the page was first placed on the Web?
- Other indications that the site is kept current?
- Is it clear when the date of any graphs/charts were gathered?

Coverage

- Is it clear if the page is/is not under construction?
- If there is a print equivalent, is it clear whether or not the entire item is on the Web page?
- If the material is from a work which is out of copyright, have efforts been made to update the material to make it more current?

CYBERSPACE STUDIOS

by Mark Haverstock

PICTURE THIS: You're watching the 6 o'clock news. Standing in a baseball park, a reporter rattles off the latest scores. Suddenly, he's standing beside a 4-metre-high athletic shoe, giving the latest scoop on track-and-field events.

The thing is, he hasn't left the television studio. It's all happening on a computer-generated virtual set.

Virtual sets are three-dimensional electronic environments constructed by superfast computers and sophisticated drawing software. Instead of sending a TV reporter to a basketball game, engineers can create a simulated court on the computer.

Actors and announcers stand in an empty room with a blue screen in the background while the virtual set appears on a separate monitor. The computer merges the two images together so you think the people on television are on an actual set.

Announcers can interact with the objects created by the computer by watching their movements on the virtual set's monitor. The computer makes adjustments as the actor moves behind and in front of images such as couches, walls, and other "props." And the virtual set can resize itself as the camera zooms in or shoots from another angle.

Television studio executives like virtual sets because wood, paint, or other building materials aren't needed. The sets are cheap to build and require very little time to make. They can occupy about the same space as a sofa in the real world but appear much bigger when you view it.

Virtual sets may also be useful in reporting late-breaking news. Reporters would look as though they were on the scene, even though they were still in the studio.

Think virtual sets are years in the future? During the 1996 college basketball playoffs, sportscasters used virtual sets to make them look as if they were right in the middle of the action.

INTERACTIVE WRITER'S HANDBOOK, Q & A

by Darryl Wimberley and Jon Samsel

Terry Borst has cowritten the interactive screenplays for *Wing Commander III* and *Wing Commander IV.* (*Wing Commander III* has been nominated by the Interactive Academy of Arts and Sciences for Best Writing and *Wing Commander IV* is the most expensive video game ever made.) His "traditional" screenwriting credits include the TV movie sequel to the DeNiro film *Midnight Run*, the independent feature film *Private War*, and an episode of the BBC action-adventure television series *Bugs*. In addition, he has performed uncredited rewrites on USA Cable movies and independent features, and developed screenplays for the producers of *The Hunt for Red October* and other independent producers in Hollywood. He is currently writing and designing a new interactive title and developing other projects in both the interactive and television arenas.

In the past, he has published both poetry and fiction, and is a member of the Writers Guild of America as well as being listed in the *Directory of American Poets and Writers.* His parchment includes a Master of Fine Arts from UCLA and a Bachelor of Arts from UC Berkeley.

INTERVIEW

What is your professional writing background?

TERRY BORST: Originally, I was a fiction and poetry writer. Professional in the loose sense of the word since generally, fiction and poetry don't really pay [LAUGHS]. I went on to film school and received a Masters degree at UCLA. Since getting out of school, it's been the usual screenwriter's route—working on a bunch of low-budget features initially—slowly working my way up the ladder.

Anything produced?

TB: One feature film called *Private War* which I cowrote. There were unaccredited re-writes on a few other USA cable-type of films as well. Right before the *Wing Commander* projects, my writing partner (Frank DePalma) and I wrote the screenplay for a television sequel to *Midnight Run* which Frank directed.

How did the *Wing Commander* assignment come about?

TB: As is often the case with assignments, it was being in the right place at the right time. A friend of ours who used to be a creative exec at Fox was working as a story editor/creative exec at Electronic Arts. She called us and said "Gee, there's this interactive project that's in need of a screenwriter. Why don't you send me a sample?" We send samples out all the time—if I had a nickel for every time I sent a sample out, I'd be a rich man and could retire ... [BOTH LAUGH] Little did we know at the time that the sample was for Chris Roberts, the designer of the *Wing Commander* franchise. He was looking for Hollywood screenwriters who could turn a completely computer-generated project into one that would incorporate a great deal of live action video. Chris Roberts liked our sample and BANG—we were hired.

How do you collaborate with another writer on an interactive project?

TB: It's no different than collaborating on any other project. Frank and I have been writing together for 10 years. We've been doing this sort of thing so long, we've got a system down. The way it doesn't work is the way people tend to think it should work—which is something out of *The Dick Van Dyke Show*. Unfortunately, it doesn't quite work out that way because it seemed like they had a lot more fun. Our methodology starts off with my partner and I in the room together. We're face to face. We try to structure the piece with index cards in order to work out each scene in advance. We see how the scenes fit together in terms of a traditional three-act structure.

Just like a feature assignment?

TB: Well, there are differences. With a feature screenplay, the number of scenes is 45–50 scenes for a two-hour movie. So that's 45–50 index cards. With interactive projects like *Wing Commander*, the number of scenes totalled 200–300 index cards. Instead of tacking the cards to a bulletin board, Frank and I had to put them on the floor. The great thing about index cards is that you can lay them on the floor and walk around the structure of your story. The cards can double as your flow chart. We have a couple of photographs of the two of us standing amid some pretty wild structures.

I'll bet.

TB: Flow charts are really a vehicle which allows us to discuss every scene in detail ... the beats of the scene, etc. By the end of this exercise we know our structure so well, we are able to go off separately. One of us can write Act I while the other person is writing Act II.

We modem stuff back and forth constantly to make changes to each other's work. The closing to our writing methodology is essentially putting all the pieces together. So you could say that our methodology has three acts as well ... the beginning is when we are together in the room, the middle is when we are off separately writing, and the end (when we have the luxury of doing so) is when we work together in the same room, dotting the i's and crossing the t's.

As a design team member, what is the writer's role in the pre-production design process?

TB: In the interactive arena, I'd say it's different from project to project. I think the biggest single factor is how close the project is to production. On *Wing Commander III* for instance, we were brought in extremely late in the process. They (Origin) had tried unsuccessfully to create a script in-house. The first day of shooting was set. Cameras were ready to roll. The gaming elements had been determined. The interface had been designed. But they still didn't have a screenplay.

How fast did you have to write this thing?

TB: We had a first draft completed in three weeks.

Yikes!

TB: That's two hundred fifty pages of material. It was insanity. We went to Austin, Texas, for three days and sat down and talked with the producer, director, and game designers about everything. From that point on, Frank and I were pretty much left to our own devices.

That was a risky venture on their part.

TB: True. But we would ship off bits and pieces as soon as we could to get feedback from the team. I think we synced up nicely under the circumstances. *Wing Commander IV* was different because we were on the project from the start. What that meant was that we were much more involved in aspects of game design. *Wing Commander* is in essence, a flight simulation. At the heart lies the missions that you fly. The design team had to come up with all new missions and our initial role as writers was to provide suggestions for the skeleton for each mission. We'd say things like "wouldn't it be great for the story if at this point we had to land on the planet surface after taking out a bunch of tanks ... maybe there's a ship landing as you're landing and you have to shoot that ship too. Things like that." Once the missions and overall story concept were agreed upon, we went off to write the treatment. After that was delivered and approved, we went off to Austin again for another three-day marathon session with the design team. So on *Wing Commander IV,* we worked much more closely with the game designers throughout the scripting process.

Did you get along with the design team members?

TB: Often times, we'd want to do things one way and the game designers would want to do things another. Frank and I do not claim to be expert game designers or puzzle-masters. We know story and we'll take no back seat to anybody in terms of story, character, narrative, and so on. Game designers know what has been done before and what will be an entertaining experience for the user. Both sides would constantly push the creative envelope. But Chris is the guy who had to make the final call. The buck stopped with Chris Roberts.

Were you able to improve upon your interactive screenplay from *Wing III* to *Wing IV*?
TB: Well, that was our goal. To provide a greater integration of character and gaming so that the experience is as rich as possible. We really wanted to integrate the story flow, the gaming flow—all of the elements.

How does the interactive writer integrate the gaming element into a screenplay?
TB: The term "gaming" has such a wide definition. I guess *Myst* is a game but there is no winning or losing. Winning and losing have always been associated with games. I guess the best way to integrate gaming into the screenplay is to first define the type of experience you're trying to provide the audience. Is it going to be a "transport simulation" experience like a flight simulation or driving simulation? Or is it a shoot-'em-up twitch game? Or is it an immersing exploratory experience like a *Myst* or *7th Guest?* Once you define the gaming genre, the trick is to develop something new and original. That's not easy to do. And that's probably why interactive projects rely on a creative team rather than on one individual.

Is the gaming element merely a diversion from the linear narrative?
TB: The interactivity should not be a diversion. This is an entirely different new medium we are working with and what it should not try to do is simply ape what previous mediums delivered. The experience of watching a live-action video, for example, on a computer screen is simply not going to compete with a 70-mm theatrical film. Why in the world should anyone sit down in front of their computer and involve themselves with this new experience? It's not because they will be enveloped in this rich, filmatic visual and sound experience. It is the interactivity. That's what is brand new. As a writer, the idea is to

explore where the interactivity can take the audience. The audience gains some control over the narrative, but not complete control. The boundaries of the world must still be created and defined by the writer/designer. What we end up with is a more collaborative experience between the audience and the writer/designer. That's exciting. My goal then as the writer is to get beyond the stop-start experience that interactivity is today. We are still trying to figure out how to do this.

How do you decide which player point of view to incorporate into your project?

TB: There are basically two models that I've seen used. First-person point of view is pretty cool but there is very little interaction possible. Your mouse or joystick has a limited amount of verbs at its disposal. I think it's six. Up, down, left, right, forward, backward. Or you're given some text choices, for example, of how to respond to somebody. The options boil down to yes, no, and maybe.

The alternative point of view has been the third person where you have an alter ego that's on-screen. By definition, that's a more distancing experience and less immersing. As an industry, we are struggling with these issues every day. Unfortunately, so often interactivity is simply a diversion. Ultimately, it should be the beating heart.

Where do you stand on interface design?

TB: One of the most exciting aspects of this new media is that there are a number of possible interfaces that can work for any given project. In film, there is basically one interface (unless you consider the option of filming in either black and white or colour). It doesn't matter if you are watching a French film or a film from Hong Kong. The grammar has been established. We understand a cut and how a montage works. In interactivity, everything is open for interpretation and manipulation. I think interface design comes down to your audience and the type of experience you want them to have. *Johnny Mnemonic*'s clean interface has its merits. A very busy interface can be a lot of fun, too. What you do want to have is an intuitive interface. Unfortunately, I still haven't met a truly intuitive software interface. Even though the Macintosh system interface is described as intuitive, it's not for someone who has never worked on a computer before. If I sat my mom down in front of a Mac, she'd still be doomed. I've seen enough people wave mouses in front of their computer screens hoping that something would work [LAUGHS].

As an interactive writer, how do you begin? Let's try an exercise. I'll tell you my story idea and you tell me how you might make it interactive: Jack and Jill went up a hill to fetch a pail of water. Jack fell down and broke his crown and Jill came tumbling after.

TB: I first need to identify three things. The audience, what you're aiming for, and what kind of genre that you're going for. There are a few questions I'd ask about my audience. Would I like to create an experience where my audience is in the world with Jack and Jill? Is this a world where Jack and Jill and the player grow as a result of their experiences together? Or are they solving a mystery of some kind? Is that more what this experience is about? Is this about the player showing Jack and Jill what he or she knows?

Next I'd try to flush out more of the story. What is it that the player is aiming for? After Jack fell down the hill, what did Jack do? Does he leave Jill and never see her again? Why were they at the top of the hill? Does our story actually start earlier? What is the goal of the experience? Once that's defined, I'd identify how the player interacts with this experience. Will the player become a character that interacts with Jack and Jill? Is the player Jack? Is the player Jill? Can the player become Jack or Jill? Is it possible that the player be Jack one time and Jill the next time? These would be my initial types of questions.

The next thing I'd do is identify the genre of the piece. Is it a twitch game? Is this a children's title? Is this an educational experience? What the experience is not going to be is as important as what it finally becomes.

But you know, the most important thing to consider before you start writing is what interests you.

FRONTIER COLLEGE

Keeping Canada Read Since 1899

Chapters

FRONTIER COLLEGE

Frontier College is a Canada-wide, volunteer-based literacy organization that teaches people to read and write. Frontier College volunteers reach people wherever they are and respond to their learning needs.

Frontier College was founded in 1899, by a group of Queen's University students concerned about the illiterate labourers working on Canada's frontiers. These first Frontier College volunteers worked side-by-side with logging crews, miners and railway workers and after work, taught them to read.

Canada's frontiers have changed. Today Frontier College literacy volunteers teach:

- *Adults in the community and in workplaces*
- *Homeless street kids*
- *Teens at risk of dropping out of school*
- *Prison inmates*
- *Children and families living in poverty*
- *People with disabilities*
- *Farmworkers and other labourers*
- *Newcomers to Canada*

Frontier College is active in every province and territory, and in both official languages. Literacy volunteers teach in factories, inner city buildings, on farms and on city streets.

Program participation is voluntary and all programs are free.

MILLIONS OF CANADIANS CAN'T READ THIS

The ability to read, especially in a country as prosperous as Canada, is a basic right often taken for granted.

Yet the words that you probably read easily – the directions on a bottle of medicine, newspapers, books, food labels – are too complex for millions of Canadians.

Two out of five Canadian adults are at risk of being functionally illiterate. One out of five Canadian adults can only read very simple material.

Illiteracy is not just someone else's problem. It affects everyone. People who cannot read face serious problems which affect us all.

- *They are more likely to be poor*
- *They are more likely to be unemployed*
- *They can't take part in workplace training*
- *They are often in poor health*
- *They can't help their children with schoolwork*
- *They can't fully participate as citizens*

CHAPTERS & FRONTIER COLLEGE: A PARTNERSHIP FOR CANADA'S FUTURE

*R*eading is a fundamental right of every Canadian. Together, Chapters and Frontier College are building a Canada-wide movement of literacy volunteers – a movement that is making a difference.

Frontier College recruits and trains Canadian university students as literacy volunteers, with tutor training workshops right on campus. Trained student volunteers serve as literacy tutors in their communities, through one-on-one tutoring, children's reading circles, homework clubs, and family programs.

Frontier College's key resource is people because one-on-one tutoring is the most effective method of teaching adults literacy skills. By supporting Frontier College as they mobilize and train university student volunteers across the country, we are helping extend literacy across Canada.

- In 1993 there were 1200 student literacy volunteers on 20 campuses. In 1998 with Chapters support there were 5000 volunteer tutors on 50 campuses
- Chapters gives Frontier College an annual corporate donation of $100,000
- In 1997 Chapters raised an additional $117,000 for Frontier College through in-store fundraising programs
- Chapters encourages their staff to volunteer as literacy tutors for Frontier College

*I*n 1998, Chapters received the Canadian Centre for Philanthropy's Imagine Award for their literacy partnership with Frontier College.

*F*rontier College literacy tutor training programs are in over 50 universities and colleges across Canada – from British Columbia to Newfoundland. For more information contact Frontier College at 1-800-555-6523.

As Canada's premier book retailer, Chapters is proud to support Frontier College. Through all of our locations, Chapters, Coles, SmithBooks, The Book Company, and the World's Biggest Bookstore, Chapters is helping Frontier College by supporting and encouraging literacy for all Canadians.

WHAT CAN WE DO TO SUPPORT LITERACY?

- Become a literacy volunteer with Frontier College.

- Make a charitable donation to Frontier College.

- Encourage your local politicians to make literacy a priority.

- Help organize literacy programs or children's reading circles in your community.

- Make reading an everyday part of your life.

Frontier College Frontière

HELPING CANADA READ

ENSEMBLE POUR MIEUX LIRE

Call 1-800-555-6523 for more information.

Please send your donation to:

Frontier College
35 Jackes Avenue
Toronto, Ontario
M4T 1E2

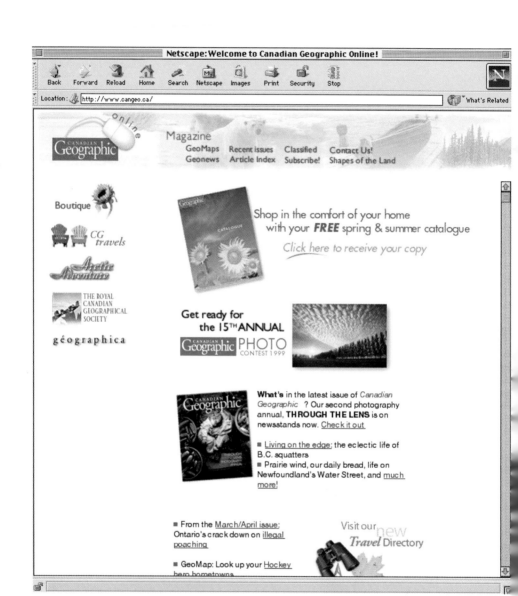

	6 p.m.	6:30	7 p.m.	7:30	8 p.m.	8:30	9 p.m.	9:30	10 p.m.	10:30	11 p.m.	11:30
(2)	News 909	NBC News (CC) 589	Entertainment Tonight (CC) 6386	Hollywood Squares 473	★★Wyatt Earp (biography, 1994) Kevin Costner. (Part 2) The portrait traces him from a boy to a lawman defending boomtowns with his brothers and Doc Holliday. 4893				Dateline NBC (CC) 3928		News 2079183	Tonight Show (TV14) 5213947
(3)	News (CC) 57763		NBA Basketball: Indiana Pacers at Toronto Raptors. (CC) (Live) 311096				Malcolm & Eddie (TVPG) 29980	First Wave: Foster investigates the disappearance of cars. (TVPG) (CC) 9134			News (CC) 2073909	Tonight Show 5200473
(4)	News (CC) 305	CBS News (CC) 657	Inside Edition (CC) 1454	Friends decision. (TVPG) (CC) 541	Cosby (CC) 5742	The King of Queens (TVPG) 6909	Raymond (TVPG) 7473	Becker (CC) 27522	L.A. Doctors (CC) 8096		News (CC) 2064251	Late Show (TVPG) 5208015
(5)	CBC News (CC) 3947	On the Road Again (CC) 4299	Royal Canadian Air Farce (CC) 7724	The Thin Blue Line (CC) 3183	This Hour Has 22 Minutes (CC) 6164	The Bette Show (CC) 5299	Life & Times (CC) 30034		CBC News (CC) 39893	Comics (CC) 48541	CBC News (CC) 96855	Children From Elsewhere (CC) 32812
(6)(41)	(5:30 p.m.) Global News (CC) 547164	First National News (CC) 5541	Entertainment Tonight (CC) 8386	The New Addams Family 1725	Cosby (CC) 7034	The Hughleys (TVPG) 6541	To Be Announced 96102	Two Guys, Girl & Pizza 74454	The Outer Limits (CC) 31763		Global News (CC) 96837	Sportsline (CC) 4306763
(7)	News (CC) 8015	ABC News (CC) 9367	Wheel of Fortune (CC) 5812	Jeopardy! (CC) 8251	20/20 (CC) 12638		Love Letters (romance, 1999) Steven Weber, Laura Linney. (CC) A man and a woman maintain a relationship through correspondence begun in childhood. 15725				News (CC) 4344725	(11:35 p.m.) Nightline (CC) 4377980
(9)(13)	News (CC) 66034		Wheel of Fortune (CC) 2744	Jeopardy! (CC) 5183	Melrose Place: McBride's Head Revisited. Peter and Eve buy the hospital. (CC) 45980		Ally McBeal: Renee's rambunctious date charges her with assault. (CC) (R) 65744		L.A. Doctors (CC) 68831		CTV News (CC) 42305	News (CC) 3098034
(11)	News (CC) 8265	Canada Tonight (CC) 1367	Love Connection (CC) 7812	Hollywood Squares (CC) 8021	Suddenly Susan 6560	The King of Queens (TVPG) 2367	Raymond (TVPG) 32928	Becker (CC) 63947	NightMan: Keyes to the Kingdom of Hell. 60299		News (CC) 14657	
(17)	Kratts' Creatures (CC)	The NewsHour With Jim Lehrer 462589		As Time Goes By 56015	Antiques Roadshow: Furniture. (Conclusion) (CC) 41744		The American Experience: America reacts to the Holocaust. (TVPG) (CC) 74675		Grape Escape Preview	Nightly Business Report	Charlie Rose 148657
(23)	Small Business 2000	Nightly Business Report	The NewsHour With Jim Lehrer: Top stories. (CC) 76454		The Visionaries (CC) 46164	Eyewitness (CC) 65299	Journey to Planet Earth: Mekong. (CC) 72638		Charlie Rose (CC) 75725		Off the Air	
(25)	Montreal ce soir (CC) 66812		Virginie: Rabaisser. (CC) 91638	La Petite Vie: Feter. (CC) 47305	4 et demi ...: Faites vos voeux! (Derniere) Francois dit adieu. (CC) 25744		Omerta, le dernier des hommes d'honneur: Vicky est en peril. (CC) 42580		Telejournal/le Point (CC) 15367		Nouvelles du sport 75251	De bouche a oreille 217386
(29)	Judge Judy (TVG) 89980	Judge Judy (TVG) 73960	Home Improvement 86305	The Simpsons (TVPG) 17304	Melrose Place: McBride's Head Revisited. Peter and Eve buy the hospital. (CC) 67744		Ally McBeal: Renee's rambunctious date charges her with assault. (CC) (R) 47980		Seinfeld (TVPG) 99676	Frasier (Part 1 of 2) (TVPG) 75096	Mad About You (TVPG) 24541	Star Trek: Next Gen. (TVPG) 955909
(47)	The Simpsons (TVPG) 770831	Frasier (Part 1 of 2) (TVPG) 761183	Lois & Clark: The New Adventures of Superman (Conclusion) (TVPG) (CC) 676676		Studio Aperto: (Italian) (CC) 870396	Melrose Place: McBride's Head Revisited. (Italian) (TVPG) 620693	Chinese Newsline: (Cantonese) 665560		Jerry Springer (CC) 679947		Married ... Children (TVPG) 6627251	(11:35 p.m.) Late Show (CC) 5415305
(49)	The Nanny (TVPG) 275522	Roseanne: A bet. (CC) 299102	Roseanne (CC) 565657	M*A*S*H: Spies gather data. 295386	7th Heaven: Nobody Knows ... Mary gets her driver's license. (TVG) (CC) (R) 660676		Rescue 77: Tunnel Vision. (CC) 640812		Jenny Jones (CC) 650299		All in the Family 910183	All in the Family (Part 1 of 3) 791270
(57)	News (CC) 238251		Seinfeld (TVPG) 756947	Friends (TVPG) 479386	V.I.P. (TVPG) (CC) 364015		Armistead Maupin's More Tales of the City: Cruisers. (TVMA) (CC) 344251		Armistead Maupin's More Tales of the City: Meetings. (TVMA) (CC) 354638		News (CC) 3073560	(11:35 p.m.) FashionTV (CC) 5162909
(A&E)	Simon & Simon: The Dead Letter File. Guest Kenneth Mars. (TVPG) 495763		Law & Order: Someone tries to assassinate a forensics expert. (TVPG) (CC) 572251		Biography: Three generations of the Heinz family help to build an international business giant. (TVG) 598299		Investigative Reports: A mobile killing unit uses crude methods to exterminate Jews. (CC) 501763		Poirot: The Plymouth Express. A wealthy man's daughter brings jewels on a train journey. (TVG) (CC) 571522		Law & Order: Murder suspect's attorney blames the victim. (TVPG) (CC) 36136?	
(BET)	(4:30 p.m.) Rap City	227	Planet Groove		Hit List		Sparks (CC)	Good News (CC)	Comicview		Tonight With Tavis Smiley	
(BRV)	Montreal Jazz Festival: Madeleine Peyroux. (CC) 263947		Bravo!Video 741015	Foot Notes (CC) 464454	Flamenco at 5:15	Ballet for Life: Costumes by Versace. 632454	★★Foreign Nights (1989) Palestinian will not let daughter dance in Toronto. 745251				NYPD Blue: Murder case.	
(CNBC)	The Edge 2853218		Business Center	Upfront Tonight	Hardball With Chris Matthews 7245812		Rivera Live 7265676		The News With Brian Williams (CC) 7268763		Hardball With Chris Matthews 1657812	
(CNN)	WorldView (CC) 695152	Moneyline News Hour With Lou Dobbs (CC) 301812		Crossfire (CC) 295396	The World Today (CC) 999725		Larry King Live (CC) 919589		NewsStand: Time (CC) 912676		Sports Tonight 256522	Moneyline, Lou Dobbs
(COM)	Royal Canada Air Farce	The Red Green Show	Kids in the Hall (CC)	Kids in the Hall (CC)	SCTV	Just for Laughs	The Larry Sanders Show (CC)	Dream On	Open Mike With Mike Bullard (TV14) (CC)		Ronnie Edwards: The Cosmic Comic (TVMA) (CC)	
(CTS)	Dr. Quinn, Medicine Woman: Herbalist. (TVPG) (CC)		100 Huntley Street		James Robison	Benny Hinn	Israel Today: (Hebrew)		Amen	Michael Coren Live		East 2 West: Interviews.

Chart 339

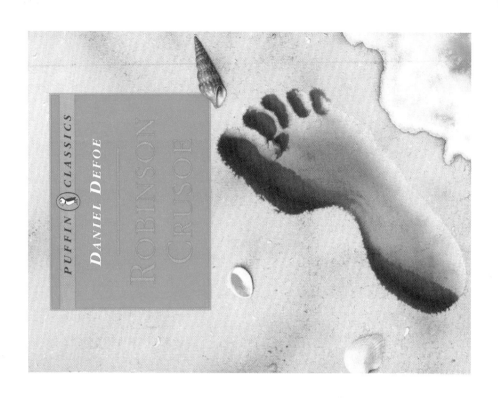

PUFFIN CLASSICS

DANIEL DEFOE

ROBINSON CRUSOE

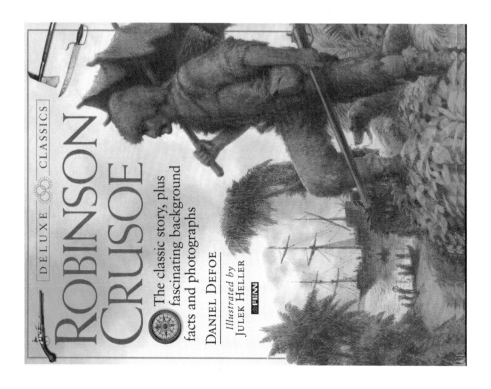

DELUXE CLASSICS

ROBINSON CRUSOE

The classic story, plus fascinating background facts and photographs

DANIEL DEFOE

Illustrated by JULEK HELLER

FENN

ACTIVITIES

UNIT ONE: SHORT FICTION
Visitors, pp. 2–10

1. Working with a small group, find and list examples of all the riddles in the story. Discuss how the author uses each of the riddles for a particular purpose at a specific point in the story. Present your ideas to the class.

2. Create a storyboard to show the first appearance of the visitors. Make sure to indicate effective camera angles and shots both in the drawings themselves and in brief notes on the storyboard. Display your storyboard on the class bulletin board.

3. Working alone or with a partner, find two or three examples of foreshadowing in the story. What do the examples suggest might happen, and what details or clues do they provide to do so? You may want to create a story map to help you illustrate the use of foreshadowing.

4. Write three or four paragraphs explaining how the details of the setting of the story contribute to its atmosphere.

Moonface, pp. 11–16

1. Imagine that this story was being made into a short film intended for an audience of 13- to18-year-olds. Create a poster to advertise the film. Be sure to choose an image or images that capture the theme and mood of the story, and include a short quotation from the story that will appeal to your audience.

2. Working with a partner, select one of the incidents in the story that includes dialogue between the two main characters. Write down this dialogue and create additional dialogue that you think the characters might have spoken. Taking the roles of the characters, present your dialogue to the class.

3. Write a short essay on the use of the moon as a symbol in the story. Be sure that your essay has a main, or controlling idea, and that you provide relevant details from the story to support your main idea.

Moving Day, pp. 17–20

1. Working with a group, identify and discuss important details in the story that convey the sense of loss and the sense of a new beginning. In your opinion, does the author keep these in balance, or is one sense stronger than the other?

2. Write a short monologue for Jenny's mother in which the mother talks about her mixed feelings on leaving Grassy Island. Present your monologue to a small group or to the class.

3. Research the background of the author, locating and summarizing information from both print and non-print sources such as biographical reference works and the Internet. Write a short report explaining how the author's background is reflected in the setting and theme of the story.

Loathe at First Sight, pp. 21–25

1. Work with a partner. Separately, identify five or six key passages of dialogue from the story that you think help to reveal important aspects of the character of each of the

speakers. Compare the lines you've chosen with those chosen by your partner. Discuss similarities and differences in your choices. If possible, reach a consensus on three of the passages for each character that you think are most revealing.

2. Working with a small group, discuss the suitability of the story's title. Create another suitable title for the story. Compare your new title with those of other groups, explaining why you think your group's title is appropriate.

3. Working alone or with a partner, write a short dialogue between two individuals to reveal aspects of their character. The individuals can be real or fictitious, from the present or the past. Follow the conventions of writing dialogue, including the correct placement of quotation marks. Present your dialogue to the class.

4. Choose a section of this story and rewrite it as a narrative either in the first or third person. Incorporate some of the existing dialogue if you wish.

Doing Something, pp. 26–40

1. Working with a small group, consider the informal style in which the narrator tells this story. Identify examples of the narrator's use of colloquial expressions and slang and discuss how they help to reveal his character.

2. Write three or four paragraphs on how the author uses similes and metaphors to achieve particular effects in the story.

3. How do you think Cynthia views Kenny and the events described? Rewrite a section of the story from Cynthia's perspective. Base your rewrite on the details that Kenny gives in his narration.

The Jade Peony, pp. 41–49

1. Write a short essay on how the character of the grandmother is revealed through her actions and through the physical descriptions of her in the story.

2. Working with a partner, identify symbols in the story. Discuss what they mean and how the writer uses them to reveal character and develop the plot. Present your ideas to the class.

3. Imagine that you are asked by a community newspaper to interview the grandmother about the differences between her life in Canada and in China. What questions would you ask? What answers do you think she would give? Write the imagined interview.

Thunder and Lightning, pp. 50–51

1. Create a story map for this myth. Identify the introduction, the opening conflict, other conflicts or events that lead to the climax, the climax, the conflicts or events that follow the climax, and the resolution of the story.

2. Working with a small group, research and discuss the meaning of the term "myth" as a form of story. Then create a two-column chart that lists, on the left side, three or four key characteristics of myth and, on the right side, ways in which this story exhibits these characteristics. Display your chart on the class bulletin board.

3. Write a short myth about a natural phenomenon such as rain or snow for a class collection of myths for primary school students. Alternatively, you might prefer to make a tape-recording of your myth for these students.

Athena, pp. 52–54

1. Work in a group. Make a two-column chart. On the left side, list all the names of the characters that appear in this myth. On the right, explain briefly what you know about any of the characters you recognize. Research the names you do not recognize, and then complete the chart. On your own, write a character sketch of one of the characters for a class collection of profiles on mythological figures.

2. Working with a partner, identify and discuss each of the conflicts in the story, how each is resolved, and how each advances the plot.

3. Create a poster for a movie of this myth for an audience of 13- to 18-year-olds. Be sure to choose an image or images that capture the main theme of the story, and include some catchy text that will appeal to your audience.

The Story of the Totem Pole, pp. 55–56

1. Write an expository paragraph for an audience of primary students that identifies and explains the moral of this story. Refer to details in the myth, but do not simply retell what happens.

2. Working with a group, find other examples of creation myths from two or three different cultures. Identify common criteria or characteristics to compare these myths and "The Story of the Totem Pole." You may want to set up your comparison as a chart. Present your findings to the class.

3. Find out about the writer/artist who has retold this myth. Check print and electronic sources that cover Canadian Native art and culture. Write a four- to five-paragraph report for a school newspaper on the writer/artist.

The Flash, pp. 57–58

1. Working with a partner, think and talk about the theme and plot elements of this short story. What elements does it include and not include? How effectively does the author structure the plot to present the theme and achieve particular effects?

2. Imagine that you are the writer of this story and want to add another page to it. Write the additional material and tape-record the expanded story for presentation to the class.

The Visitation, pp. 59–63

1. With a partner, compare the plot of the story with a similar plot of a movie or an episode from a television series that you've recently seen. Which plot do you think is conveyed in a more effective manner? Why? Present your ideas to the class.

2. Imagine that you are a detective who's been assigned to solving the mystery of Gustavo's disappearance. Make a list of the characters in the story you would interview. Next to each of the names, write the questions you would ask that character. Present your list and questions to the class, with an explanation.

3. Why do you think the narrator decides not to say anything to anyone about what he observes? Prepare a short monologue in which he reflects on his decision.

Lysandra's Poem, pp. 64–73

1. Write a paragraph identifying and explaining what you consider to be the main theme of the story. Exchange paragraphs with a partner. Have you both identified the same theme? If not, try to agree on what the theme is.

2. Working with a partner, write and tape-record an interview between a journalist and Lysandra for a radio program on authors and writing. Focus your discussion on influences on her poetry. Base the interview on details provided in the story.

3. Make a list of any unfamiliar words or phrases that you encounter in the story. Use a dictionary to identify the meaning of the words and whether they are examples of standard or nonstandard Canadian English. Discuss how effectively the words and phrases are used in the story.

A Mad Tea Party, pp. 74–80

1. What is the main form of conflict in this story? How does the writer use it to develop the action?

2. Working with a group, choose a section of the story and rewrite it as a script, including stage directions and instructions for the use of props. Assign the four roles and perform the script for the class or for a group of younger students.

3. Working with a group, find examples in the story of the different ways in which the writer plays with words. Discuss how this use of language contributes to the story. Present your findings to the class.

4. Write a short essay on what specifically is "mad" about this tea party. Describe and explain the actions of the characters involved, including the way they speak to one another.

Save the Moon for Kerdy Dickus, pp. 81–92

1. Working with a partner, find in the text the source of the title of the story. What does it mean? Discuss the significance of this title for the meaning of the story as a whole. Present your ideas to the class.

2. Using the headline and the decks (sub-headlines) from the *National Enquirer* report referred to in the story, write the report as it might have been written for such a tabloid. Base your report on the details referred to in the story below the headline, expanding on them as necessary (e.g., What did the flying saucer look like?).

3. Storyboard a sequence from the story. Include a variety of camera angles and shots to show what is happening from different points of view. Display your storyboard on the class bulletin board.

Green Grass, Running Water, pp. 93–98

1. Working with a partner, discuss the effectiveness of the writer's use of the third-person, or omniscient, point of view to tell the story. What are the advantages of his choosing this method? Are there any disadvantages?

2. Choose a section of the story and write a monologue from Lionel's point of view, retaining the humour of the original story. Present your monologue to the class, either directly or through a tape recording.

3. At the beginning of this excerpt, the writer mentions that Lionel has made three mistakes in his life. For a class collection of story sequels, write a short continuation of this story in which you tell about Lionel's second or third mistake.

4. Write a short report on the background of the author, locating and summarizing information from both print and non-print sources. How is the author's background reflected in the setting and theme of the story?

The Other Family, pp. 99–103

1. In the role of the daughter, write a diary entry that you make after your mother's outburst. Give your point of view on what has just happened and outline what you plan to do about it.

2. Work in a small group to discuss the mother's response to her daughter's drawing. Identify specific words and figurative language (similes and metaphors) that express the mother's emotions. Discuss how effectively these details convey the way she is feeling.

3. Write a sequence of expository paragraphs in which you analyze the effectiveness of the opening paragraph of the story. What words, images, and ideas does the writer include in this paragraph to create a mood, or atmosphere, and to set up the main theme of the story?

The Tell-Tale Heart, pp. 104–108

1. Identify the points in the narrative where the narrator addresses the reader directly. What effect does that have on you as you are reading the story?

2. Write a short essay on the ways in which the writer creates suspense in the story. Refer both to the way he structures the plot and to his use of stylistic devices such as imagery.

3. Write a poem based on this story. Tape-record it, adding appropriate sound effects.

4. Create a poster to advertise a film of this story for a general audience. Be sure to choose an image or images that capture the theme and mood of the story, and include a short quotation from the story that will appeal to your audience.

Unit Two: Nonfiction
On Love and a Lake, p. 110

1. What is the gift the author has been given by her father? Using examples from the selection, explain why you think the author feels this way.

2. Skim the text to find three effective adjectives. Explain why these adjectives are effective and how they contribute to the description.

3. Using this text as a model, write a descriptive paragraph about a place you love. Then compile a photo-essay to accompany your descriptive paragraph.

The Goal Post, pp. 111–112

1. Find examples of humour in the text. Discuss how the author creates this humour with his choice of diction. What other methods does he use to create amusement?

2. Identify examples of slang, and language that reflects a particular culture. How does the use of these words contribute to the tone of the text?

3. Where do you think the author grew up? Cite clues in the text as evidence for your conclusion.

4. Although the text is humorous, it has a serious point to make. What is the author's purpose in writing this memoir? Support your answer with quotations from the text.

Pages from a Diary, pp. 113–114

1. List any unfamiliar words used in this selection. Try to define these words without a dictionary, using instead the context in which they are found. Then check their meaning in a dictionary and use each word in a written sentence of your own.

2. Find three different tones of voice in this diary passage. Explain how each tone is created by diction, giving examples to support your opinion.

3. Choose one tone of voice from activity 2 and use it to write a short diary entry of your own, exploring how you feel about being a teenager.

Early Days, pp. 115–118

1. Describe the structure of this excerpt. What thematic links do you see between the sections? Explain why you think the author divides this section of her autobiography in this way.

2. Discuss the author's last sentence in this selection. Discuss why the author might feel this way, using examples from her story.

3. Recast in the form of a storyboard the author's experience of her trip to the store the last time she was frightened by Wolverine. Determine what aspects of the story have been strengthened or weakened by this adaptation.

Everything It Carries Away, pp. 119–120

1. Scan the text to find and list unfamiliar words in this essay. Then define the words, either from context or using a dictionary.

2. Find words that help to convey the mood between father and son that frames this essay. Explain how this mood contributes to your understanding of the father-son relationship.

3. What else is the author's father forsaking besides the flood? Why do you think the author says that he "will one day do the same"?

Tom Longboat, pp. 121–122

1. Do you think the author has made a good case for Tom Longboat as "the greatest Canadian star"? Give examples from the text to support your answer.

2. Create two posters advertising a race in which Tom Longboat competes—one poster which might have appeared in the early 1900s, and one poster for the present day. Use the information in the text but adapt it for the two time periods. Explain the differences in the text and treatment of the posters.

Anna Lang, pp. 123–129

1. Make a plot graph to trace the main events of the story that is told in this report. Identify the setting and characters; the problem; and the sequence of events.

2. The author has used the characters' own words to tell much of the story. Choose a section of the story in which this technique is used, and rewrite that section in the third person. Compare the effect of the first-person and third-person treatment. Tell which you prefer and why.

3. Do you agree with Anna Lang that she did not deserve the Cross of Valour? Write a letter nominating her as a recipient.

Cudjoe and Nanny, Heroes of the Maroons, pp. 130–133

1. Locate the words in italics for which the author has provided an explanation. Find the word that has entered the Jamaican language in a variety of terms. Make a list of words from other languages that are used in Canadian English.

2. Write a speech that Cudjoe or Nanny might have given to inspire the Maroons. Practise delivering your speech effectively before presenting it to the class.

3. Assume you are a journalist during the time of these events. Write a news report of any one of the events described in this essay. Revise your work to ensure that the sequence of events is clearly developed and that you have provided enough detail. Then edit and proofread your work carefully.

Hesquiaht, pp. 134–135

1. Why do you think the author feels that the place she is writing about—Iusuk—has "enriched and replenished us once again"? Give examples of words and phrases she has used to express her feeling.

2. Assume it is your job to attract young people and adults from around the world to the rediscovery program at Hesquiaht. Create a brochure or web page to attract participants and to provide information about the program.

Through the Looking Glass, pp. 136–137

1. Reread the first sentence of this article. How is it structured to highlight the theme and determine the audience? Share your conclusions with the class.

2. Brainstorm a list of both the good points and the bad points about concern for one's appearance. Organize your ideas in a two-column chart. Then use your chart to write a letter to the author in response to her article.

Paddle to the Amazon, pp. 138–143

1. Skim the text to find five effective transitions between paragraphs. What makes them so effective? How do they contribute to the mood of the description?

2. What might Dana have been thinking about his father and about the events during the experience described in the narrative? Write a diary entry from Dana's point of view.

3. In what ways does this narrative resemble a short story? In what ways is it different?

Letters from Vietnam, pp. 144–151

1. How are Tom's letters to Bob different from those to his parents? Create a chart to compare the letters to his parents and to Bob. Consider content, language, form, and tone. Share your findings with the class. Discuss what effect is produced by the differences between the two sets of letters.

2. Work with a partner to prepare a dramatic reading of one of Tom's letters. If possible, tape suitable background music and sound effects.

3. The notice of Tom's death is placed at the end of the letters. Do you think the letters would have had a different effect on you if you had known about his death from the beginning? Tell why or why not this would be so.

Mr. Preston (and Mr. Rawat) Go to New Delhi, pp. 152–154

1. Make a chart to compare the experiences of Mr. Preston and Mr. Rawat in New Delhi. Choose headings that will allow you to compare a range of their experiences before, during, and after the conference.

2. Find examples of sentence fragments and paragraphs ending with short, simple sentences. Discuss the effect of these examples.

3. Prepare a speech that Mr. Rawat might give to the conference. Practise delivering the speech and make a recording of it.

Covering the Sports Beat, pp. 155–158

1. Identify the thesis of this essay. Give supporting details that the authors use to support their thesis.

2. Make a list of the criteria for a good sportswriter using the selection as a guide. Create an advertisement for a sportswriter with these criteria in mind.

Sniglets, pp. 159–160

1. Divide each word into a prefix and suffix, to see how its meaning has been derived. Then, using the same technique, create a list of ten sniglets of your own, complete with definitions.

2. Work in a group to create a dictionary of sniglets. You might wish to illustrate some sniglets with appropriate visuals.

Exposure to Secondhand Smoke, pp. 161–165

1. Explain why the following elements are used in this selection a) charts and graphs, b) footnotes, and c) boldface headings.

2. Make a poster or brochure to make people more aware of the dangers of secondhand smoke. Use information from the article to support your message.

A Mother's Heart Aches, pp. 166–167

1. Discuss whether you think the cultural background of the author has influenced the information and ideas she expresses.

2. Write a journal entry in which you respond to Carol Cayenne and the issues she raises.

3. Write your own letter to the editor of your local paper. Address a social issue that concerns you. Revise, edit, and proofread your letter carefully before mailing it.

Dogs and Books, pp. 168–170

1. In the body of the article, the author begins each argument by making a statement and then supporting it with a concrete example. Find evidence to support this view.

2. Highlight key words and phrases the author uses which you feel are particularly effective in expressing her love of books and dogs.

Review: Canadian Geographic Explorer, p. 171

1. How do the reviewers convey enthusiasm for the software program? Consider sentence structure, diction, and punctuation.

2. Do you think this review tells you everything you need to know before making a decision on whether or not to buy or try the software described? Work with a group to establish criteria for a review of computer software or a CD-ROM, based on your response to this review.

We Are Concerned About the Poor All Over the World, pp. 172–174

1. What makes this speech effective? Make a list of techniques used by Coretta Scott King and supply examples for each.

2. Make a poster or flyer attracting an audience to Coretta Scott King's speech on April 8, 1968. Remember that her husband, Martin Luther King, has just been assassinated.

Unit Three: Poetry
Lineage, p. 176

1. In which line of the poem does the poet compare herself to her grandmothers? Why do you think this line is placed where it is? Discuss your response with the class.

2. Use a literary dictionary or other resource to define the term *sensuous imagery*. List all the examples of sensuous imagery you can find in the poem. Is this kind of imagery used effectively in the poem? Support your opinion with examples.

3. Write a one-paragraph character sketch of someone you know. Include descriptions and images that appeal to a variety of senses. Ask a partner for suggestions about how to make your writing more effective, and then revise your paragraph.

Identity, p. 177

1. What is the poet representing through the symbol of flowers? of weeds? What clues in the poem support your ideas?

2. Using the descriptions in the poem, make a list of the pros and cons of being a weed and of being a flower. Do you agree with the poet's ideas? Did his choice surprise you at first? Which would you choose? Why?

3. Using your own words, write a sentence that expresses the main idea of the poem. Then suggest some other symbols, besides flowers and weeds, that could be used to express the main idea.

An Early Start in Midwinter, p. 178

1. What perspective or point of view does the poet use in this poem? Whose experiences is she describing? What effect is created by the point of view in the poem?

2. Describe the mood of the poem. Is it consistent or does it change? Identify words and images that help to establish mood.

3. Write a poem or narrative paragraph to describe what your morning is like. Choose words and images that help to create an appropriate mood.

When Dawn Comes to the City, pp. 179–180

1. Work with a partner or small group to discuss how the poet uses diction, sound, and repetition to create contrast between the two environments. Use examples from the poem to support your ideas.

2. Choose four images from the poem and describe them from the point of view of someone who loves the city and hates the country.

3. Write a two-minute speech about your favourite place. Rehearse it and read it to a classmate. Talk about how you could improve both the writing and the delivery.

Your Buildings, p. 181

1. Who is the intended audience of this poem? Find evidence in the poem to support your opinion.

2. In a group, discuss the meaning of the term "alienation." Then explain how the poet communicates and develops the theme of alienation in the poem.

3. What do you think is the message in the last two lines of the poem? Write a sentence or two giving your interpretation.

4. Do some research to find out more about Rita Joe. From what cultural perspective does she write? In a journal entry, describe how your research affects your understanding of the poem.

The Shark, p. 182

1. Choose what you think are the two most effective adjectives, verbs, and adverbs in the poem. In point form, explain why you think each is effective.

2. Identify and discuss with a partner all of the ways in which the poet compares the shark to metal. How do these comparisons relate to the theme of the poem?

3. Use both print and non-print sources such as the Internet to research sharks. Identify the type of shark that you think the poem describes. Prepare a fact sheet to share information about the type of shark you chose. Ask a classmate to proofread your fact sheet for errors in grammar, usage, spelling, and punctuation.

4. Using details from the poem and other references, create an illustration that could accompany the poem.

Fireworks, p. 183

1. Use a dictionary to define any unfamiliar words in the poem. List all the references to colour. Why is colour important in this poem?

2. Read the poem aloud and listen for the rhythm. Copy the first three stanzas in your notebook and mark the accented syllables in each line. What patterns of rhythm do you notice? What effect does this pattern create?

3. What elements in the poem suggest that the relationship between the two people might not be as simple as the first line suggests? How would you describe the relationship? Why?

Little Boxes, p. 184

1. From what perspective or point of view is the speaker looking at the situation? How do you know?

2. Examine the poet's use of repetition and note examples. Organize your examples into categories such as diction, syntax, etc.

3. Why might the poet have chosen to use such simple language? How do simple language and repetition reinforce the theme?

4. Find the meaning of tone in a literary dictionary or another appropriate resource. How would you describe the tone of this poem? Identify elements in the poem that help to create this tone.

5. This poem criticizes a life based on conformity. What do you think: Is it more important to conform with others around you, or is it more important to express your individuality? Write a short essay giving your views. Revise and edit your work carefully.

Stopping by Woods on a Snowy Evening, p. 185

1. What is the effect of the repetition in the last two lines of the poem? How does the repetition help to reinforce the meaning?

2. Using clues from the poem, compare and contrast the attitudes of the woods' owner, the horse, and the speaker.

3. Write a modern version of this poem. You might wish to use an urban setting. Ask a classmate to give you feedback on your first draft, and then revise it. Rehearse effective ways of reading the poem and present it to the class.

The Song My Paddle Sings, pp. 186–187

1. Define *alliteration, assonance,* and *personification.* Find three examples of each poetic device.

2. Explain how images and sound work together to communicate feeling in at least three different stanzas.

3. Work with two classmates to prepare and present a choral reading of three or four stanzas. Experiment with different techniques for making your reading effective.

4. Find and read other poems by E. Pauline Johnson. Choose one and compare it with this poem in terms of subject, style, and poetic devices.

"my father hurt," p. 188

1. How did you feel as you read this poem? Identify words and phrases in the poem that helped to create this feeling.

2. Why are the pronouns important in this poem? How do they help to create meaning?

3. What might the poet mean when he refers to "*the* father"? Explain why you think so.

4. Why might the poet have chosen to write using very short lines? Do you find this technique effective in the poem? Why or why not?

5. Write a formal letter of apology to someone you hurt, either intentionally or unintentionally.

The Wreck of the Edmund Fitzgerald, pp. 189–190

1. In chart form, list examples from the poem of each of the following: *metaphor, simile, personification.* Include in your chart a place to note the effect created by each example.

2. Imagine you are a crew member on the ship and write a journal entry that might have been written as the storm grew in intensity. Use language consistent with the language used in the poem. Exchange entries with a partner and make suggestions for improvement. Revise your entry and keep a copy of each draft in your writing folder.

3. Work with two classmates to prepare a choral reading of three stanzas from the poem. Experiment with different choral techniques, such as varying the number of voices reading certain lines and phrases. Use facial expressions and gestures to add drama. Ask some classmates to give you feedback on your performance.

[You are reading this too fast.], p. 191

1. Work with a classmate to discuss the meaning of four or five lines that you find difficult to understand. After the discussion, express the meaning of each line in your own words.

2. The poet writes using the second-person pronoun *you*. What effect does this create? For comparison, think about how the poem would sound written from a third-person perspective:

   People are reading this…
   Unless *they* live with it…

3. Do you agree with the poet's advice and his observations about poetry? Do his ideas apply to all poetry? Write a well organized expository paragraph to express and support your opinion.

4. Write a poem to express *your* ideas about poetry. Topics might include how you define poetry, why you like or dislike poetry, or what kinds of poetry you like or dislike. Ask a classmate to comment on your first draft.

Tichborne's Elegy, p. 192

1. Research the literary terms *elegy* and *epigraph*. How are the two connected in this poem?

2. How does knowledge of the poet's situation affect the reader's understanding of the poem?

3. How would you describe the mood expressed in the poem? Use references to the poem to support your opinion.

4. Define the word *paradox*. What is the effect of the poet's use of paradox? With a partner, discuss whether or not the poet's statements are contradictory.

Sonnet XVIII, p. 193

1. Research the characteristics of a Shakespearean sonnet. Using specific references, show which of these characteristics are present in this sonnet.

2. Find two lines in which Shakespeare comments on the nature of poetry. What ideas does he express?

3. Use informal contemporary language to write a paraphrase of this poem in free verse.

4. Some people find this sonnet very moving, while others find it overly sentimental. Using references to the poem, explain your reaction.

A Poison Tree, p. 194

1. With what does Blake compare the speaker's anger? What clues in the poem support your answer?

2. Why is the poem's title important in understanding the meaning of the poem?

3. Define the literary term *symbol*. Explain the symbolic meaning of the apple.

4. If this poem were a fable, what would be an appropriate moral?

The Solitary Reaper, p. 195

1. List any words in the poem that are unfamiliar to you. Use context to predict their meaning, and then use a dictionary to check your predictions.

2. Why might the speaker of the poem offer the instruction to "Stop here, or gently pass!"?

3. What verb tense does Wordsworth use to describe the scene? What effect does this verb tense create?

4. Imagine you are the speaker of the poem, writing about your experience in a post card to a friend. In five or six sentences, try to capture the meaning of the poem.

Song, p. 196

1. Identify examples of archaic language in the poem and provide a modern equivalent for each.

2. How would you describe the mood of this poem? Use specific references to the poem to support your answer.

3. Define the term *epitaph*. Based on what the poem seems to tell us about Rossetti, write an appropriate epitaph for her.

One Perfect Rose, p. 197

1. Define the literary term *irony*. Explain the irony in the poem's title.

2. Compare the language used in the first two stanzas with that used in the third. List examples that highlight the differences. What effect does the poet create through this use of contrasting language?

3. Define *tone* as applied to writing. Describe the tone of this poem, using specific examples from the poem to support your ideas.

4. What attitude toward romance and romantic customs does this poem reveal?

5. Imagine you are the person who sent the rose. Write a letter to an advice column describing your loved one's reaction to your gift. Then write a response to your letter.

"adieu foulard..." p. 198

1. Explain the meaning of this poem's title. What image does the title suggest? How is this image related to the situation described in the poem?

2. Find two examples of comparisons used to create visual images. Which one do you think is most effective? Why?

3. Making reference to diction, structure, and mood, explain how the last line provides contrast. Do you think this line provides an effective ending to the poem? Support your opinion with specific references to the poem.

4. Write a descriptive paragraph describing a place you love and how you feel when you have to leave. Try to use metaphors and similes to create vivid visual images. Ask a classmate for suggestions on how to improve your paragraph.

What Do I Remember of the Evacuation? pp. 199–200

1. Find a definition of the literary term *free verse*. What characteristics of free verse do you find in this poem?

2. This poem is written using a conversational style of language. Do you think it is effective, considering the subject matter? What effect does it have on the reader? Discuss your views in a small group.

3. Rewrite this poem as prose. Think about where new sentences and paragraphs might begin, and use correct punctuation. Compare the two versions. Which one do you think is most effective? Explain why.

4. Imagine that you are planning to make a film about the events described in the poem. Create a storyboard using sketches to illustrate four or five important moments or events. Add a caption to describe what's happening in each scene. Choose a piece of music that you think would create an appropriate mood.

Belly Growls, p. 201

1. Identify the adjectives in this poem. Identify the verbs and verb forms. What effect does each create? Share your responses with a partner.

2. Define *onomatopoeia*. Find examples of onomatopoeia in the poem and explain your choices.

3. Describe the mood of this poem and identify words and phrases that help create the mood.

4. Write a poem that describes how you feel when you're very hungry. Try to use vivid images and language that appeals to the senses.

Tractor-Factor, p. 202

1. How does the shape of this poem help to communicate the idea?

2. Research the characteristics of concrete poetry. Which of these characteristics are found in this poem?

3. Write a poem in which the shape helps to communicate the central idea.

UNIT FOUR: DRAMA
Chagall, pp. 204–222

1. Explain the effects of the following stylistic devices.

   a) *alliteration:* "dangerous, dreaded, death-defying dive"

   b) *simile:* "I felt as if I was the brush"

   c) *metaphor:* "in art class ... I was king"

   Find other examples of stylistic devices and explain their effects.

2. Which character do you like most? Choose some of his or her lines and practise reading them aloud. If possible, work with a group to perform part of the play as Reader's Theatre.

3. Create a poster or playbill advertising the play for a specific age group. Include the play's setting in your poster or playbill.

4. What is the play's theme? Is it one of the following—or something else?

a) Follow your dream.

b) Don't be afraid to be different.

c) There's more to life than being practical.

State what you think the theme is. Then write two paragraphs supporting your viewpoint.

The Hitchhiker, pp. 223–235

1. Explain how the playwright creates and maintains suspense. Why, for example, does Adams say near the beginning: It will keep me from going mad? Why does the hitchhiker appear again and again? Why does he always have rain spatters?

2. Reread the Girl Hitchhiker's lines. Identify and explain examples of colloquialisms and slang. Why do you think the playwright has the girl speak this way?

3. Choose a section of the play and study the stage directions, printed inside parentheses (). Using these directions, find or develop music and sound effects that effectively portray the setting. If possible, work with a group. Some of you can produce the music and sound effects; others can read the dialogue aloud.

4. Briefly note two or three questions the play raises in your mind. Rewrite the ending in such a way that it answers at least one of your questions.

Monologues for Teenagers, pp. 236–238

1. Compare the two monologues. What could be the setting of each? Which is more like a story? What story elements does it include? Which is more like a supported opinion essay? How does the author support the opinion expressed?

2. From each monologue, choose two or more sentences that convey emotions. Practise reading them aloud, using facial expressions, intonation, and gestures to help express the emotions. If possible, share your oral reading with a partner or the class.

3. Choose one monologue and rewrite part or all of it as a dialogue between two or more characters. "Larry," for example, could be a dialogue between Larry and a cousin. "Marcie" could be a dialogue between Marcie and a close friend. Use appropriate punctuation marks.

Words on a Page, pp. 239–258

1. Compare and interpret the play's main characters. Make and complete a chart like the following.

Character	Life Experiences	Values and Goals
Lenore		
Pete		
Connie		
Miss Walker		

2. Use Lenore's written story or her dream as the basis for a poem, song, or other piece of writing.

3. How might various readers' backgrounds influence how they interpret the play's language? How, for instance, might some interpret the words white and Native? What alternative words might some prefer? Why?

4. Pretend you are making your own televised version of this script. Choose some of the scenes and draw sketches showing how you would set them up.

Weird Kid, pp. 259–282

1. Identify examples of informal language and slang. Explain why the playwright uses them.
2. The plot includes a number of flashbacks created by the actors themselves. They are introduced with words such as:

   a) Remember that first day.

   b) So that was one situation. Okay. Who remembers another one?

   Identify the flashbacks and explain why the playwright uses them.
3. Pretend you are a character in the play, other than Babs Story. In role as that character, write a letter or e-mail of apology to Babs. Use proper letter or e-mail style and punctuation.
4. As suggested by the actor at the end, predict what will happen in the principal's office once the students get there. Express your ideas in a short script or, if possible, work with a group to role-play what happens.

Unit Five: Media
Anatomy of an Article, p. 285

1. Locate an article of interest in a magazine or newspaper. Write an analysis of the article, using the information in "Anatomy of an Article" as a guide.
2. Examine sources such as newsmagazines, newspapers, and the Internet to locate two articles in which opinions are presented as fact. Highlight the relevant sections. Then for each article, explain what kinds of facts should be provided to support the opinion.
3. Choose a topic with which you are familiar. Write two short articles on that topic— one that is factual and one that states an opinion.

Invaders from Mars, pp. 286–288

1. What does this article tell us about the media's ability to create "reality"? Have you seen or heard something that was incorrect in the media? How did you know? Discuss your experiences with the class.
2. List media sources you consider either reliable or unreliable. With a partner, discuss what makes a source reliable or unreliable. Then compile a list of ways in which you can verify a source.
3. Work in a group to develop a short radio play on a topic relevant to present times. Consider how to use elements such as dialogue, plot development, and special effects to enhance the radio play. Tape-record the play, using appropriate sound effects.

Rap, pp. 289–290

1. From the information in the article, create a chart classifying the characteristics of different types of rap music. Tell how each type communicates a point of view about social issues important to our times.

2. Choose a rap song or video and classify it, using the information in the article. Write about one of the following:

   - What elements of the song reveal its intended audience? Which of these are explicit? implicit?
   - How might the background of the listeners or viewers influence their interpretation of the music or the lyrics?
   - Analyze the lyrics, looking at how the singer's diction, phrasing, or use of similes or metaphors are important to the song's message.

3. Rap "articulates views that would otherwise remain unheard." Select a topic or point of view that is "unheard" and write a song or poem in which you clearly express an opinion.

Chasing Down the News, pp. 291–293

1. Write a story for your school newspaper. Before you begin, identify several focus questions that will help you gather the facts you need. What key words can you use as search terms for electronic research? Consider the information you collect and discard material that may be irrelevant or inaccurate.

2. Watch several newscasts on different television stations. Look for examples of Canadian, American, and international stories. Record the differences in a chart that includes the following headings: Topic, Information, How Presented, Why the Story is Considered Important, Other Information Implied. Discuss your findings with a partner. What generalizations can you make about the different sources of news?

The News, p. 294

1. In an expository paragraph, explain the point, or message, of the cartoon. Ensure that your paragraph has a topic sentence, supporting sentences to develop your main idea, and a concluding sentence.

2. Watch a TV newscast. Record the topics of the stories, how much time was dedicated to each one, and what visuals were used. Evaluate the truth of the cartoon in light of the information you collected.

3. Create a cartoon of your own that makes a statement about the role of media in your life. Think carefully about design elements you can use to help you make your point.

Lights, Camera, Frostbite! pp. 295–299

1. What did you learn about the Canadian North from this article? Choose one aspect of the North that made a particular impression on you and use it to write a descriptive paragraph or poem.

2. What questions about Native culture (e.g., legends, food, art) do you have after reading this article? Conduct research to find answers to one of your questions. Present your findings to the class.

3. Write a letter to the editor in which you argue about the importance of government funding for filmmakers who record and communicate different aspects of Canadian culture.

My American Cousin, pp. 300–310

1. In a small group, prepare a dramatic reading of the script using only voice and sound effects, as if it were a radio play.

2. In this script, the story is told from Sandy's perspective. Select one of the other characters. Script the story from that person's point of view. Rehearse and then present your story orally, in role.

3. With a partner, discuss the role that media play in Sandy's life. How does it compare with the role that media play in your life?

Some How-to's of Making Videos, pp. 311–316

1. By yourself or with a partner, watch or tape a TV show or a movie to find an example of three kinds of shots described in the article. Present samples of your findings to the class.

2. Create an ad or promotional campaign for a "how-to" video. Think carefully about which medium you will use (e.g., TV commercial, radio spot, newspaper ad). Explain how your ad will encourage people to view the video.

The Making of a Car Commercial, p. 317

1. View the storyboard carefully. For each frame, note the content, the variety of shots, and the way in which the shots create continuity.

2. Create your own storyboard for another product. How does your storyboard differ from the one for the Trans Am? Explain how each has been designed to achieve its particular purpose.

3. Write the script for the voice-over that would accompany your storyboard. Take care to use language that will be appropriate for the product and your message.

High School Rules, pp. 318–320

1. How accurately has the writer captured the culture of your high school? Write a paragraph to present your opinion.

2. With two other students, create short scenarios to dramatize the three elements of integrity, passion, and attitude.

3. Analyze how teens are depicted in two or three TV shows. Keep a list of accuracies and inaccuracies you notice. Write a letter to the producers of one of the shows, giving your opinion of the way teens are depicted in it.

Einbinder Flypaper, p. 321

1. List the conventions used by the writers of this selection that demonstrate it is a parody.

2. With a partner, select a familiar product, rename it, and write your own parody "spot" about it.

3. You are presenting an advertising proposal to the CEO of the Einbinder company. Outline your plans for a print ad campaign for Einbinder flypaper that demonstrates the effective use of advertising strategies. Consider all print media and outline all facets of the campaign.

A Product Advertisement, pp. 322, 333

1. Examine the two versions of the Unico ad. When would using a black and white ad be more effective than a colour ad? Discuss your ideas with a partner.

2. Create two ads for the same product of your choice, one in black and white and one in colour. Explain the purposes for which the company might use each kind of ad.

3. Write a script for a TV or radio spot for a food or beverage product. Begin with a storyboard. Polish the text, rehearse it, and then present it dramatically to the class.

Evaluating a Web Site, pp. 323–324

1. Evaluate a Web site using the criteria presented in the article. Organize your findings under the headings used in the article. Assume there are 20 points for each category. What score would you give the Web site as a whole?

2. Using the article and adding ideas of your own, create a checklist of 10–15 questions you should ask yourself when using the Internet to obtain information.

3. Create your own factual Web site about a sport or hobby you enjoy and know well. Decide who your intended audience will be. How can you check your own work for bias?

Cyberspace Studios, p. 325

1. List some ways in which virtual sets could distort truth.

2. Prepare an argument, pro or con, for a debate on one of these topics:
   - Using virtual reality sets in place of actual locations or studio sets is fine for entertainment purposes but not for delivering the news.
   - The use of computer technology is getting out of control.

3. Write a short story set in the future, showing the effects of virtual reality. Exchange with a partner and offer constructive ideas for how the story might be improved. You might also check one another's work for complete sentences, variety of types of sentences, and consistent point of view. Revise your work.

Interactive Writer's Handbook, Q & A, pp. 326–332

1. Work with a partner to plan a scene for a short story, using the process described in the article (index cards, flow chart, etc.). Share your work with another pair. In what ways is your scene like and unlike the original story?

2. Working with two or three classmates, choose two episodes or game stages from a video you are familiar with, and analyze them for both content and "message." For example, examine scene changes, point of view, or special effects. Does the game portray violence? What messages do you think the game conveys about how people interact with one another?

3. Using both images and text, create an advertisement to sell *Wing Commander*. What design elements would help to get your message across to your audience?

Frontier College Brochure, p. 334

1. What is a brochure? What is the purpose of this Frontier College brochure? Identify three or four main ideas about Frontier College that you obtained from this brochure. How does the brochure format help to convey these ideas?

2. Create a brochure for your school. Before you begin, choose an intended audience and list ten questions that the brochure will answer. Be sure to use design elements that are most appropriate to your purpose.

3. Use the information from the Frontier College brochure or a school brochure to make a video or radio ad. What new information might you need to include? How does the video or radio ad communicate differently from the written brochure?

Star Wars Poster, p. 336

1. With a partner, discuss the poster and its elements. Identify five pieces of information about the movie that the poster gives you. How does the use of colour, symbols, and setting reinforce the message?

2. With a partner, list the characteristics of a "blockbuster" movie. Then make a chart to show how *Star Wars* fits the blockbuster mould.

3. Create your own movie poster for any work you have studied in this course. Before you begin consider: What audience do you have in mind? What aspects of the work will you feature? What kinds of visual images will best help you convey your message?

The Circus Cyclists, p. 337

1. With a partner, discuss the following questions: How would you describe the colours used in this picture? How do they make you feel? How well do they suit the idea of a circus? Are they realistic? Is it important for them to be realistic? How do the colours reflect how Chagall sees the circus?

2. Write a brief paragraph explaining how the ideas in the play "Chagall" (pages 204–222) are demonstrated in this painting.

3. Using oil pastels, create a piece of art inspired by Chagall's style. Plan it in your mind before you begin. Think about the subject, how you will arrange the elements on the page, and the colours and shapes you will use. Share your work with a partner and explain how you incorporated what you learned about Chagall's style.

The *Canadian Geographic* Home Page, p. 338

1. Write a paragraph to answer the following questions: What is the purpose of this Web site? How does it use colour, format, images, and text to serve that purpose? How successful do you think the page will be in achieving its purpose?

2. Look at the home page of another well-known magazine and compare it with this one. List five similarities and differences. Write a paragraph to tell which home page you feel is more effective and why.

3. If possible, find the March/April 1999 issue of *Canadian Geographic* in a library. Does seeing the magazine change your assessment of the Web page? If you were the designer of the Web site, what changes would you have made? Discuss your ideas with a partner.

The *National Post*, p. 339

1. Work with two or three classmates to examine the information in this chart. On paper, or using the computer, rearrange the names of the shows to categorize them by genre. What kinds of shows are broadcast most frequently? Why do you think that is so?

2. Now rearrange the names of the shows by rating. In each case, is the time slot appropriate for the rating?

3. Rearrange the shows one more time, this time by target audience. How many shows are aimed at children? teens? older adults? Is the time slot appropriate for the audience?

4. Create your own TV listings based only on shows of interest to teens. In what order would you show them? Why?

Two Covers of *Robinson Crusoe*, p. 340

1. Make a chart to compare the two covers. Use categories for comparison such as colour, font, text, visuals, or target market.

2. Choose a book that you think has an uninteresting cover. Design a new one, taking into consideration the categories suggested in the preceding activity. Write a brief paragraph to explain why your cover works better than the original.

3. Create two ads for the same product but aim each ad at a different market audience (e.g., teens and adults). Share your work with a partner or the class and explain the choices you made.

Kathleen Arnott   Born in Britain, Kathleen Arnott spent many years as a missionary teacher in Nigeria. During that time she became fascinated with Africa and its oral histories. She began to retell these stories in her own books. With more than 20 books published, Arnott is credited with making a valuable contribution to the folklore of Africa.

Ingri and Edgar Parin d'Aulaire   Edgar d'Aulaire was an artist and Ingri Parin d'Aulaire was an illustrator/writer when they met in Paris. After moving to the United States, the two began a lifelong collaboration writing and illustrating children's books.

Himani Bannerji   Born in India in 1942, Himani Bannerji was educated and taught in Calcutta. She came to Canada in 1969, where she has published poetry, short stories, critical articles, and reviews.

William Blake   The great English mystic poet and artist was born in 1757, and died in 1827. His visionary poetry and symbolic paintings and engravings had a great influence on English Romanticism.

Christie Blatchford   Journalist Christie Blatchford was born in Rouyn-Noranda, Quebec, and graduated from Ryerson Polytechnic in 1973. Her career as a reporter began at *The Globe and Mail*, where she was part of the first wave of female sportswriters. Since then she has written for all of the Toronto daily papers and is currently a columnist with *The National Post*.

Italo Calvino   Born in Cuba in 1923, Italo Calvino spent most of his life in Italy. A novelist and short story writer, he was famous for the collection of Italian fables he edited, as well as for the fables he wrote himself.

Maria Campbell   Native Canadian Maria Campbell is of Cree, Scottish, and French descent. She was born and raised on a trapline near Prince Albert, Saskatchewan. Her childhood was spent in a world of poverty and racism. Campbell told her story in the book, *Halfbreed*, which was published in 1973.

Lewis Carroll   Lewis Carroll was the pseudonym of Charles Lutwidge Dodgson, the nineteenth-century British author of the classic children's fantasies, *Alice's Adventures in Wonderland* and *Through the Looking Glass*.

Carol Cayenne   Ontario resident Carol Cayenne's letter to the editor, "A Mother's Heart Aches," was first published in the *Toronto Star*.

Karen Charleson   Karen Charleson is a writer and member of the Hesquiaht First Nations. She lives in Hot Springs Cove, British Columbia.

Wayson Choy   Wayson Choy was born in Vancouver, British Columbia, the setting for his novel *The Jade Peony*. His short stories have been published in a number of anthologies.

Warren Clark   Ottawa native Warren Clark has spent the last 25 years working for Statistics Canada as an editor of *Canadian Social Trends*, a publication that looks at social issues such as religion, education, and health.

Ellen Conford   American writer Ellen Conford is the author of many popular novels and short stories for children and young adults. She has also contributed stories and poems to a number of magazines and books.

Liz Crompton   Liz Crompton is a Canadian writer whose work appears in *Up Here* magazine.

Carman Cumming   A former parliamentary correspondent, author Carman Cumming recently retired from his position as a professor of journalism at Carleton University. He is also the author of several books on the craft of journalism and its history.

Cyril Dabydeen   Cyril Dabydeen was born and grew up in British Guiana (now Guyana), and emigrated to Canada in 1970. He is the author of several volumes of poetry and short stories and his work has appeared in several anthologies.

Renée David   At the time this piece was written Renée David was living in rural Ontario with her mother, stepfather, brothers, and her dog.

Rex Deverell   Rex Deverell was the resident playwright at the Globe Theatre in Regina, Saskatchewan, from 1975 to 1990. During this period, he wrote over 35 plays. Much of his work has a regional theme, written with the Globe's audience in mind.

Bob Elliott and Ray Goulding   The comedy team of Bob Elliott and Ray Goulding entertained radio, television, and film audiences for over four decades. By poking fun at people's facades and pretensions, they produced a unique and timeless humour, which is still enjoyed today.

Sarah Ellis   As a children's librarian, Sarah Ellis read many books before writing her own. Her short stories and novels often deal with family issues.

Lucille Fletcher   Lucille Fletcher Wallop was born in Brooklyn, New York, in 1912. Writing under the name Lucille Fletcher, she is best known for *Sorry, Wrong Number*, a suspense novel which was made into a successful play and film.

Robert Frost   Poet Robert Frost was born in San Francisco in 1874. He grew up and lived in New England, finding the inspiration for much of his work in the natural beauty of the countryside there. He won the Pulitzer Prize for Poetry four times.

Barbara Frum   Barbara Frum's career with the Canadian Broadcasting Corporation spanned many years. She was best known as the host and interviewer on the award-winning radio series *As It Happens*.

Jack Granatstein   Historian and author Jack Granatstein was born in Toronto, Ontario. He has written over 30 books and published a variety of articles on political history, defence, and foreign policy. He served in the Canadian army from 1956 to 1966 and is currently the Distinguished Research Professor of History Emeritus at York University in Toronto.

Rita Joe Micmac poet Rita Joe was born in 1932 in Cape Breton, Nova Scotia. Her early life in foster homes and residential schools became recurring themes in her work. She received the Order of Canada in 1990.

E. Pauline Johnson Emily Pauline Johnson (Tekahionwake) was born in Ontario in 1861. A member of the Mohawk Nation, she was a poet, short story writer, and lecturer. She is remembered for her contributions to First Nations literature, and is often called the unofficial poet laureate of Canada.

Roger Karshner American musician and playwright Roger Karshner worked in the recording industry in California before turning to writing. He is the author of several plays and collections of monologues for actors.

Richardo Keens-Douglas Born in Grenada, West Indies, Richardo Keens-Douglas is an internationally known storyteller and actor. He now lives in Canada, and has written several books for young children, as well as short fiction and plays.

Coretta Scott King Coretta Scott King is the wife of slain civil rights activist Martin Luther King. She has spent most of her career affiliated with the causes that her husband championed and has become an important figure in her own right in the civil rights movement.

Thomas King Thomas King is of mixed German, Greek, and Cherokee descent. His first novel, *Medicine River*, was published in 1990. King mixes dark humour and unusual characters in a unique storytelling technique praised by readers and reviewers.

Thomas Kingsley Thomas Kingsley was an American soldier who was killed during the Vietnam war.

Joy Kogawa Born in Vancouver, British Columbia, in 1935, Joy Kogawa spent time in a Japanese internment camp during World War II. She is best known for her novel *Obasan*, which is based on this experience.

Keith Ross Leckie Keith Ross Leckie was born and still lives in Toronto, Ontario. He worked in film and television before becoming a novelist.

Gordon Lightfoot Born in Orillia, Ontario, singer/songwriter Gordon Lightfoot rose to stardom in the 1960s and 1970s on the strength of such hits as "For Lovin' Me," "Early Morning Rain," and "If You Could Read My Mind." He has received multiple recording awards and was invested into the Order of Canada in 1970.

Amy Lowell A tireless advocate of contemporary poetry, American writer Amy Lowell wrote and published over 650 poems in just over a dozen years. A collection of her work, published posthumously, won the Pulitzer Prize for Poetry in 1926.

R. P. MacIntyre   Born in Saskatoon, Saskatchewan, R. P. (Roderick Peter) MacIntyre has written radio and television plays, poetry, and short stories. Several of his plays were produced by CBC-Radio and CBC-TV.

Claude McKay   Claude McKay emigrated from Jamaica to the United States in 1912, where he became a key figure in the Harlem Renaissance, a prominent literary movement of the 1920s. A poet, short story writer, and novelist, McKay won recognition as the author of *Home to Harlem,* the first commercially successful novel by a black writer.

Catherine McKercher   Ottawa-born Catherine McKercher is an associate professor at the School of Journalism and Communication at Carleton University. She has also written for the *Ottawa Journal* and for The Canadian Press in both Toronto and Washington.

Rick McNair   Canadian playwright Rick McNair has worked in Canada and Britain, directing and writing plays. He has been artistic director of four Canadian theatres.

John Melady   Canadian writer John Melady was born in Seaforth, Ontario. He is an award-winning author who specializes in historical fiction. He has published several books for adults and young people including the popular *Cross of Valour.*

Todd Mercer   Canadian author Todd Mercer writes and edits material for educational publishing houses.

Kat Mototsune   Toronto resident Kat Mototsune is Sansei, a third-generation Japanese Canadian. Mototsune has worked primarily as a writer and editor for educational and children's trade publishers.

Julio Noboa   Born in New York City in 1949, Julio Noboa is the son of Puerto Rican immigrant parents. He is an educator, journalist, and writer whose research, articles, and papers focus on areas of bilingualism and cultural diversity. He lives in San Antonio, Texas.

Joanna Norland   Joanna Norland is a young writer whose article, "Through the Looking Glass," appeared in the teen scene column of the *Ottawa Citizen.*

Ken Norris   Born in New York City in 1951, Ken Norris lived in Montreal for many years. He has published several books of poetry and edited a number of poetry anthologies.

Dorothy Parker   Humourist Dorothy Parker wrote poetry, essays, short stories, and screenplays, as well as being a regular contributor to *The New Yorker* magazine for over 30 years.

Sylvia Plath   American poet and writer Sylvia Plath published her first piece of poetry at the age of eight. By the time she took her own life at 31, she was already becoming a legend. She was awarded many honours including the Pulitzer Prize for Poetry.

Edgar Allan Poe   Poet and short story writer Edgar Allan Poe was born in Boston, Massachusetts, in 1809. The author of many classic tales of terror, he is considered the father of modern mystery and detective fiction.

Helen Porter   Helen Porter was born in Newfoundland, and is the author of several plays and collections of short stories. She collaborated with two other authors on *In This Place,* an anthology of women's writing from Newfoundland and Labrador.

E. J. Pratt   Canadian poet E. J. (Edwin John) Pratt was born in Newfoundland in 1882. He is highly regarded for his long narrative poems, and in 1940 he won the Governor General's Award for *Brébeuf and His Brethren.*

Malvina Reynolds   Born in 1900 in San Francisco, Malvina Reynolds was a political activist, writing and performing protest songs in the 1950s. Her famous song, "Little Boxes," is a comment on the conformity of modern society, and has been performed by many folk artists.

Bill Richardson   Writer and media personality Bill Richardson lives in Vancouver, British Columbia, where he hosts a popular radio program, *Richardson's Roundup* and a television show called *Booked on Saturday Night.* He is the author of a number of books and has received the Stephen Leacock Medal of Humour for his work.

Christina Rossetti   Born in England in 1830, Christina Rossetti began to write verse when she was a child. She published collections of poetry for children and adults.

Robyn Sarah   Robyn Sarah was born in New York City in 1949, and now lives in Montreal, Quebec. She has written several volumes of poetry and contributed to a number of anthologies.

William Shakespeare   Born in 1564, in Stratford-upon-Avon, England, William Shakespeare is universally recognized as a great playwright and poet. Plays such as *Romeo and Juliet, Macbeth,* and *Hamlet* are regularly performed all over the world.

Edward Smith   Edward Smith has had a successful career as both a teacher and administrator. He is well known in the province of Newfoundland for his popular column "The View From Here," in which he uses his easy-going style to describe the world around him.

Fernando Sorrentino   Fernando Sorrentino is an award-winning Argentinian short story writer, whose work has been published in English translation. He is also the editor of collections of Spanish-American stories.

John Stackhouse   Writer and editor John Stackhouse was born in Toronto, Ontario. He has written for a numbr of magazines and newspapers including the *Toronto Star* and the *Financial Times of Canada.* In 1991 he won the National Magazine Award Gold Medal for Business Writing. Stackhouse is currently a senior writer for *Report on Business* magazine.

Donald Starkell   During his paddling career, from 1948–1996, Donald Starkell paddled some 80 000 kilometres. He swam solo across Lake Winnipeg in 1973 and is a two-time Guinness Record holder. Starkell was the first ever to make a kayak voyage through the North West Passage. He has written a number of books about his adventures.

Doug Stewart   Doug Stewart is the founder of Youth Culture Inc. of Toronto, and publisher of *Watch* magazine and *Bang*.

Norman Tait   Norman Tait is a Nisga'a artist. He has been a carver for more than 30 years.

Chidiock Tichborne   Chidiock Tichborne was a pseudonym of William Harrison Ainsworth. Born in England in 1805, Ainsworth was a novelist, editor, publisher, and solicitor.

Fred Wah   Fred Wah was born in Swift Current, Saskatchewan, in 1939. He has published many collections of poetry, and in 1985 won the Governor General's Award for *Waiting for Saskatchewan.*

Derek Walcott   Born in 1930, in St. Lucia, West Indies, Derek Walcott is a poet, essayist, and playwright whose work blends Caribbean, English, and African traditions. He was awarded the 1992 Nobel Prize for Literature.

Margaret Walker   Born in Birmingham, Alabama, in 1915, Margaret Walker was one of the youngest African-American writers to publish a book of poetry in the twentieth century. This collection, *For My People*, and her historical novel *Jubilee* are considered major works in black American literature.

Ben Wicks   Born in London, England, in 1926, Ben Wicks now lives in Toronto. The many jobs he held after leaving school provided him with an understanding of people which serves him well in his career as a syndicated cartoonist.

Budge Wilson   Born in 1927 in Halifax, Nova Scotia, Budge Wilson has worked as a teacher, librarian, newspaper columnist, and photographer. She began writing her short stories for young adults at the age of fifty.

Sandy Wilson   British Columbia–based filmmaker Sandy Wilson wrote and directed her first feature film, *My American Cousin,* in 1985. Based on Wilson's own experiences of growing up in the 1950s, the film won six Genie Awards.

Darryl Wimberley and Jon Samsel   Darryl Wimberley is an author and screenwriter, and has taught screenwriting at the University of Texas. Jon Samsel currently teaches digital arts and lives and writes in San Francisco.

William Wordsworth   Poet William Wordsworth was born in England in 1770. Considered by many to be the father of English Romanticism, he was appointed poet laureate in 1843.

Tim Wynne-Jones   Born in England, Tim Wynne-Jones lives in Canada and has written novels and short stories for adults and young adults, as well as several popular children's books.

CREDITS

"**Visitors**" from *Back of Beyond* by Sarah Ellis. Copyright (c) 1996 by Sarah Ellis. A Groundwood Book/Douglas & McIntyre, Toronto. Used with permission. "**Moonface**" (c) 1994 by Richardo Keens-Douglas from *Fiery Spirits: Canadian Writers of African Descent* edited by Ayanna Black. Published by HarperCollins Publishers Ltd., Toronto, Ontario. "**Moving Day**" by Helen Fogwill Porter from *Baffles of Wind and Tide* edited by Clyde Rose. Published by Breakwater Books Ltd., 1974. Reprinted with permission of the author. "**Loathe at First Sight**" from *If This Is Love, I'll Take Spaghetti* by Ellen Conford. Copyright (c) 1983 by Ellen Conford. Published by Four Winds Press, an imprint of Macmillan Publishing Company. "**Doing Something**" from *The Blue Camaro* by R.P. MacIntyre. All rights reserved. Reprinted by permission of Thistledown Press Ltd., 1974. "**The Jade Peony**" by Wayson Choy from *Vancouver Short Stories* edited by Carole Gerson. Published by University of British Columbia Press. "**Thunder and Lightning**" from *African Myths and Legends* retold by Kathleen Arnott, 1962. Reprinted with permission of Oxford University Press, U.K. "**Athena**" from *D'Aulaire's Book of Greek Myths* by Ingri and Edgar Parin d'Aulaire. Copyright © 1962 by Ingri and Edgar Parin D'Aulaire. Used by permission of Random House Children's Books, a division of Random House, Inc. "**The Story of the Totem Pole**" retold by Norman Tait from *Totem Pole Carving: Bringing a Log to Life*. Used with permission of Douglas & McIntyre. "**The Flash**" from *Numbers in the Dark and Other Stories* by Italo Calvino. English translation copyright © 1995 by Tim Parks. Published by Vintage Canada, a Division of Random House of Canada Limited, Toronto. "**The Visitation**" by Fernando Sorrentino from *Celeste Goes Dancing and Other Stories* edited by Norman Thomas di Giovanni. Copyright © North Point Press, N.Y. "**Lysandra's Poem**" from *The Leaving* by Budge Wilson. Published with permission of Stoddart Publishing Co. Limited, Don Mills, Ontario. "**A Mad Tea Party**" from *Alice's Adventures in Wonderland* and *Through the Looking Glass* by Lewis Carroll. Published by Oxford University Press, U.K. "**Save the Moon for Kerdy Dickus**" from *Some of the Kinder Planets* by Tim Wynne-Jones. Copyright © 1993 by Tim Wynne Jones. A Groundwood/Douglas & McIntyre book. Used with permission. "**Green Grass, Running Water**" from the novel *Green Grass, Running Water* by Thomas King. Copyright © 1993 by Thomas King. Published by HarperCollins Canada. "**The Other Family**" by Himani Bannerji from *Other Solitudes: Canadian Multicultural Fictions* edited by Linda Hutcheon and Marion Richmond. Published by Oxford University Press Canada. Used with permission of the author. "**On Love and a Lake**" by Renée David. From *Canadian Living*, June 1998. Reprinted by permission of the author. "**The Goal Post**" by Edward Smith from *Take it, it's good for you*. Published by Jesperson Press. Reprinted with permission. "**Pages from a Diary**" by Sylvia Plath is an excerpt from *Letters Home by Sylvia Plath* edited by Aurelia Schober Plath. Copyright © 1975 by Aurelia Schober Plath. Published by HarperCollins Publishers. "**Early Days**" from *Halfbreed* © 1973 by Maria Campbell. Reproduced with permission of the publisher, McClelland & Stewart, Toronto. "**Everything It Carries Away**" from Oddball@Large by Bill Richardson. Copyright © 1998 by Bill Richardson. Reproduced with permission of Douglas & McIntyre Publishing Group. "**Tom Longboat**" by Jack Granatstein from *Maclean's*, July 1, 1998. Reproduced with the permission of the authors. "**Anna Lang**" from *Acts of Courage*. Copyright © 1998 by John Melady. Reprinted by permission of Scholastic Canada Ltd. "**Cudjoe and Nanny, Heroes of the Maroons**" by Kat Mototsune. Copyright © 1990 by Nelson Canada. "**Hesquiaht—A People, A Place and a Language**" by Karen Charleson. Published in *Canadian Geographic* July/August